Blue Denim Press
P.O. Box 1181
Baltimore, MD 21203-1181

Due to writers whose integrity and originality are lacking, similarities to others work may appear. Rough drafts of my work were acquired by unnamed parties. Note that my work has been copyrighted since April 2001. I have decided against changing names, places, themes or ideas to remain true to my story. Thank you for your support and enjoy *Liquid Dreams*.

Written by Tiffany A. Womble
Edited by Nichole M. Stewart for Gemini Brown Publishing,
gemini_brown@hotmail.com
Cover designed by Grayson M. Williams, graycolors1@juno.com
Lyrics provided by Sir Robinson, Sir Reigns@hotmail.com
Photo courtesy of Celebrity Photo Shop

ISBN 0-9719793-0-8

# XOXO's

The Most High... Mommy, it's been a journey...I am b/c you are. Remember, you're my horse if you never win a race. There's no world like the ones that lie in the pages of a book. Thank you for keeping me in Enoch Pratt. This is for you! Troy, my brother & friend, I spent so much of my early life on your shoulders, now it's your turn to take the ride. I Love You. Linda, if I ever missed having an older sister, you make up for it. You define wife, mother & most importantly—friend. Thank you for Taylor (my Babylove) & TJ...Ti Ti loves you so much. Eric, I'm so glad you carry on the spirit of Daddy. Always give Lil' Eric the love we received, love you both. Shanny, my lil' big sister, as long as you dream it, it's yours. You're my heart. Big Mama, if there was ever a person I could have the chance to meet, it would be you. Your presence lives in us all...R.I.P. Big Daddy, The Carter Family, my Aunts Cynthia (aunts are really the best friends a girl could have), Delores, Pat, Peggy (a true soldier), Margaret, Dell, Trudy, Sheila & Narvis, my Uncles Doc, Bus, Junior (hey ugly!) & my older cousins who've been more like aunts & uncles, Deena, Bridget, Earl, Jaconda, Stan, Judy, Renee, Eric, Derrick, Sarah & Brenda—all 200 & counting...Vernon, Chris, James, Dominique & Tosh who've been more like brothers/sisters, ummwah! The Womble Family, Ma-Ma, nobody makes greens or punch with as much love as you do, Granddaddy, Aunts Evonne & Evette, Uncles Elliott, Quentin & Darryl, & cousins...The Clarke Family, Nana, a nana's love is the best kind, Holly, Bonnie & Derrick, The Lewis Family, Iva, Stevie, Tamicka & my sisters in FL, April, Cora & my 2$^{nd}$ fam @ 2512... Teachers are often taken for granted, all of mine deserve an ovation. THANK YOU... Kevin, for being there since FCH, watching me grow, & showing me what love & real friendship is about. More than anything, *Liquid Dreams* is about sisterhood, & to all mine, 1 Love: Morgan (my earliest childhood friendship), Sharon (Ms. Cheryl), Cherrice (T & Chantel), Danielle S., Laini (Coppin camp), Shannon (Ms. Tracy), India (Ms. Anita), Mikia (A. Greta, Quiana, Pupa, Vonda & the Mills Family), Quiana (Ms. Marlene), LiLi (the 1$^{st}$ friend I made @ Western), Tamboo (your contagious laughter got me through many "yawn" periods), Vikia, Estrelita, Layla, Leah, Randi (kisses to baby Cam'), Janel, Lila, Dara, Latia, Leatrice, KiKi, Shani ("we here"), Keisha C., Trice, Shawntell, Toi, Maria (Outkast), Shea Oschino (the realest chick in VA, Holla!), and finally Shalynn, who else but you can brighten up a person's life w/your ridiculous sense of humor & open heart. Creative Geminis like you make the world go 'round. Can't wait to hear the CD & thank you for being there from chapter 1. Dedicated to all my sisters reppin' Western's c/o '99(it's too many of y'all), our big sisters in '97 (Chíc, Joelí & Kenyetta) & '98, our lil' sisters in '00 & '01 (my lil' sis Kristina), & the entire Western Family, "Dear Western," Temple U.'s Spring 2001 Creative Writing Class, the friends I made @ Notre Dame, The entire Baltimore & the people who make it a proud place to call home. Thank you for embracing me... Nichole, Nic, "Cookie," *no one* could've told me that we'd become long lost sisters after that 1$^{st}$ day of school. We've done it all from DC to March Madness. Thank you for blessin' LD w/your editorial skillz. Can't wait to read your masterpiece (Peg & Candy), Sir Reigns, all I'll say is HOTEP, keep spittin', DJ Lil' Mic & all the friends I've made @ 5 Seasons, Grayson, I am forever grateful for you bringing LD to life & making the girls a reality. You define greatness...456, XOXO, who would've known that a chance visit to DC would bring back someone from a past lifetime. If ever you need an umbrella...Unconditional BPL, Forever B215

Daddy, Thank You for sending those white butterflies—even in the winter, Forever in My Heart...Your soul rests so that I may live, I Love You Always

# Liquid Dreamers

# "Liquid"
## Love is Questionable, Us is Destiny

Dreams are liquid/that means it's a paper chase/so get ya' capers straight/ain't ballin out da gate/but poverty is hard to face/so now I sit here and write what she accepted/Innocently molested/age 7, pops was arrested/it was crazy/niggas missed her thunderous cries/she roll wit' E. Badu/had bags under her eyes/sex was her profession/so she sung sad dick/tion of all used women that used to swallow **street fiction**/stability missin'/so now it's on to a lifestyle that right now represents a nocturnal night owl/Behind doors/slip diamonds inside her drawers/remove tags in the store/no worries about the blue boy/true story

**Hook**

A divine mode/well-designed clothes/earlobes froze/around her brothas couldn't keep they eyes closed/her mind shows/study for class between the strip shows/stick a dollar in her thong/and then you pull ya' dick close/a quick blow/will hop on top like 10 ponies/all her friends were men 'cause 'dem women been phony/a symphony/of small dicks and false hopes/drench pillows/false horoscopes so when she spoke I quote

**Hook**

**Bridge**
When we met it was like/midnight and daylight/I blazed mics/she got stage fright/but stayed tight/opposites attract is what they say right/we the living proof of that/a man that really loves you I guess you gotta get used to that

**Hook**

Beautiful package/pure love minus the sadness/perfect madness/**Hot/EP**/peep how it happens/immortalize your essence/you were destined to hear this message/because I love you wit' out no questions no second guessin'/as long as love lives/we never die/Revolution time we carry weapons side by side/you can say we co/inside/your soulmate/I hope your soul can relate/double four chambers control the whole state/it's so great/fate never changed/**Sir Reigns**/tat on the breastplate/this is soul food/Place these lyrics on my best plate/especially since I know you listen to these words/**Liquid Dreams** never dry/never listen to these birds/that's my word

Written & Performed by Sir Reigns
Hear 'Liquid' on *Epiphany Hot/EP*, a spoken word, hip-hop experience coming in Fall 2002

# Liquid Dreams

Liquid 1. The state of matter in which a substance characteristically flows readily, has little or no tendency to disperse, and is relatively difficult to compress. 2. Articulated without friction. 3. Readily converted into cash

Nikola Parrish

Jaded Vision/ 1

It is often said that three things rule the world—money, power and sex. What about the cases when those three things can rule a person's life? I've constantly wondered about the hustlers who seem too dumb to pull out of a lifestyle that will either bring prison time or death and the gamblers who seem to gamble everything away before they realize it's too late.

But then it became apparent that everything seems to take second place to that feeling of winning. Knowing you're a winner while the pockets are fat will make you forget about the other shit that comes with life. And let's face it, once you're in the game, whatever the hustle may be, it's for life.

My lifestyle has left little room to care for the small, yet big things normal, 9-to-5 people concern themselves with. For the last two years I have been a slave to money through sex, and the power that comes with getting and having dough pushes me to make it a constant factor in my life.

It was at my high school graduation when I thought I had finally figured the world out. I looked into the faces of the girls who were Black, White, Spanish and Asian and realized that it didn't matter what color our skin was. Shit, the sun was beaming so hot that by the end of the ceremony, all of our complexions were close in shades.

No, race didn't matter because the white girl Jessica who sat to my left lived in the same kind of ghetto most of my black friends were acquainted with. Keisha, who was to my right, drove a Lexus to school even before she had a provisional. That bitch lived in a phat-ass house on the secluded streets of Towson, MD that was only familiar to the lily white girls that played lacrosse and shit.

Point blank, who gives a fuck about color? When everything is said and done, the only thing that matters is the haves and the have nots, and if you have not, you're shit outta luck. So, I decided then that college didn't matter. Why waste four years to get some piece of paper? A piece of paper that would decide my income, now that's a joke.

And if I wasn't planning on engineering, aerodynamics or some shit, I would be fucked because the average job wasn't bringing in any real money. Nobody gives a fuck about the teachers or the doctors. They put up with the most bullshit and never see the payoff.

They used to be the shitty careers everybody wanted when asked that stupid-ass question, "What you wanna be when you grow up?" Not me, I just wanted the wealth without the work, and now it's beginning to catch up to me. I know now that

2

*nothing* comes easy without a struggle or letdowns. And sooner than later, when shit hits the fan, you discover that some things come at a price higher than money can buy.

It was an early Saturday in March and every type of insect seemed to be out of hibernation. Bright yellow Queen bees buzzed loudly outside the second-floor window in search of mates and flowers with any leftover pollen. And though the sun's rays gave off comfortable warmth throughout the middle room, it could not calm all of our jumpy nerves.

I had been working on Chelsea's neck-length hair all morning. Now that the wedding had arrived she was crying over her recent haircut, which in my opinion, fit her square face perfectly. It took off a couple of years but added that needed maturity she had lacked and complained about since we had reached adulthood.

After setting her hair for what seemed like the hundredth time, we finally settled on a body wave. Instead of giving her the outdated fingerwaves that stuck to her scalp like paste, I had taken the wide-tooth comb and dipped it throughout her hair like huge surfer waves. I didn't have to look at her face in the mirror to know that she was frowning. I saw the huge dimples in her cheeks sink in as she pursed her lips together.

It didn't matter that I had been doing her hair since we met. Chelsea continued to worry that I would make her face look too fat or her head too big, but I was willing to ignore the whining since it was her day. When her hair was finished only hints of the waves would be visible, although I knew she wasn't thinking about the end product. She never did.

While I combed out the loose waves and waited for the flat irons to heat on the small silver-plated stove, Chanel applied the bronze MAC foundation to Chelsea's high cheekbones. She had to use a darker foundation on her pale skin since we had all received tans from our trip to Aruba in early February.

Now, Chanel was a completely different case when it came time for her to get her wig done. Chelsea was the complainer, but Chanel had to put her fingers in her hair whenever she wanted to explain some minute detail I wasn't performing correctly. It didn't matter if I had her turned away from the mirror. She would find a way to face it, and insisted on looking into it throughout the entire hair process. Once I burnt her hand to show her how irritating it was for her to tell me how to do my job. She didn't speak to me for two weeks but the small mark reminded her whenever she slipped.

Since her hair was too long to fuss over and too thick to wait for drying, I had it pinned up with soft tendrils that accented her round face. She liked that I had given her a soft and delicate look and that was hard since Chanel had the nastiest attitude and quickest tongue of us three. Me, I was happy with my snatchback. I hated doing my hair since it hung past my shoulders, and the chignon was simple yet elegant. Chanel and me were Chelsea's maids of honor so I had intertwined the same small pink and red roses throughout our hair that was in her veil.

3

From the time I knew her, Chelsea thought she was 'Miss Pretty in Pink.' If Chanel and me weren't there to hold her hand while she planned the wedding, it might have looked like an accident with Pepto Bismol. Everything seemed to be drenched in cough syrup already, including the pink six-layered cake that would be served to the slew of people at the reception.

It should have been a rare and exciting occasion, but the truth was we were used to big events like weddings and parties where half of the people were friends of someone else. Frankly, none of us cared about the people. The one thing we *were* concerned with was the event itself. Us three were all the friends we needed and it had been that way since high school. We had made the promise to all get married within the same year and because Chelsea's happened to be the first, it would be a wedding no one forgot.

This would be the first time since high school we got to show off for all the bitches from our alma mater, Western Prepatory. Western was the only all-girl public high school besides the one in Philadelphia. Back when, we weren't good enough to hang with the cliques who wore their designer gear, and we were too hip to hang with the nerds. Our clique was the only thing we had.

I met Chelsea and Chanel the first day. Public school was a new ballgame for me. I had been attending Catholic school my whole life and went from a student body of 150 boys and girls to 1,500 girls.

It was the first time I'd caught public transportation, and when the bus pulled up to the curb I was scared to get off. The butterflies in my stomach would not settle and as soon as I looked around, I wanted to go home and forget about school altogether. There were girls who looked like they were dressed for work or dinner at *The Palm* instead of high school. I immediately felt intimidated and like an outsider.

I had never experienced the hustle and bustle of switching classes throughout the day and the upperclasswomen didn't help. When it was time to eat lunch someone gave me directions to the gym. I got there and was embarrassed when a teacher told me in front of her whole class that the cafeteria was the other way. I guess my face had that lost look written all over it.

I had never made a big deal out of my clothes on the first day of school, but I wish I had that day. Having to endure the same uniform of a navy skirt and blouse from pre-K to eighth grade left me with no sense of fashion. My clothes were nice, but they were void of the DKNY and Polo emblems that marked so many of the girls' garments at my new second home.

When I finally made it to the cafeteria, the food lines seemed to go on forever. Instead of waiting, I headed to the much shorter snack line for a honey bun and the nastiest cup of fruit punch made by the private food service. I don't know if it was real sugar in the potion, but the taste stuck to the roof of my mouth like cheap cough syrup.

I looked around and there were tables of girls who sat according to color contacts, fly basement weaves and too-tight tittie tops with Calvin Klein and Versace emblazoned on the chest. I found a spot at the end of a table and was greeted with the fakest smiles from a group of girls whose conversation was centered around "that nigga wit' the phat Lex," or "the one wit' the laced Acura." There was enough space between the fake-eye clique and myself at the long white table to separate themselves from my then shoulder-length wrap, navy T-shirt and outdated Gap jeans.

Although I felt out of place and was disgusted with the way they sucked their teeth when they talked, I wanted one of them to speak to me. I hated that I was sitting at the end of the table alone while everyone else was catching up on their summer happenings.

I finished off the honey bun with extra icing and realized that I had nothing to do with my hands besides sip the cough syrup, but after that first gulp I wasn't taking my chances. So I opened the notebook and calculated the money I would need for my art supplies. All I had was an 80-page spiral notebook and a black Papermate flex grip. I wished I had brought the latest issue of *Vibe* because I was tired of pretending not to gaze into the faces of Black girls with violet and blue contacts.

I opened my spiral and looked at my seven classes. My final period of the day was an Intro to Drawing and Painting class, but I knew nothing except stick figures. No matter, I was psyched—I had always wanted to carry around a large sketchpad like I was a designer since I took such an interest in creative hairstyles and trends. My designer dream was interrupted by a figure that I noticed in my peripheral.

A thin girl with the same pink and white Lerner outfit I had seen on two different girls that day took a seat at my end of the table. I didn't care about her outfit. I was just happy to have someone sitting across from me. Now, if my face said I was nervous, hers said she might piss her pants. Her hair was pulled into a long ponytail and the silver studs in her ears made her look like an innocent church girl. She quietly introduced herself and after an awkward silence I could feel myself becoming more assertive. She was obviously more scared than I was.

We talked about the mix-ups with our schedules and the tiring eight-period day. The bell soon rang and we were off to seventh period. I was glad that I had someone to walk and talk with in the halls and saw she wasn't quiet at all, she just looked the part.

Looking down at our red half-slips of paper with our schedules on them we saw we were headed to the same history class. I was more confident with Chelsea at my side as I walked into the classroom. I was no longer self-conscious about my outfit and my hairstyle that wasn't as ghetto fabulous as the other girls. It didn't matter. I had made a friend.

There were five sets of desks on each side of the classroom with rows of three in each one. Chelsea sat by the window and I in the middle. We were both happy to have the other to converse with.

Our teacher, Ms. Jones was writing her name on the board while she told us about the quaint town in Wisconsin she called home. She definitely looked like it. She wore brown leather clogs and a floral print sundress. Her blond hair was cut into a short pageboy and she had the warmest and sincerest smile I had seen all day.

While she introduced herself, a girl walked in who fit the mode of most of the girls I had silently envied that day. Her hair fell over her shoulders and it looked like she had just had it dyed with a fresh, black rinse. It was cut neatly with tapered bangs and her large gold hoops made her look older than the average fourteen-year old.

All of the other seats were occupied except the end seat next to mine, and I saw in her face that she had probably hoped to sit next to someone else who shared the same taste in fashion. Her white and sky blue Armani T-shirt matched her dark blue jeans and though I couldn't see the label in the strappy shoes, I was sure they read the logo as well.

Instead of making everyone stand and introduce themselves like we had done so many times already, Ms. Jones gave us all fifteen minutes to learn each other's names and numbers. Western had adopted the buddy system. We would use the numbers to call and ask for missing assignments or recaps from the classes we missed. Western was a college preparatory school and the curriculum had us practicing the things that awaited us in college.

I was so anxious to become *buddies* with the new girl that I almost forgot Chelsea. Since I was in the middle I introduced Chelsea and myself to the new girl who gave us a half smile. The mocha-colored girl didn't have much to say and when we exchanged numbers, I was surprised when she gave me her pager number only.

*A beeper number.* The only people I had associated beepers with were important people and drug dealers. It was becoming a fad among teenagers, yet I had never known someone my age to carry one. I would later learn that half of Western's population owned them. And though they were illegal to have in school, students simply put them on vibrate and led the class into a coughing frenzy whenever the actual beeping sound went off mistakenly.

During the fifteen-minute introduction we talked about our previous middle schools. Well, actually Chelsea and I did while the newcomer Chanel maintained an unimpressed look on her face. I had given up on any chance of us becoming friends and dismissed her as a snob until she asked me where I got my hair done. The last time I had escaped into a bathroom to check my hair it looked okay. I was scared to answer her for fear that she might laugh.

Reluctantly, I told her that I had done it myself and held my breath for her response. She was impressed that I had cut my own layers in the back and hesitantly asked if I would do hers. She said she hated having such thick hair and wanted her wraps to have more body. I couldn't wait to try out my skills on her since I had been doing my own hair and others for the past two years.

6

On my way home I was feeling good. I had planned on coming home and asking my mother to enroll me in the Catholic high school we had visited during the summer, but I had made two new friends. Though they were complete opposites, they would both offer the same true friendship.

Growing up I would often ask my mother about my name—Nikola Parrish. It sounded so proper and bourgeois, yet we had no wealth. Not the kind I could see anyway. Since I could remember, she was an avid reader and would tell me she got my name from the bride-to-be in one of her favorite romance novels. And instead of giving me my father's last name she gave me hers because she said the Foster name had no couth or class.

I enjoyed hearing the story before I went to bed and it later became a favorite of mine when I grew out of books with pictures. The young girl had grown up poor and met a wealthy man who gave her the world as well as undying love. There were more details but that was the gist of things. I always carried the story with me. Who knew that it was only a story.

After she finished reading, my father would come in the room and kneel with me while we said my prayers. My home was filled with that kind of love until age ten.

They separated after Mommy found out he had a girlfriend on the side, who we later discovered had a daughter the same age as me. Mommy didn't know how it was possible for him to have a secret family she knew nothing about. *Secret* was the operative word.

I didn't know it then, but he had two and three other women besides my mother. He was definitely a womanizer with his jet-black curly hair and smooth skin. He used the most expensive cologne which would linger in a room minutes after he left and was known for wearing tailored suits all the time.

After he was gone, we were forced to move into a small apartment complex in West Baltimore. I was glad that we had stayed in the same general area but I missed our big house. The shiny, hardwood floors and the soft, expensive couches in our huge living room were off limits to my childhood friends.

I always looked forward to the weekend visits with him. We would stay up late and watch his collection of old movies. I got to eat junk on top of junk, and since money never seemed to be an issue with him, I would return home with shopping bags full of clothes, games and dolls.

Soon my visits with Daddy went from every week, to every month and finally every year if I was lucky. I learned to erase him from my mind and went as far as cutting him out of photo albums. Mommy and me only had each other, and as I got older we switched roles. The breakup was sometimes too much for her and I found myself covering her up at night numerous times after she had cried herself to sleep.

Just like the regular visits that disappeared, so did the weekly envelopes of money. They had covered our rent, Saturday visits to Ms. Lynn's hair salon and anything else we were used to when he was doing for us. Mommy ended up taking on two jobs just to keep me in private school and pay our bills.

My love for Daddy went from dislike to hate and the slightest things would trigger it. I would come home from school to cook something and the only thing in our refrigerator were bottles of ketchup, mustard and old jelly jars that we kept, scraping what we could from the sides. The school lunch I never had to eat before was now sometimes the only meal I had unless I found enough change to buy two or three bags of 25 cent chips at the corner store.

The white walls above the stove had turned yellow from the greasy cooking and I often wished she would take him back. But I would quickly regret my tears when I saw my mother come home from her day job as janitor at one of the downtown buildings. Her pretty caramel skin that was the same shade as mine suddenly looked so old and fine lines were forming around her round eyes that had stopped dancing a long time ago.

I stopped speaking to my father and when he did call the house he was surprised when I said, "Sidney, my mother and I would appreciate if you didn't call here anymore." He got quiet and hung up, and I hoped that I had hurt him the same way he had done us for so long. We were struggling, yet I heard he had no problem supporting his new family and had actually named his illegitimate daughter after him, Sydney or something.

My father had controlled all the money. My parents married straight out of high school so all my mother knew *was* cleaning since "housewife" had been her title. Even at twelve and thirteen it was depressing to see her work so hard. I begged her to take me out of private school to bring some extra money into the house, but she wasn't having it.

She said she refused to see me without a top-notch education and dared anyone to try and take it from me. Education was important to me as well because I certainly wasn't cleaning anybody's toilet except my own. But school wasn't feeding us. It didn't take me long to realize the power behind money, and going without for so long taught me how to make ends meet anyway I knew how.

Mommy would give me a fifty to shop with at the store every two weeks and I would carry one or two shopping bags like I had been to the mall and fill it with a month's worth of food from the local market. So I wouldn't seem suspicious, I would still buy ten dollars worth of snacks or something and walk out. Mommy only questioned me once about all the food in the fridge. When I told her I had just clipped coupons out of Sunday's paper, she sent me to the store to do the shopping all the time. It felt good to know that I had lifted one of her biggest worries off her shoulders.

We had stopped our visits altogether at Ms. Lynn's when I started doing hair. I would go to the local Rite Aid, lift the hair magazines off the shelf, put them under a spiral notebook I carried in my arms, and walk out as if I had paid for them. I got so used to it that I stopped hiding them and walked out with them and anything else I needed. When I got home I would stand in the bathroom mirror and practice the styles I had studied in the magazines.

In the beginning I wasn't successful. I used too much holding spray or too much gel and my head would feel heavy. I learned to find the right products—the good shit, that is. Soon, me and Mommy's hair was looking better than most women who faithfully stayed in the salon. The women at her jobs were asking her for her stylist's number and when she told them about me I had no problem making two or three hundred dollars a month.

The extra money helped us move from the small apartment into a nice rowhouse in Reservoir Hill, one of Baltimore's safer neighborhoods. We were still struggling but suddenly it didn't matter. We were decorating our house and however small, it was ours. I was proud that I was only in the eighth grade and helping out.

It was a new beginning for us. The basement was left for me to turn into a makeshift salon. It was my spot in the house. We traveled to different thrift stores and lucked up on two overhead dryers and swivel chairs. They were ancient, but they got the job done. I also nailed various mirrors and framed pictures of black models onto the walls to give it that Saturday morning salon feeling.

By eleventh grade I had formed a nice clientele with many of the girls at school including Chelsea and Chanel, who were eventually getting their hairdos on the house. But then again, money was never an issue with us. When we hung out and one of us didn't have, we were covered by the other two.

Doing hair suddenly brought me enough money to dress in the Donna Karan and the other trendy gear I admired on the other girls at Western. When they saw my high-priced clothes, the stuck-up stares were replaced with smiles. I was invited to exclusive parties and asked to join clubs where the prerequisites were hair to my ass, designer clothes (of course), and a boyfriend or various male friends who picked me up after school in a phat Lex or laced Acura. I had all except the latter, but I *had* made progress from that first day of school.

My newfound world of popularity was halted in my last year of school when nice clothes and a nice ride were the most important. My mother's doctor had discovered tumors on her uterus and after her surgery she was forced to take off work for weeks that ended up turning into months.

She had switched jobs so many times that she couldn't receive any sick leave. I was still doing hair, but it barely covered our mortgage and the other bills that came with the house. Therefore, I was back to wearing the same clothes from junior year and I was also looking for the friendship I had lost in Chelsea and Chanel. My clothes had outdone anything Chanel was wearing and Chelsea still had that baby face that made her look too young so I had stopped hanging with them.

When the high-fashioned girls saw my outdated clothes they slowly distanced themselves from me. I was walking the halls alone again. I knew Chelsea and Chanel had the same lunch period so I prepared my ass-kissing speech and began walking toward their window table in the Senior Lounge.

Chelsea was beginning to fill out her clothes and she had discovered makeup. Chanel looked the same, only older. I forgot how much I missed them and suddenly felt stupid for the way I had treated them junior year. I felt bad for purposely ignoring them in the halls when I saw them coming my way and making up excuses when it was time for us to hang out on Friday nights. No matter, I found the courage to say something.

I sat next to Chanel, and at first they ignored me for five minutes until I told them about Mommy. They had always treated her like a second mother so they were more than willing to look past the shady way I had been treating them to come and visit her.

They sat with her for two hours and we laughed and caught up. It was almost like we had never been apart. I was still feeling guilty so I told them they were in need of a wash and style. I knew that would further break the ice.

The basement was not only the place for hairdos, but it was the place where we all came after hanging out all night and where we had intimate talks that lasted until the sun came up. It was where we smoked weed for the first time and shared life-changing experiences such as our first dick-sucking moments (well Chanel and me did anyway) and stories about anal sex. We all agreed that it was something we never wanted to try. That day of reconciliation led to something that would change our lives forever. Senior year was coming to an end and graduation was around the corner. It's funny when I look back because out of everything we had ever talked about, we had never discussed what we would do after school.

I was reclined in the black leather chair I used to sit clients under the dryer. Chelsea was stretched out on the makeshift couch and Chanel was sitting in one of the swivel chairs with her face towards the ceiling. Chanel was passing me the Dutchie that was filled with what seemed like the best weed the earth had produced when I sparked the life-altering conversation. "Damn, it don't even seem like we've been in school for four years does it?" I asked after exhaling the smoke.

"*Hell no*. Seems like yesterday when we sat in Ms. Jones' class and got our seats moved 'cause we talked too much," Chanel said before closing her eyes.

Chelsea took the blunt from me and looked at it for a long time before inhaling. "I'm glad it's almost over 'cause I'm tired of getting up, writing exegeses, and answering to teachers about why the shit is late." Me and Chanel both sat up to look at her. We had never heard her talk about school in that way. When we wanted to hook periods or leave school early, Chelsea was the one who talked us into staying. "*What?*" she asked, like we shouldn't have been surprised. "I'm tired of it all. The books, deadlines, and then college... I'm not looking forward to four more years of bullshit."

She must've felt really strong about the whole thing because I had never heard her curse like that before, and if any of us were going to college I always assumed it would be her. Her face was frowned up and her cheeks were turning red. All I needed now was Chanel's opinion before I put my idea out there. So I turned to her and asked, "What you plan on doin' after Western?"

"I ain't even gave college a thought. The way I figure is that I'll find some dumb nigga to take care of me." I wasn't surprised at her response. Of us three, Chanel was the one with the *fuck dem niggas* attitude so I knew she would back me up if Chelsea needed persuasion. "Why all the questions yo?" Chanel asked.

"Well, I was thinking about shit lately, and I just don't see any point in goin' to college, gettin' a dead end job that I'll end up hatin'. I mean look at these mutherfuckers out here. People don't realize just how much of a joke life is. You got people who *live* for their jobs. They don't realize that they wasted their life punchin' the clock. They get up and do the same shit everyday, never reapin' any real benefits," I said, shrugging my shoulders. "Sure they might take their lil' vacations to Virginia Beach, Six Flags and shit, but is that it? What about trips around the world and just being able to get up the next day and sayin' *'fuck it, I'm going to St. Lucia'* or some shit."

"I don't know too many mafuckas who can do that shit," Chanel said like she was really deep into thought.

"That's what I'm sayin'. So I was thinkin' we take easy living to another level."

"Easy living without working? Whatever you're talking about has to be illegal, 'cause I can't see anything easy coming without working," Chelsea said.

"Okay, let me ask y'all this, how much free pussy have we given away?" I waited for them to respond. "If we put all of our experiences together including our first times, how much?"

They looked at me like I was crazy, but I was so serious that even the effects of the weed couldn't mellow out my mood. Although the looks on their faces said that they seemed confused, Chanel was the one who really seemed to be thinking about the shit. Of us three she was the smartest because I knew she was getting whatever she had to, however she could since her mother wasn't doing anything for her. Chelsea just thought that every fuck she had with a mutherfucker was out of love.

Me, I have to say that I was probably the dumbest, though I would never admit it. I had had sex with almost five niggas in my whole eighteen-year old life, and after the first guy, I knew that there was something I should have been asking for. Shit, something I should have been demanding.

My mother and me were struggling and I was fuckin' for free. The more I sat and thought about it the angrier I became, and it only fueled more fire in our conversation. "You totaled the shit up yet?" I asked them.

"Shit, I don't know," Chanel said.

"What about you Chelz?"

"I'm no whore. Whatever I did was because I loved them and they loved me," she said like she was trying to convince herself.

11

I was upset after she said that so I pulled her cards. "They loved you Chelz? You really believe that shit?"

"Well, yeah."

"Okay, well if any of that shit was love, why when that stupid nigga Derrick got you pregnant, me and Chanel had to pay for it? He wasn't tryna give you shit and even said it wasn't his. But that's love, right?" I laughed flippantly.

I knew I had blown her high, but I wanted her to look at things from my perspective and if it meant playing on her emotions it was just something I had to do.

"I guess that wasn't love, but *I have known it* and if you're saying that I should have been receiving something in return for sex, well then that's your opinion. Now how much, I don't know."

"I know you don't know, because there ain't a price. Just like that Mastercard commercial, the shit is priceless."

I had their attention and for a moment the air was silent. Chanel had turned her chair to face the mirror and was fixing her hair, but there was nothing wrong with it. Chelsea was flipping through a magazine. I could tell that they didn't know what to say and were avoiding the conversation so I tried something else—another route.

"Chanel yo, look at yourself. What are you thinkin' while you look in the mirror? That you sportin' a fly-ass roller wrap, a cute face and the same outdated clothes you had on a month ago."

"Fuck you, Kola. You got a lot of shit to say. Pointin' fingers and shit, but look at you. You've been fucked too and ain't received a damn thing in return. The one thing *I do remember* is you gettin' fuckin' crabs. And for the record I don't see you sportin' nothin' that says Gucci bitch."

What she said hurt for a second but I brushed it off because I had sat up plenty of nights and thought the same things. "You're right, but what I'm sayin' is not to hurt you. I just want you two to realize some things. One, is that there is a world we know nothin' about. I'd like to be able to afford some Gucci shit, I'd like to take a trip somewhere outside of Baltimore, and two, we need to realize that we can't do those things if we broke."

"So what you sayin' we do Nikola?" Chanel asked. I knew she was still pissed at me because she rarely called me by my full name.

"There is one thing that will always hold true and that is, there are two things that people will always pay for no matter how illegal—drugs and sex. All I'm sayin' is that we have to stop bein' stupid. Layin' on our backs for pleasure that more often than not ends in pain… Niggas that really don't give a fuck about us, who only want to stick their dick in somethin'."

"Damn, you a lesbo or some shit?" Chanel asked.

"The shit ain't funny. That's why we don't have shit 'cause we don't take sex as seriously as we should. We need to have that same mentality as them niggas. They sling their dicks around like bitches owe them the pussy when they really need to be owin' *us* shit," I said, never stopping to breathe. "We gotta make shit liquid."

"*Liquid*? You mean like assets and shit?" Chanel laughed.

"Exactly. Somethin' needs to be liquid 'cause the pussy sho' been flowin' like water around this bitch "

My joke leavened the mood. We were all laughing.

"I feel you. So what's next?" Chanel asked.

"First, are we on the same page?" I asked while looking at Chelsea. I could tell that she was thinking about the abortion because her face had that lost look like she was trying to comprehend something.

"Yeah, we are," she said.

"So, this is the deal. We all cute as hell and our bodies are bangin'. Our hair stays tight. The only thing missin' is the clothes and the phat ride, 'cause niggas wit' bankroll ain't givin' bitches no dough who ain't got all their shit together. And I'm not talkin' no Express or Gap shit, I'm talkin' Prada and Fendi."

"How are we going to get things like that, Kola? I can barely afford the Gap shit I buy and *I work there*," Chelsea said.

"See I was thinkin'…. At the counter y'all have those sensor removers. What's gon' happen is me and Chanel are goin' to come in there and buy some shit. After you remove the sensors off the last outfit, you slip the gun into one of our bags."

"I don't know Nikola," Chelsea said with that same uncertain voice I had become accustomed to and all around annoyed by.

"What part don't you know about? The shit is going to be brilliant." I felt like Vivica in *Set it Off*. "After we have it, we'll be straight. We'll head right to stores like Nordstrom and we in there."

"You make it sound so easy," Chelsea said.

"'Cause it is. It will be," Chanel spoke up for me.

I guess Chelsea felt like it was two against one, but the truth was, from then on we were in it together. And whatever problems that came with the life we were about to lead would be handled as a whole, because we were all we had and nothing would change that.

I couldn't believe it. Chelsea would be walking down the aisle in less than one hour. We had finally gotten the hair issue together and of course, she was happy with the end result like I knew she would be. On the way to St. Bernardine's on Edmondson Ave. we all had our fingers crossed that the wedding would go on without any problems.

She was marrying this guy named Charles she had met in Philly and he had bank like that. He had told her he was in the music industry and owned a couple of barbershops, but even Chelsea knew that meant drug money. Shit, she certainly never saw any entertainers or plaques on his wall.

We had all made the promise to get married within the same year, but whoever the guy was, he had to be set for life. We weren't trickin' forever. And we weren't taking any shorts when it came to spending a lifetime with a mutherfucker. If he didn't have shit and couldn't offer us shit ten years down the line, he wasn't worth the fuckin' time. The wedding was going to be a good thing for Chanel and me as well. There would be enough big ballers in the house to whet both of our appetites.

I could tell Chelsea was nervous 'cause she was talking too much and she kept pulling the pink bustier over the tit job that she had had done a year ago.

"Chelz yo, what's the problem?" I finally asked.

"I'm scared that Charles might've found out about my past. What if we get to the church and he's stood me up? I'm not tryna look like a fool."

I had toyed around with the thought myself. I had thought about all the niggas that would be there and I knew without a doubt that there would be at least twenty that I had fucked. I didn't know about Chelsea or Chanel but I wasn't going to let it fuck with my plans. We had traveled up and down the East Coast so frequently and attended every big event that there wasn't a doubt in my mind. We all had skeletons that would show their faces, if not at St. Bernardine's then later at the reception on the *Bay Lady* where the real party would begin.

Instead of reassuring Chelsea, I looked over at Chanel who was staring out the window and I did the same. She too seemed to be deep in thought, but I had to keep my cool. And I silently promised myself that if I had anything to do with it, nobody was fuckin' up Chelsea's day or our paper.

Chanel Gilmore

My first time was with one of my mother's boyfriends. I was thirteen and inexperienced but I knew it would happen with one of them eventually. My mother's bedroom was like a revolving door for men who made it known I was really who they wanted. I was in my room sitting at the desk listening to Mary J. Blige's *My Life* CD when the door opened. I thought it would be my mother telling me she was home from the hairdresser's. Instead it was her latest boyfriend, Ronnie.

At that time my mother was thirty-one so she was still into young niggas. Ronnie looked like one of the guys I would see at the corner store who tried to holler whenever I went to buy my mother her Newports and pack of Doublemint. At thirteen I attracted men with my thick legs, double C's and ass from nowhere. I was aware of the power behind a bangin' body, but I never asked for the attention Ronnie would give me that day.

I was singing the words to 'Be Happy' at the top of my lungs when he walked up on me. He stumbled in and came behind me, pretending to look at the *Right On!* Magazine I was skimming. He used to do this thing with his tongue that turned my stomach. He had a gold crown in one of his front teeth and would click his tongue against it like he was trying to clean food out.

When he leaned over my shoulder I could smell the Hennessy. I knew this because all I ever saw him drink was the dark liquor with Coke. Ronnie tilted his head and ran his tongue over my ear. I don't even remember him saying anything to me. But I could see the lust in his eyes.

Now, I had kissed a couple of guys before and had even let them rub my titties or stick their fingers in my pussy so I knew what was supposed to turn me on. All he was doing was making me sick.

I got up from the desk and sat on the edge of the bed not knowing what to do. What was I supposed to say, *don't do it?* I guess I could have, I could have fought him, but I was scared that he might lie and tell my mother I had tried something *with him*. She already thought I was fuckin' no matter how many times I had told her the opposite. So he would have no problem convincing her.

Before I knew it, I was on my back. Even with all the thoughts racing through my mind I was still aware that he was forcing his dick into my small hole. It's crazy, 'cause despite the shit that was happening I could never forget what I had on.

It was a little after ten so I was wearing the XXL Orioles T-shirt that belonged to my brother Rico before he got locked up. Underneath I had on some light blue panties with butterflies that he had pulled off after he told me he was going to make me feel like a woman.

After spreading my legs apart he placed his mouth over my pussy and sucked it like it was a piece of fruit. I had seen stuff like that on nasty flics my cousins and I used to sneak and watch, but I didn't feel the need to holler and scream like I had heard so many of the chicks do in the movies.

I remember laying there for what seemed like an eternity. The whole time I was biting down on my bottom lip thinking about how much fun I was going to have at Wild World amusement park the following week during my eighth grade graduation trip. When he was finished, he got up and stuffed his dick into his pants. And he even had the nerve to lean over and kiss my forehead.

I listened for his keys and when I heard the door lock, I slowly got up from the wet spot where he had just laid over me. I sat on the edge of my daybed and looked at the pieces of cracked paint on the wall and thought about how dirty I felt. I could feel the sweat from his face on my neck, and on my face I smelled his musty cologne along with my own scent. I tried to stand up but my stomach was cramping and my shit was burning.

I just sat there and thought about Rico and wished in that moment, he was there to come and put his arms around me. He was only seventeen, but he was doing time with the big boys out in Hagerstown, MD for murder and robbery. True, I had seen him and his friends do some cruel things to the rats roaming our alley when I was younger, but murder? I know for a fact that if he murdered anybody it's 'cause he had to.

I hadn't seen him in over two years and it hurt. He was my everything and there I was, getting raped. *And where was my father?* Shouldn't he have been there to prevent shit like that? I had never seen him except in pictures, but from what I saw it's obvious that me and Rico got our high cheekbones, chocolate skin and slanted eyes from him, and if I was a nigga, me and Rico could pass for twins. It's a shame, the mafucka never did shit for me and I looked just like him.

Nevertheless, I sat there feeling just so lonely and low. The tears fell without warning and I knew at that moment, my innocence was gone. *Would my mother know when she saw me?* The thought of her made me rush into the bathroom, forgetting any kind of pain I was feeling. I let the water hit my face and tried to forget everything that happened. I scrubbed my inner thighs and breasts so hard that as dark as I was, my skin had turned red.

I didn't see my mother until the next morning when I was on my way to school. She was sleeping in her room and of course she had some no good nigga laid up with her, but it wasn't Ronnie. I found out later that he told her he couldn't see her anymore. Maybe he felt like shit or was too embarrassed to look me in the face again.

Seeing her with someone different didn't affect me like it should have. I was used to hearing the moans escape from her bedroom. I had stopped covering my ears with pillows a long time ago. I was about eight when she brought home the first no good mafucka.

I was getting ready to watch *The Wonder Years* like I always did on Wednesday after I finished my homework. When I walked into the living room she asked me what I wanted, and I looked at her like she was crazy. *What did she mean*, I had been doing the same shit every week. The old-ass man sitting next to her on our black pleather couch looked sneaky, like all he wanted to do was fuck her and bounce.

But my moms was telling me to go to my room 'cause *she had company*. I felt betrayed, even at eight years old. She was definitely on some new shit. Looking back, this was around the same time she put Rico out for selling drugs and getting into trouble with the police. Funny though, she had no problem spending his drug money.

At that time I didn't know much about sex, but I knew that's what went on late at night when she thought I was asleep. That first night with that sleazy-looking nigga I was awake reading *Jet* when I heard the screaming. At that age it's no doubt that I was going to go see what was going on. With all the noise, her moans and his groans, I still felt the need to tiptoe across the hallway. When I pushed the door open the things I saw sent me into shock. It has stayed with me to this very day.

My mother was bent over taking it in the ass like a fuckin' dog. Of course I thought he was hurting her, so I immediately went for him. Before I knew it I was hitting him on his nasty, sweaty back and yelling for him to get off of her. The stench of sex was in the air thick and I would come to hate it. In my adult life I made it a priority to shower after sex.

She pulled me off him, grabbed me by my arm with her nails digging in my skin and walked me into my room, scolding me like I was wrong. When we were back in my room she looked like she wanted to punch me in my face. "What the fuck is wrong wit' you Chanel?" I couldn't believe she was asking me that, but I had no response. My tears spoke for me. "Don't *ever* barge in my fuckin' room without knockin'," she continued. "As a matter of fact, when I got company you stay ya fast ass in your room." She walked out and I laid down, feeling sick on my stomach while I choked on my tears. Minutes later the same cries from her bedroom could be heard again and they lasted until I had rocked myself to sleep.

I continued to go without sleep, especially after that. I became very quiet and when I did speak, it was always on some smart shit. I never thought before I spoke and the reality was I really didn't give a fuck. My behavior in school was a reflection of what went on at home. Since my mother kept me up all night with her screaming and moaning I was falling asleep in class and just growing up too fast. But she didn't care.

She never showed her face at a PTA meeting and when my teachers called the house, she cussed them out. She never tried to talk to me, or at least make an attempt to explain her behavior. As long as she was getting hers, she was cool.

The incident with Ronnie left me numb to everything going on around me. High school was a new chapter in my life that I looked forward to. I never thought I'd be going to Western. I was very intelligent, but my grades in middle school were up and down. I was constantly late to school and had been suspended at least five times for fighting. I couldn't smack the shit out of my mother so I terrorized the bitches I went to school with.

Western wasn't having that. In fact, I heard there weren't any fights there ever. I just knew that record would change when I got there. Yeah, the angels must've been looking out for me 'cause if I hadn't met the two friends who have been more like my sisters, I might've been dead.

The summer before I started at Western I was seeing this guy Petey. I had met him when I was staying at my cousin Quiana's house over in East Baltimore. Sitting on the white asphalt steps, I was getting my hair braided when he pulled up to the corner to collect some money from some niggas.

He was driving a white two-door Legend with tinted windows and gold trimming. As he got out my eyes could not leave him. He was a red nigga with defined muscles and dark curly locs. Nobody else in the hood wore their hair like that, especially the niggas. That made him even more intriguing. His legs looked like he ran track, they were so strong, but what I liked most was his height. I had just turned fourteen in June and was already 5'6." He looked to be taller than six feet. Quiana told me he was one of the niggas who had just come up on the streets and that made me want to see what he was about.

There was going to be a party later on at this girl Tyeesha's house and it went without saying that everyone from Barclay St. would be making an appearance. Tyeesha was known for having the best parties and young, grown-ass girls like me and Quiana knew that niggas like Petey would be there representin' their respective crews.

By the time she finished my hair it was around six in the evening. We started getting ready immediately after. Quiana was my first cousin but the only time we got together was during one of our infamous slumber parties or during the summer breaks since I lived over West on Baker St.

The party was about ten minutes away but we needed a whole two hours to get dressed. I swear Quiana is ghetto as hell. To this day she will still put tons of powder around her neck. It's almost like she doesn't realize how dark we are. We're both the same complexion but you couldn't tell her that.

We were dressed alike with booty shorts, DKNY T-shirts we had bought from Renee the booster and fresh, white Reebok Classics. The summer was coming to an end and there was this feeling in the air that said that everyone was going to make the most out of Tyeesha's last house party. On the way there, we hooked up with other girls from around the way, niggas we had grown up with, and from there, just traveled together.

When we got to the door, Tyeesha's mother, Ms. Carolyn was taking dollar bills and putting them into a jar. She was going to make a killing because she not only made space in her basement and her backyard, but also in her upstairs living room. And she dared anybody to fuck with the plastic on her couches.

Their cousin was a local DJ so they had no problem with the music. As soon as we hit the doorway, we could see the club music taking its effect. We were early but there were still enough people in there to have fun. Niggas was competing against girls with the old dances like the Percolator and the Tap. Me and Quiana got our cups of punch and headed downstairs to stand on the wall while we waved to people still strolling through the door.

We were talking to Trina and Peaches, the neighborhood freaks when he walked in twenty-deep with his boys. Petey had changed his outfit and was wearing a black Nike sweatsuit with matching Jordans. He flashed me this grin and I was embarrassed for an instant for being caught staring at him so intensely. I continued to watch him until we made eye contact. To my surprise he motioned for me to come over. I walked like I was under hypnosis or some shit.

He told me he had been watching me for the past summers that I had been staying with Quiana and Aunt Charlene and he could see that I had turned into a big girl. *Could he tell that I had had sex?* I was getting so lost in his light gray eyes that if he had told me to hop on one foot that night, I would've turned that shit into a new dance.

He asked if I wanted to leave the party and chill with him. *Hell yeah I did*, so I told Quiana where I was going, and of course her and all the other broads standing against the wall were showing nothing but green on their faces. Outside he asked if I was hungry and since I had only eaten a chicken box earlier, I was ready to grub down.

I had never been inside of a nigga's car, so when he opened the door and I sat down, I didn't know how to act. I kept repositioning myself in the seat and looking at him out the corner of my eye. I didn't know where we were going and throughout the whole ride we kept to ourselves unless we commented on a song we both liked. He did say that he couldn't believe I was only fourteen. I couldn't believe I was out with a nigga that was twenty-two.

We pulled up to the IHOP on Loch Raven Blvd. and I waited for him to open my door the same way he had done before we left the party. When he got out he looked back at me waiting for him and laughed. I guess he thought I was like one of those other dumb hoes that would've been happy just to ride in his shit.

Months after that we would laugh because he said I must've assumed he was a gentleman and shit. But I didn't care how many bitches he had dealings with, I made sure he always opened the door for me.

After we did IHOP we went out and had drinks at his friend's bar. I pretended like I had been drinking before, but I think he figured it out when I ordered a Shirley Temple. It was okay because he said he never touched alcohol and that it was poison. He just came to the bar for the atmosphere.

I didn't get home to Aunt Charlene's until three that morning. I thought Petey was going to expect sex but it never came up and he turned out to be as cool as a brother or male cousin.

There were about two more weeks before high school would start when my mother started flippin' out. Me and Petey were still hanging out and she had started complaining about me coming in late and was basically giving me the same shit she did with Rico before she put him out. I didn't have a problem coming home at a decent hour, but I was tired of laying down and getting only three or four hours of sleep 'cause I would spend four tryna tune her ass out. So I started staying at Petey's house and sleeping in his bed while he did what he had to at night.

One night I came home to my mother's house and it was only about twelve when she started her shit. "Chanel, I told ya fast ass about comin' through my door all times of night. This is *my fuckin' house* and you will do as I say."

It's no wonder where I get my foul mouth. She could never talk to me without using some curse word. By this time I was calling her by her first name. She wasn't treating me like a mother should, so I didn't respect her as my mother. "Rochelle, go ahead wit' all that shit 'cause I'm not tryna hear it tonight."

"Go on wit' that shit? Oh, you a grown lil' bitch now, huh?"

Before I could turn around to answer her she was slapping me in the face and pulling my hair. It was like I became another person because within seconds, thoughts of her shitty ways triggered something in me and I had her on the ground *slapping her and pulling her hair*. She told me to get the fuck out and to never come back until I showed her some respect. *Me show her respect?* I laughed in her face and paged Petey *911*. He was there in ten minutes. Suffice to say my address changed. The time we had been spending together had created this level of comfort that made moving in with him the best choice.

We were living in his apartment on Belvedere Ave. and I felt so much older than fourteen. My living situation with him made sex unavoidable, and it wasn't that I was scared, I had just come to believe that it was something dirty. About a week after my move we were laying in bed watching videos when he started caressing my titties. He must've felt my body tense up because he asked me what was wrong. I felt like I had been through so much with my mother and Ronnie that all I could do was cry.

He looked scared but he held me and asked if he could show me what it was supposed to feel like. I agreed that he could and he was really gentle. It didn't feel like he was trying to take something from me. After that we only did something if I wanted to and that was only because he had taught me how to suck dick.

I am forever grateful to Petey for that shit. I think it's the one thing that has gotten me where I am today. After I mastered the art of sucking dick that's all he ever wanted. And I say mastered because he was packin'. I thought big dicks like his only existed in the flics but his told another story.

He told me that a bitch's pussy wasn't worth shit if she didn't have bombin-ass head to go along with the package. I can agree to that 'cause I don't know how many niggas I've met that complain about the tired head they've received.

School had started and I felt like I belonged when I looked at my surroundings. Western was covered with girls that looked just like me, only they weren't sitting in a car as phat as I was. Petey had pulled up to the school with his bangin-ass system. All that belted out the speakers when I was with him was Nas, Public Enemy or anything dealing with the struggle.

"Don't you get tired of playin' this?" I asked him. "We been doin' *Illmatic* and *It Was Written* all fuckin' summer."

I was sitting there beside him like it was my shit and he was my chauffeur with my lips poked out. If he was going to blast Nas I had asked him to play 'Street Dreams.' He said he refused to glamorize the streets. When he looked in the mirror didn't he realize he *was* the streets?

"Stop talkin' slick baby girl," was the only response he gave me until 'Black Girl Lost' finished playing. We sat there until the bell rang and I saw the throng of girls heading inside. Petey turned down the radio and turned to me like I was his daughter or some shit. "Aight baby girl, here is some money for you. I'll be waitin' when you get out."

I looked down at what he handed me and noticed that there was at least $500 in my hand. *Where the fuck did he think I was going?* "Petey, why all the money?"

I knew I shouldn't have asked any questions. Shit, most bitches would've been happy with fifty dollars. Forget that—even five.

"I don't know, just in case. Girl go 'head in there. Everybody is already in the building and you sittin' here questionin' me. Oh what, you don't want it? Well give it back."

"Nigga, is you crazy, yeah I want it," I said, playfully licking his ear.

"I told you about that *nigga* shit. That's not a positive word to use when referring to the brothas."

I rolled my eyes once again to let him know how tired I was of hearing his conscious rhetoric. Petey's parents were Five Percenters. They had passed that Black Pride, *I am God* mentality onto him. When he wasn't hustling, he devoted his time to books on Black thought and throat-choking frankincense-burning sessions.

It wasn't that I disrespected that aspect of his life, I was just never exposed to it. When I questioned his love for *his people* and his coinciding need to sell drugs, he said he only distributed to the crackers in Pigtown. I didn't know how much of a truth that was, but if it gave him a clear conscious at the end of the day, I could care less.

"Okay Petey X," I joked him. "Me and my five bills are off to a first day of school."

"You bein' funny now? Give it back," he said, jokingly putting me into a chokehold and tickling me.

"Stop! You messin' up my hair," I yelled.

"Let that pretty stuff grow natural and kinky and you won't have to worry about *messin'* it up," he said, moving his neck around like a girl with attitude.

"Neva that!" I said and leaned over to give him a deep kiss.

"Hmm, give me one more and give me my money back," he said, holding my chin.

"Tah! See you at three," I said and reached into the backseat for my notebook. I squirmed away from him, kissed his cheek and slammed the door.

*Was he crazy?* I was pumped as hell that he would give me that much money and I was already happy with all the clothes he had been buying me. I went from Reebok Classics to Anna Sui and other designer shit I had never heard of. On that first day of school I had on nothing but Armani, but it didn't blow my mind like it would have done for most girls. I was just happy to have a place to stay and I think he knew that.

When I got to homeroom all eyes were on me and I knew most of them were the same ones that had been watching me while I sat in the car. They were going around the room introducing themselves and when they got to me, there was nothing but silence. Everybody wanted to hear what I had to say, only I wasn't pressed for them to know me.

After that embarrassing shit was over I turned to my right and listened to this girl Latosha who was really a sophomore making up the Spanish class she had failed the year before. I could tell she liked hearing her voice. All she talked about was her boyfriend who was coming to get her after school in his new Suburban. *Big deal*, he was probably fuckin' the girl she was talking to.

Before I left homeroom and first period several girls had asked if I had anybody to eat lunch with. High school was supposed to be about friendships and all that, but I wasn't feelin' them. They only wanted to get close to me because of the clothes I had on and the car I had stepped out of that morning. I never gave them a second thought. Besides, I was so used to being alone with my thoughts that eating lunch solo wouldn't bother me in the least. The school day was coming to an end when I met the two girls who became lifelong friends.

I was on my way to seventh period when I got a page from Petey. His code was *01.* Western had pay phones near the cafeteria so I went to use one. He told me he wouldn't be able to come and get me until four so I could wait or catch a cab. Fuck that, I wasn't waiting a whole hour, so I told him not to worry. I would get home. Only I didn't know how to get to our house from Western.

Of course I was late getting to seventh and when I walked in there was only one empty seat next to a girl I had seen earlier during lunch when I stood behind her in the snack line. The reason I remembered her is because she had long healthy hair, the kind that only needed a perm once or twice a year. If there was a hairstyle I would have liked to copy, it was hers. I sat down wanting to ask her for her stylist's number, but she was talking to the girl sitting to her left.

23

The other girl's hair was pulled into a long ponytail. She already had the cat eyes and dimples, and with a little makeup she would actually look like she belonged in high school. I sat down and they both looked over at me and smiled. It wasn't like the other phony shits I had been getting all day.

The one with the hair, Nikola, introduced herself and the other one as Chelsea. *Were they sisters or something?* They had the same prissy names, but I was one to talk with a name like Chanel. I know I must've seemed like a bitch but the truth was, I was surprised that they were asking me something besides, *where I got my Armani T-shirt*.

We exchanged numbers and Nikola acted surprised when I gave her my pager number, but it was only because Petey didn't like for a lot of people to know the house number. Chelsea gave me her number. I noticed the first three digits and made a note to ask her if she lived near Belvedere.

Nikola had finally stopped talking when I got the nerve to ask her about her hair. She got real quiet like she didn't want to tell me. I found out she did the shit herself and I knew I wouldn't be going back to my regular hairdresser Wendy unless I needed her to do a tight-ass weave.

I ended up meeting Chelsea at her locker and we caught the #44 together. Turned out, she lived ten minutes from me on Fenwick. I liked her right away. She was quiet like me, but when she started talking, she had a lot to say about shit going on with the world or whatever.

Nikola was sweet too but she talked a lot, sometimes too much. We got into it a lot because I would simply tell her to shut the fuck up. Now that we're older, she knows it's out of love.

I loved them both and again like I said before, if it wasn't for them I might be dead, 'cause when family turns their backs on you, all you have is friends. But that's something I had to learn the hard way.

It was the start of my junior year and I had learned a lot from Petey in those two years that we had been together. I made runs with him and saw how he made his money. I always got a rush cruising the streets with him at night and got excited when I saw him enforce power on niggas—mental or physical—who tried to fuck with his paper. I got real good at playing mind games to get what I wanted.

Another Monday rolled around, and I wasn't looking forward to school. My body was relaxed from the night before. Some bitch named Missy had called the house, claiming to have his baby. I went off on her and then him. Petey was never the one to argue. His Libra ass was too calm and balanced to even take it there with me. By the end of the night he had fucked me so good that I forgot what I was fussing for. I swear there is no better sex than make up or angry sex.

Anyway, winter had arrived and it was brick outside. If Petey couldn't take me to school I wasn't going. There was *no way* I was catching a cab in zero below weather especially since he had taught me how to drive. I still needed to get my license, but I knew that if I asked I would have a whip, license or not.

I was cuddled up against him and wasn't trying to move from my warm side of the bed. I had a habit of burying my face in his chest while we laid up. There was always a trace of myrrh on his neck that found its way to my nose. Even the black and white posters of Bob Marley and Malcolm X were telling me to go back to sleep. I lifted my head a little to see the television and saw that Channel 13 had a listing for school closings. I couldn't believe the superintendent was closing schools for a suspected winter storm. We would normally have to go even with six inches. The privileged county students always had a guaranteed day off whenever anything fell out of the fuckin' sky.

I sat up from the circular bed and looked outside. The snow was coming down thick and heavy. I waited for my school to show up 'cause sometimes they tried to get slick and would have us come in that bitch two hours late. I looked at the bottom of the screen and saw Western flash three times with the rest of the school closings. Satisfied, I turned over and took my tired ass back to sleep.

I was having the strangest dream where it felt like I was falling. I couldn't believe how real the shit was. Next thing I knew, I was being pulled off the bed by a nigga with a black mask and bubble coat. I didn't know where Petey was. I hadn't even heard him leave. I didn't know what was happening.

"Bitch, tell me where that nigga Petey keep his stash. Crack slick and you won't be around to tell him I was here." His voice was raspy and cruel.

It was happening so fast that the stash was the last thing on my mind. The only thing I did know was that the silver-plated steel against my temple was real. All I could see were my brains against the wall. I didn't think about my life, what I could've been, the stuff people say they see when they know they're going to die. All I saw was the nothingness of death, and if I thought about anybody it was my brother.

"What?" Was all I could say. My voice, my hands, everything was shaking.

"Don't fuck wit' me! I know the shit is in here."

He took the gun from my face and turned towards the closet. He was knocking boxes of shoes off the shelves and breaking all my good shit that was around the room, just going crazy. I pulled the sheet over my chest and backed up against the headboard.

I thought for a second and then my mind regained clarity. I remembered that the shit was in the closet under a weak board in the floor. I had discovered it one day when I hooked school to wait for a FedEx package of weed. There were large Ziploc bags of cocaine and vials. Curious, I had dipped my index finger inside and rubbed the powder on my gums. It was like an instant reaction, like an injection of Novocaine. The sudden effect scared me and I quickly snapped the bag closed.

Hearing the glass vase shatter on the floor brought me back to the situation at hand. I knew I should've picked up the phone to dial the police, but because Petey really did have some shit in there, I would've been fucked too.

*What did he want from me?* I was still staring off, shook and speechless when he stormed back into the bedroom. He answered my question when he yanked the sheets off me. I had started sleeping without clothes since me and Petey had become more intimate. So when he saw that I was naked, I already knew what was about to happen. I tried to inch to the other side of the bed but he grabbed me by the right ankle while he held the gun in his left. All I could see was his scary-ass eyes plotting to do whatever he wanted with me. He took the gun and pointed it between my legs.

"Open your fuckin' legs!"

I couldn't believe the shit was happening to me again but I did it. Only this time I spread them wide like I wanted him. He took the gun and ran it up against my legs and thighs before jamming it into me. It felt like all the wind had been knocked out, and it was then that I prayed. I prayed that whatever he was going to do would end quickly.

"Bitch, I'm gon' let you live this time, but you tell that mutherfucker that I'll be back. And the next time this gat is goin' inside his mouth instead of his bitch's pussy."

I just laid there lifeless afterward, like I didn't know or give a fuck if I was dead or alive. I heard the phone ring and sat up, startled, and realized it was over. I still had my life. I let it ring and grabbed the gray sweatsuit that was near my foot and started getting my thoughts together.

Whoever the nigga was, he said he would be back and I wasn't taking any chances on him bluffing or really shooting my ass the next time. I knew Petey would be out doin' dirt until the evening since he had changed his routine. I wanted to page him, but there was no way I was letting him talk me into staying. I would have to talk to him later. Instead, I called a Yellow cab and the dispatcher said someone would be there in forty-five minutes. I thought that was too long but figured I might be waiting even longer if I tried to catch a hack.

I went to the kitchen, stepping over broken glass and turned over furniture to grab some trash bags. I looked at the door and it was locked like always. When I saw the opened window I knew that was how he had got in. I locked and slammed it shut before I ran back to the bedroom. I grabbed everything I could pick up from my side of the closet and then the stuff from the floor. Packing up, I had six large bags of clothes and shoes, most of it was stuff I had never even worn.

The only personal thing I had was a picture me and Petey had taken at *Kingsdominion.* That's all I had left of Petey 'cause I didn't count on seeing him again. It was obvious that shit was thick, and because I hadn't talked to him or even began to comprehend the threat on my life, I could only imagine what he was experiencing or about to face.

I was scanning the room when I heard the horn honking. I almost shit on myself, I was so jumpy. I had four of the bags in my hand while I kicked the other two to the door. I was so scared the cab was going to pull off that I almost tripped over them going down the steps. Finally inside the cab and away from the cold air, I told the driver to take me back home to Baker St.

I didn't have anywhere else to go and I couldn't go to Aunt Charlene's. She had Quiana and was taking care of Quiana's older sister's kids—all five of them. There was no way I was being cramped in that house. Mafuckas were already sleeping on the floor.

While he drove away I looked back at the apartment and let out a long sigh of exhaustion. Things were finally sinking in. I could've been killed. The tears were falling without me realizing as I thought about Petey. I was scared for his life more than anything. He was still in the streets probably unaware that someone was out to get him. Choking on tears, I wiped them away and told myself to be strong. That was something he would've told me if he was near.

The snow was coming down heavier than before, and his driving didn't seem to be getting me anywhere. I looked at the meter and it seemed to jump from nine dollars to 15 within seconds and we weren't even over West yet. I reached into my pocket and counted all the crumpled up bills. I had about $1,300 left. Since Petey had been giving me at least two hundred everyday, I had been spending like crazy—on dumb shit too. I only had what I had left because of the weather. It was too cold to go anywhere and spend.

When he pulled up to Rochelle's house I gave him a fifty-dollar bill. If I didn't have so much shit to carry I would've left his slow ass with an unpaid fare. I still had the key to my mother's dilapidated rowhouse so I went to unlock the door. I heard the bottom lock click and I thought about what she would say. *Would she let me back in even though I hadn't seen her in two years?* When I went to unlock the top lock, it wouldn't turn. So she had got the shit changed on me. Figures.

I was so cold that I couldn't even feel my fingers. In my rush I had thrown my coat into one of the bags. I banged on the door with my bare hands and when that didn't work I started kicking. I knew she was in there 'cause I saw her move away from the upstairs curtain. "I saw you already, so open the door!" I screamed.

I couldn't believe she was going to make me stand outside in a fucking snowstorm. There was a pay phone at the corner, but I wasn't about to carry all my shit for five blocks so I sat all but two bags in front of her door. I didn't think anyone would bother them and thought they'd be mistaken for trash.

After sliding and falling several times on my ass I reached the phones. Nikola picked up on the first ring.

"Kola yo, I need a favor. I don't have anywhere to go and my fuckin' mother won't open the door for me."

"Where are you?" she asked.

"I'm at the corner of Baker and Poplar Grove."

"Do you have a ride?"

"I can get one."

"Okay, I'll tell my mother," she said. "You remember my address?"

"2055, right?"

"No, 2045."

"Aight, see you."

Now, that was fucked up. I couldn't even go to my own mother. I had to call a friend. But the thing is Nikola never asked me any questions, she was just there. She didn't even ask her mother first. I guessed she figured she would deal with all that later. My hair and face were being whipped so hard by the wind that my runny nose never had the chance to drip. I turned and walked back to get my clothes before hailing a cab and I saw that my shit was gone.

I didn't see anybody else walking around so I assumed that my mother had taken it. Fuck her, if she was that sleazy to take my shit, she could have it. I walked back to the main street and had to wait twenty more minutes before I saw another cab.

When I got to Nikola's, her mother Ms. Diane answered the door. She had the friendliest smile I had ever seen and I wanted to run into her arms and tell her about everything that had happened. I stood on the top step and waited for her to tell me I couldn't come in.

Instead she grabbed my bags and waved to the cab driver. Inside, their house smelled like burnt cinnamon and hair caught in a flat iron. I figured Nikola was doing someone's hair in the basement. I swear that I have never felt as safe as I did at that moment. Ms. Diane never asked me what happened and told me I could stay there until I got things together. Her voice was so soft and I don't recall ever once hearing her yell. Unlike my house where my mother thought screams and curse words was the only way to communicate.

Nikola opened the basement door moments later with a worried look. The beauty mark beneath her left eye always seemed to jump when she was stressin'. I followed her to the extra bedroom in the back where Ms. Diane kept her sewing machine and ironing board. She pulled a towel and washcloth out the closet and told me I could keep my things there.

"What happened Chanel?" she finally asked in a cautious tone.

"This nigga tried to kill me, that's what!"

"Who, Petey?"

"No, somebody looking for him."

I told her the story and cried. She listened quietly like she was reliving the whole experience with me. When I finished I was so tired and could only see a hot bath and a bed. She hugged me awkwardly and told me she was going downstairs to start some lady's hair and that she would see me later.

Even with her subtle concern for me, Nikola was still the same standoffish person I had become used to. I had never seen her show any real emotion unless someone was preventing her from getting what she wanted. No matter, I knew her concern was real and started taking my things out of the two trash bags that my mother didn't take. There was so much to sort.

I wanted the time alone, and I needed to call Petey to tell him what happened, but I didn't want to disrespect Ms. Diane. I had only been in their house for thirty minutes and I was about to page the nigga who had put me in the situation. No matter, I had to know something.

I reached for the cordless on the wall when Ms. Diane walked in. "Chanel honey, I changed the sheets on the other bed in Kola's room for you, okay?"

"Umm okay, thank you Ms. Diane."

She was really showing me love so I felt like I had no choice but to offer her something. I pulled the money out of my pocket and peeled off six notes. "Here, Ms. Diane. I appreciate everything."

"Chanel I don't need that. You keep your money baby. You're only sixteen and I don't expect you to pay rent around here. As long as you're in school, you can stay here as long as you need to. We can even turn this room into your own space if you want."

I hoped she didn't think I was a charity case or something. True, I had a mother who didn't give a fuck if I had a place to stay or not, but I didn't want her to feel sorry for me.

She looked at me like she was reading my mind. "Chanel, everybody needs help sometime, I just hope you won't let your pride get in the way."

"I won't Ms. Diane."

"Okay sweetie, I'll be in the kitchen if you need me." She cupped my face lovingly with her tender fingers before she walked out.

When I heard her taking pots from the cabinets I went to her room and placed the money on her night table. I knew her sentiments were genuine, I just didn't want her to have any reason to put me out or tell me I wasn't pulling my weight in her house.

I went back to my room, got the cordless and took it to the bathroom. I ran my water and I paged Petey *911* along with their house number. As I waited, I called time so that I could hear the phone beep when he finally called back instead of allowing the phone to ring.

With the phone resting on my shoulder, I listened to the operator repeat for the third time that, *at the tone the time would be 6:13.* I was pouring the Avon bubble bath under the running water when I heard the beep, signaling that it was him calling back. My heart started racing. *Would he be mad at me for leaving? Had he seen the apartment?*

"Hello," I said softly.

"Hey baby girl, it's me."

"W'sup Petey, you alright?"

"Yeah, I'm fine. Listen, I know you had to do what you had to and I know I put you into a sticky situation, but shit is hot right now."

"I'm okay," I said, glad that he wasn't mad at me for leaving.

"Did that nigga hurt you?"

Yeah Petey was shook. Hearing him use the word *nigga* was unusual. "No, but he said he would be back."

"Well, I already picked up the shit he wanted. You got any money on you?"

"I got like six left. Why, you need it?" I asked.

"Nah, but I thought you might need somethin'."

"Where are you?"

"Tryna get the fuck outta dodge, but I wanna bring you somethin' before I leave. Where are you?"

I gave him the address and he told me he would be there in the next hour. I spent the time in between soaking and reflecting on the things I had been through that day. I cried again when I thought about Rochelle. My mother wasn't a mother at all. She had left me out in the cold—literally.

I got dressed and waited downstairs for Petey. After fifteen minutes I saw the black tint and threw on the blue Miu Miu puff coat he had bought me before we went on the ski trip two weeks before.

Upon reaching the door his face looked so tired, like he had been through some real shit as well. I opened the door and sat in my seat.

"You look so tired baby girl."

"I was thinkin' the same thing about you," I said.

He reached over and grabbed my leg while he rubbed his nose on my neck like he was smelling me for the last time. "Chanel, I'm gon' miss you but you understand that I have to go, right?"

It was just like him to get to the point. I knew not to question him. Whatever he had to do was for a reason, but I had to know why I was almost killed. "Petey who was that nigga that tried to kill me?"

Whatever response he gave, I couldn't be mad. I was living with a hustler and incidents like that came with the territory.

"Don't even worry about him. He won't be around to point that gun at anybody else, *ever*."

I understood then that the matter was taken care of so I turned to him and tried to tell him everything that was on my heart and on my mind since I didn't know when I would see him again, but the words never came. It was like my heart was keeping me from saying what I really felt, so I leaned over and kissed him with everything I had left and hoped that he understood what I was trying to say. I was saying thank you for showing me the only love I had ever known.

After I pulled away he reached into the backseat and handed me a quilted, black leather bowling bag with shiny gold Chanel emblems on both sides. "A Chanel bag for Chanel," he joked. I could tell he was attempting to cheer me up. I held the heavy bag and wondered what was inside. "It's about ten G's in there for you. Sorry I couldn't give you more but I had debts to pay before I bounce. You understand, right?"

I had no choice but to understand. All I could think about at that moment was all the money I was holding in my lap. I was only sixteen, *what would I do with it?* I nodded and leaned over to hug him once more while I let my hands run through his soft locs for the last time.

"Will I hear from you again?" I asked.

"You know there are no promises baby girl. Don't worry about me though, do what you have to. Take care of you and don't expect *nobody* to look out for you, *but you.* Take no shorts wit' these niggas out here and look both ways."

That's the last thing I remembered before I fell asleep that night. I prayed for Petey but deep down I knew that no prayer could change the path he was on. He was caught up and I didn't know it then, but I would be following close behind him, only I would be playing a different kind of game.

We were walking through Towson Town Center after leaving the Gap. Me and Nikola did enough shopping to fill five large bags with clothes and Chelsea was at the counter like she said she would be. The caper went smoother than I expected. I could see that she was nervous as she slipped the sensor remover in my bag like it was nothing. Before we went to Nordstrom we stopped at the bathroom and condensed what was in our bags. Nikola moved the metal device from my bag to hers and we were on our way.

Entering the store's upper level I looked around and remembered the shit Petey used to lace me with. It was nothing for him to come and waste five G's. Now we were about to lift enough shit to double that amount.

I looked at Nikola. Nobody would ever know she was the mastermind behind the shit we were about to do. She looked like the typical college student. Her light brown hair was pulled back with a red headband and she wore a denim dress with red stitching and red and white shell heads.

I guess I didn't look like I was about to participate either. I had on an almost identical khaki dress and my hair was pulled back into a neat bun. The huge diamond hoop earrings made the ponytail okay. They were a gift from a guy named Maurice I had met shortly after Petey left.

Maurice was a lot older, probably thirty-five. He was too nice though, so all I did was dog him and treat him like shit. I didn't even have to give him any pussy. After our first date he seemed so pressed to be out with a pretty bitch like me that he gave me whatever he had. He was one of the top agents at an insurance company (yawn) and had a wife and kids, but I think me being only seventeen and still in high school got him off.

I told him I wanted the earrings but I didn't know he would go and blow two paychecks on the fuckers. They were priced at $6,500. When his wife asked him about the missing money, he started telling me his problems. I ain't give a fuck! I told him we couldn't see each other anymore and that he could take that crying shit to his wife 'cause I didn't need it.

We were walking through each section when Nikola stopped at Prada. I was a Gucci girl myself so that's where I headed. We would be going to Jay-Z's *Hard Knock Life* tour that was coming to town. It would be the first time we put her money-gettin' plan into action. Everything we discussed in the basement was about to be put to the test.

I picked up a pair of black mink hot pants that were just long enough to cover my pussy. I didn't have to look to see that they were worth a good stack. While I searched for a top, a white bitch with a pointy nose came over like she was tryna get in my business and shit.

"Can I help you with something?" she asked in her nasal voice.

"Did I call you?" I said with much attitude. Her pale face turned all red on me but she took her happy ass back to the counter. What I really wanted to say was, *Bitch did I call you*, but I wasn't tryna fuck up the plan.

I found a matching top and a black floor-length coat with mink trimming and was off to find something for Chelsea. She wasn't very fashion-conscious and I thought she would've been happy either way with a T-shirt and jeans, but I eventually found a girly type of dress by Christian Dior. Not exactly my style, but the built in bustier would accent her breasts since that's something she was always complaining about. Plus, the size 2 ensemble was pink, so I knew she would go crazy when she saw it.

I began looking for Nikola. She had started shopping for Chelsea too 'cause when I got near her she was holding up a Prada leather handbag, the same color as the dress. I showed her the dress and she laughed out loud.

"Yup, that's her," she said, fingering the pink material.

Nikola held up a black lace dress with a silky material underneath that would cover her essentials. The dress looked more like a shirt but that was cool with me. The only one who would have on actual clothes was Chelsea, but even her dress was revealing as fuck.

"Bitch I hope that shit comes with a skirt or something," I said.

"No, but there's some lollipop shorts attached that says Prada on the right ass cheek. The shit is off the hook!"

We were getting excited over things we weren't even paying for. Nikola looked at what I had in my hand and frowned her face.

"*You know* you gon' have to grab some other shit."

"For what?" I whispered.

"*Because*, it'll be a front for what we really want."

"Okay," I said.

She was the expert so I took her word for it and went to look for some other stuff. There were plenty of fly things I wanted so I had no problem finding *other shit*. Feeling a little fidgety and guilty, I followed her to the dressing room when I saw that she was finished.

Let Nikola tell it and she would say the world owed her. She had no qualms about lifting whatever she wanted. Her favorite saying when it came to lifting was "The best crimes are the ones done in the open." It could be something as simple as a pack of gum. She wasn't paying for it if she didn't have to. We had all been out shopping together when she said she was broke. Who else but Nikola came away with the most things—the most expensive too. Said the government was a bunch of crooks anyway and that it was better she robbed them before they got her. Petey would've agreed with her completely. He used the same theory when he would explain the drug game.

We were in the mall on a Tuesday afternoon when it wasn't that crowded. I guessed that was the reason no one was monitoring the dressing room. "Okay Chanel, give me what you and Chelsea are wearin'," Nikola said, bringing me out of my nervous daze.

I handed her the things I had in my left arm. So I wouldn't seem suspicious, I still tried on the other stuff I had taken in there. There was a linen Michael Kors dress that fit me perfectly. My titties were sitting out like two big melons. I bent over in the mirror like I was Marilyn Monroe. Kola heard me laughing and asked me what was so funny. I threw the dress into her fitting room and told her I wanted it too.

While trying on a pair of Frankie B's, Nikola knocked on the door. "It's time to go, Chanel."

I thought something might be wrong so I quickly changed my clothes and met her in front of the dressing room entrance. I just knew security was waiting outside to take our asses away.

"W'sup?" I asked her, heart skipping beats.

"Oh, nothin'. I just took care of everything. Now, how much money did you bring wit' you? Please say you brought at least five hundred." Seemingly her round eyes were more expressive than ever. The rush of stealing had distorted her facial features.

"Yeah, I did."

"Okay, so let's go over it again. We have to seem as normal as possible, so we're goin' to buy other miscellaneous shit like shoes and accessories."

"Cool. Now am I payin' for Chelsea's shit or are you?" I asked.

"I brought about five hundred too so we can go half if her shoes are too much."

I looked down at the bags she was carrying and they looked the same. She packed our shit away with mad skills, yet from the time we left the dressing room to the time we made it to the shoe department my heart felt like jello.

It didn't take long to find Chelsea's shoes. Me and Nikola reached for the same matching Via Spiga's that were leather like the handbag. We agreed that $185 wasn't bad and started looking for our own stuff. Chelsea was going to look as sexy as she had when we went to our senior prom.

Nikola found some black Donna Karan stiletto sandals with feathers in between the thongs. I knew they were gonna set her back at least $350. She made me sick the way she could slide her size 7 into any fuckin' shoe, but she didn't have anything on my pretty feet, size 9 and all.

I just knew I was going to have a problem finding something for me. The size nines always seemed to go first. My eyes landed on the thigh high Richard Tyler's and I didn't care if I had to pull out extra dough. They would set the shorts and jacket off lovely. I took a deep breath before I picked up the display and exhaled when I saw that they were only $400. They were worth it, seeing that they had the same mink trim as my jacket. I was glad I had brought eight hundred with me.

It didn't matter that my toes wouldn't be out, those boots said one thing, *I was a bad bitch*, and with a price tag like that, I could make a nigga wish he *could* lick my toes. Fuck it, the boots were so tight somebody was licking the stilettos on those mafuckas.

We sat down with our shoes and waited for someone to come and help us. I was surprised when we looked up and saw Lila, a girl who had graduated with us. Lila was my same beautiful dark complexion and was representin' for the thick bitches. Most chicks her size would've been scared to wear the short shit she put on, but she wore it like she didn't have that natural thickness to her thighs or the extra handles on her stomach. I wasn't mad at her 'cause I flaunted my thickness around too, every chance I got.

"Hey ladies, how are you today?" she said with the infamous Western smile, half-phony and half-surprised. And where did that proper tone come from? The bitch knew she was from Lexington Terrace.

"W'sup Lila," we said together.

Nikola handed her the shoe she wanted along with Chelsea's size 8. I asked her to bring my boot and crossed my fingers that there was at least one pair in the back. She came back with the three boxes and Nikola and me were both relieved.

I pulled the boots over my thighs and walked back and forth in front of the mirror five or six times. They were hot! And they were going to make me the hot shit right along with 'em. We took them to the counter and Nikola started scheming again. "Check this out Lila, you think you can give us the Western hookup?"

Lila let out a loud hesitant laugh but she knew what we were talking about. "I don't know. The cameras in here are off the hook," she said.

I knew a way around it so I put my idea out there. "How 'bout you charge us clearance price and we slip you $150. That's more than you get wit' commission, right?"

She hesitated again but the fast money was sounding good to her. "How you gon' give it to me wit' all the cameras?" She had dropped her overly proper dialect *real* quick.

Picking up the closest shoe on display, I instructed her to bring me out any size. She came back and I opened the lid, pretending like it wasn't the shoe for me. I set the shoe in the box and I placed the money behind the tongue. Lila wasn't slow 'cause I saw her peepin' my move.

Our total only came to $175. Now that was what a Western hookup was about. Sisters looking out for sisters. We had more money left over than we thought so we accessorized and stopped at the MAC counter. I got some powder that was as close to Chelsea's complexion as possible. She was practically white so any color along those lines was good for her.

We walked out and I held my breath once again. I prayed Nikola had gotten rid of all the sensors and hoped there weren't any silent ones. She walked out like she had been doing the shit forever. *Me?* I felt that old familiar rush of adrenaline I used to experience when I was with Petey taking care of his business.

Passing the Gap, I waved to Chelsea. I could see that she was glad we weren't being escorted in handcuffs. I pointed to my watch to let her know we would be back for her at 10:30. The mall closed at 9:30 but the Gap would have her in there another hour folding shit that would only get messed over the next day. I didn't have the patience for that bullshit. And as easy as Nikola's plan had gone, I was beginning to understand the logic. *Why the fuck was I going to work so hard for some shit that didn't pay off?*

After that first time of putting one of Nikola's plans into action it was hard for me to doubt anything she said. When she sat and thought shit out, no matter how ridiculous things seemed at first, she always ended up making me feel like I could face whatever came my way. That was the first of many schemes. Two years later Nikola was still plotting and Chelsea's wedding had to be the ultimate. But even she couldn't prepare herself for that day in March when so-called great plans started unraveling and falling apart at the seams.

Chelsea Victor

Before I knew about a favorite color, mine was pink. It seemed so perfect and I even went as far as choosing cartoons like the Pink Panther over the Smurfs. On my eighth birthday my mother surprised me with a pink and white cake, and to me it resembled a smaller version of a huge wedding cake. In each corner there was a small pink bow and in the center my mother had asked the decorator to include a picture I had taken on a class trip. It was so cute how in the picture I had on a shirt that had pink bows connecting the shoulder straps.

The party was one of my happiest memories. Of course there were pink balloons and pink streamers connecting every wall. When it was time to blow out the candles my demon brother Michael beat me to it. I cried until Daddy hit him upside the head and lit them again. Later I opened my gifts that included a pink *Let's Get Physical* workout outfit, tape and everything.

My five closest friends were allowed to stay for the sleepover that night and we stuffed our faces with chocolate ice cream and candy. We were only in elementary school but stayed up late talking about our weddings and our future husbands. Back then I swore that whoever my husband was he would have to look and act just like my Daddy. Yeah, I was a true Daddy's girl even after his demeanor seemingly changed overnight towards me.

My father, Reginald Victor was tall, very dark and handsome. Before I even knew what to look for in boys, I liked to look at his face. He towered over my mother Clarissa who was 5'11." My maternal Grandmother Cleo was Italian and had given her the same olive skin and green eyes. I was happy to have the same piercing eyes and my mother's deep dimples, but I wish I had inherited my daddy's smooth chocolate skin. It made him look strong and I always saw my paleness as another sign of timidness, along with my petite frame.

At thirteen I noticed a change in my body. I got my period and my body went from straight up and down, to curves from who knows where. I was still thin, but I could finally wear a bra and my butt helped me graduate from the junior section at Macy's. Daddy saw the change too because I went from his princess to Chelsea. We stopped playing games like Scrabble and Clue and he was focusing more on my brothers Reginald and Michael.

They were big like him so they used the male bond to their advantage and started playing football and basketball. I saw that he was into them and sports so I started running track. All throughout middle school he never missed a competition but when I got on Western's track team I can only remember him coming out to see me twice.

My mother was never into sports but she was always there cheering me on. She didn't have to work since my father had his own repair shop on Greenmount Ave. called Victor Autocare, which was very lucrative. I was always disappointed to see her sitting in the stands without him. We had no connection. Maybe I saw so much of her that I disliked in myself. She never spoke up if she firmly believed in something. My father always had the first *and* last say. And I always thought she should be doing more with her life than just cooking and cleaning.

I had seen the pictures of her before she met my father and she was a virtual bombshell. An international model who had done shows in places like Milan and New York. She was living in New York when she met my father at *Junior's* while he was up there visiting my Uncle Stevie.

He saw her sitting at the bar and told her immediately he wanted her to be the mother of his children. My father was such a family man and so intense most of the time that I could never picture him using a pickup line like that, but back then being with Uncle Stevie, I guess anything was possible.

Uncle Stevie and my father both have that color complex, only my father settled down and married the woman he was attracted to physically, and mentally I assume. Uncle Stevie, who is now forty or so has never married and at every family gathering introduces us to a new girlfriend who is always as close to white as possible.

I think they've passed that preference onto my older brothers because Reginald, who is the oldest and looks just like daddy brings home girls who look like me. Mikey, two years younger than him and the same complexion as me, brings home the darkest girls he can find. But maybe it's not a color complex at all and opposites really do attract. I'll never forget the first time he met one of my best friends Chanel.

She was staying at my house for about a week while she waited for her apartment to be renovated and it was like Mikey was possessed. I could see where any man would be attracted to Chanel but for him it seemed like fatal attraction at first sight. He went out of his way to sit next to her during breakfast and dinner and even let her use the bathroom before him. Mikey thought he was so pretty that I don't ever remember him letting *me* into the bathroom first for as long as we lived in the same house. Her attraction to him was undeniable as well, I even think she gave him some that week. Chanel was my best friend and Nikola was the other. I had always wanted a sister and when I met them I had two for life.

When I got to Western I could feel the decades of tradition in the hallways. My mother had graduated in 1965 and when I saw her graduating class' banner on the wall I wondered how she must've felt on her first day at the prestigious school.

I wasn't nervous. My feelings were more of anxiety. I was looking forward to switching classes and making new friends. The girls around me looked like they had put more time into getting ready than putting together their notebooks, some of them were even empty handed.

My parents, especially my father, had put so much emphasis on me receiving the best grades in order to get into the "right" colleges that I had based most of my life on academics. My grades were the one thing that still got his attention. Even after I had quit the track team at Western I looked forward to progress reports and showing my father that I had maintained a 4.0. I was in desperate need of his approval.

Most of the girls at Western seemed to have one thing on their mind—fashion. The ones who were into books like me looked too nerdy. When I saw Nikola I thought she had the smarts like me but lacked the dryness I didn't desire in a friend. Her facial expression was bold and void of intimidation or weakness.

She was sitting alone writing in her notebook when I came to the table. She looked up and I saw that she had the most expressive eyes. They were telling me to sit down and that she was in need of a friend. I noticed that as she talked she seemed to think a long time before she spoke—like she wanted to control the conversation and let me know only what she wanted me to. I learned just from that day that her eyes said whatever she was feeling.

I was glad we had U.S. History together with Ms. Jones. I was never fond of history and if the discussions ever got too boring I would have someone to slip notes to. We were reintroducing ourselves when Chanel walked in. If Nikola's eyes were full of expression, giving her character, Chanel's gave her beauty. They made her look older than most of the girls in the class and they told a story like she had been through a lot. Her eyes, a chestnut brown that were probably just accented by her already mocha skin, were seductive and dreamy.

Chanel joined us and I wanted Nikola to stop talking long enough for me to hear this new girl's voice. I wanted to see if it went with her face. She finally spoke and it was brief and to the point. I was almost jealous when her and Nikola started talking about hair. It was like they had found common ground and I was left out of the picture. I thought I would have to start at square one with new friends until class was over.

Chanel wanted to know where I lived and asked if I knew my way home from Western. She met me at my locker at the end of the day and we caught one of the MTA shuttles waiting outside the school.

Sitting next to her during the ride, I felt important and mature, like there was more to me than good grades and pink ribbons. She seemed interested in my family and astonished that I lived with two parents, like the thought was foreign to her. I found her life just as fascinating. My jaw almost hit the floor when she told me she lived with her boyfriend. I didn't even get a real boyfriend until tenth grade and she was living with hers in the ninth.

After I got to know her better, I started riding to school with her and her boyfriend Petey. He never said too much in the car. I think he felt like I was invading their space because when we pulled up to school in the morning, they always sat in the car and talked for another fifteen or twenty minutes.

I had always thought life was about going to school to get a good job and live the perfect life, but when I met Chanel and Nikola I was exposed to other things. It was actually exciting to get in trouble every now and then. I even met my first boyfriend through Chanel.

His name was Derrick Mayers and he went to Poly High School, which is connected to Western. A long time ago it was an all boy's school before it turned co-ed. Some people say their curriculum is more strenuous than Western's. They focus on math and engineering and many of the graduates go to the best engineering schools in the world. Not that engineers and mathematicians are boring, but Western is known to produce some of the most interesting women who end up taking on society with noteworthy careers such as writers, politicians and filmmakers.

I saw Derrick during lunch when we went outside in the quadrangle. For most of the girls the lunch period was the highlight of the day. It was the only time we got a chance to interact with the opposite sex. The schools shared a quad that connected them to each other.

When I saw him I thought he was so fine. He was a little taller than most of the guys at Poly who were usually suffering from short-man syndrome and all of his features were dark. He was on the football team so he was always surrounded by a swarm of girls.

I was too shy to even look his way long enough to catch his eye. Luckily Chanel was friends with his cousin and called him over. He looked at me with those sleepy, brown eyes and I forgot about being shy and asked him for his number. If Chanel wasn't there I don't think I would've been so bold. We talked on the phone that night and every night after that.

I was a sophomore and he was a senior so I felt that made me have something over all the other girls. I knew most of them were envious of me because he played on Poly's Varsity team and had his picture in *The Sun* every week during the football season. When his team went against the opposing City High School I was right there cheering him on with Chanel and Nikola. I finally felt like I belonged to something bigger than me. I wasn't innocent Chelsea anymore, I had a boyfriend. Derrick and I were really getting attached when we started talking about going to school in New York. He planned on studying film and I wanted to be a journalist.

His prom was coming up and he asked me to go. I was more than ecstatic. Most sophomores envisioned themselves at someone else's prom but never got the chance. Me, I was getting ready for my first with the football team's quarterback. My father had met Derrick before and liked him, especially since they both loved sports and the fact that he had such detailed future goals. My mother was just sucked in by his looks.

The night of the prom Nikola was doing my hair and Chanel was doing my makeup when they brought up sex.

"So Chelz, you givin' up the booty tonight?" Chanel asked.

I loved when they called me by the nickname they had given me in ninth grade. Nikola knew I hated how proper Chelsea sounded so she shortened it to *Chel* and Chanel added the z. She said it gave me a little ghetto flavor.

"I thought about it but you know I always said I would wait until I got married," I said so adamantly.

"Married!" Nikola said, like she couldn't believe I had let the words escape from my lips. "Come on now, be real."

"Well if not when I'm married, at least at my *own* senior prom."

I knew the issue would come up sooner or later. Derrick and me had been on a lot of dates and things had gotten pretty physical. The furthest we had gone was the night we had stopped at his house after a movie. His parents were away on their annual vacation to Europe. I told him about my plans to wait and he respected that, but that night he told me he could do something else that would make me feel good and it didn't involve actual intercourse. I loved him so I trusted that whatever he was talking about would be okay.

His room was in the basement so it felt like we were in his own apartment. He told me to lay back and he unbuttoned my shirt. I looked up at the ceiling and prayed that what I was doing wasn't a sin. I wasn't fond of Catholic mass but I believed that prayer was a part of cleansing the soul.

I had on fitted jeans so when he started taking them off I had to help him. I lay back down and realized I only had on a bra and panties. Thank God I had worn one of my best pair. I was so nervous since nobody besides my mother had ever saw me without clothes. He kissed my stomach and told me how beautiful he thought my body was, and when he unhooked my bra he kissed my breasts and said he had never saw a pair so perfect.

Now if there was ever a lie I had heard, it was that. My mother had told me I was built like a model and that basically meant I had no breasts. A cute little butt maybe, but the breasts area was seriously lacking. I felt so exposed so I covered them with my hands while he kissed my forehead and eyelashes. Suddenly, he had my panties off and was placing my hands on his chest. Shortly after, he was making his way down my stomach with his lips and when he reached my wetness I could only let out a gasp. He was licking it slow and before I knew it my legs were clamping his neck and shaking uncontrollably. After that I felt closer to Derrick and in the back of my mind I knew that sex would be the next thing to happen.

At the prom I felt like I was on top of the world. We stayed on the dance floor the whole night and I felt safe, his arms were my shield. I wanted to hold onto that feeling so I didn't protest when he suggested we get a hotel room. He got us a room at the Marriott, the same hotel where the prom had taken place earlier. There was a huge bed and a view of the picturesque Inner Harbor. I remember thinking how beautiful the city's skyline was.

Derrick dimmed the lights and stood behind me as I gazed across the water. I was still caught up in the moment so when I felt his erection I didn't tense up like the numerous times before when I had felt him get hard against me.

The next thing I knew we were on the bed and our clothes were off. He was whispering in my ear and telling me how much he cared about me.

"Chelsea, you know I love you, right?"

"Yeah," I said with hesitation in my voice.

"See, we've been together for awhile and I want to be your first."

"Derrick, you know I want to wait."

"I know, but tonight has been so special that I want to make it last forever."

Before I knew it my nails were digging in his back, and I was letting the good sensation take over me. I had plenty to write about in my journal when I got home. Two weeks later my period was late and I had even *more* to say to Chanel and Nikola.

We left school during lunch to go to Nikola's basement. Not before the hall monitor Mr. Tibble hemmed us up though. He would write a student up even if they had a pass. The reason *we* always had such a hard time getting by him, was because Nikola joked his swept over, thinning hair every chance she got. I told him I needed him to walk me to the nurse's office so they could sneak pass him and leave out one at a time.

To my horror the test came out positive. I sat in Nikola's basement and cried. Not because I was scared, but because I was shocked at how quickly my future plans were washed away. Chanel came up with the solution I wasn't quite ready to hear.

"Listen Chelz, it'll be okay. Shit like this happens everyday so before it's too late we can go and take care of it."

"Take care of it? I can't kill my baby! It goes against the Catholic religion."

"Well ya father will kill you first anyway," Nikola said.

I hadn't thought about that. She was right. This was Reggie's biggest fear—a knocked up daughter.

"Okay, I'll think about it but I have to talk to Derrick first. I didn't do this by myself."

I spoke to him and he too acted like he was in disbelief. He said we would talk it over during lunch, but when I saw him at school the next day he avoided me and acted like I wasn't there. Chanel wasn't having it. I told her about his reaction to the whole thing and she was in his face that same day pushing him around while Nikola cursed him out. His friends and everyone in the vicinity was wondering what was going on and asking questions.

Two weeks later I had an appointment at Planned Parenthood and we were all hooking school again. Derrick never returned my calls. I won't dwell too much on the experience because it's something I've forced myself to forget. I was cramped up for three days afterward and blamed it on the flu when my parents asked me why I wasn't doing homework or getting up for school.

My broken heart healed over time. I told myself I would try not to love so hard the next time. But when you least expect it, love comes your way without warning, like a smack in the face—and leaves a sting that is never forgotten.

I met Charles Somerset in the fall of '00 when the girls and I took a trip to Philly for a hair show. I had stepped outside of the convention center to get a whiff of the autumn air. The calm crispness of the air in the months of September through November had made it my favorite time of the year. Chanel and Nikola were inside checking out the new hairstyles and sampling hair products. It was one of the times we were just bonding and not out to "make shit liquid."

I was admiring the trees' foliage. The bright orange and red hues of autumn had my full attention when this black Escalade jumped the curb. I knew what it was because Chanel and Nikola were like the highway patrol. They knew the make and model of a car even if it was blocks away.

I almost jumped out of my skin because I thought that my actions were catching up and it was someone's girlfriend or wife coming after me. Then I remembered we had come to Philly on a whim and erased the thought. No one would know we were there.

I looked to my left and when I saw him step out, my heart picked up its pace. He was dark and thick like chocolate, just like I liked them—or "thicker than a Snicker" as Chanel put it. His resemblance to Steve Harris made me look twice. I wasn't much of a TV watcher, but I never missed an episode of *The Practice*. When he got closer I noticed his pearly white teeth and knew that I could do him without accepting a dime.

That was one of Nikola's rules when we formed our club. Well, actually I couldn't call it a club, it had become more of a way of life, but there were rules to follow:

1. Never get emotionally attached.
2. Demand cash and/or gifts before any sexual interaction.
3. Strap 'em up to avoid pregnancies and any unwanted STD's.

Those were just the first three. There were many that followed, and I was about to break the first one. Nikola always stressed that I appear nonchalant, but I couldn't help but return his wide smile as he got closer. He was over six feet and walked with this domineering swagger.

I heard his voice and it didn't seem to complement his huge frame. Even though it was very deep, it had this calm and gentle tone to it.

"I'm sorry if I scared you ma, but there was so much traffic and if I didn't pull over like that, well you know, I might not ever see you again."

"*Really?* Well now that you've met me, tell me your name," I said, not bothering to hide my own girlish grin and surprised at my boldness.

"Charles, and please tell me you're not standin' here waitin' for ya man."

Just then a gust of wind snuck up on us and his eyes began to water. It was then that I noticed how sincere they were, like he didn't have anything to hide.

"Well, no I'm here at a hair show with my friends," I said, paying closer attention to his face and full lips.

"You don't sound like you from here. Where do I know that accent?" he asked.

"Baltimore."

There was a female officer serving tickets to illegally parked cars. He looked back at his truck and continued the conversation when he saw her continue down the block. "Baltimore, huh? And you come all the way to Phil-a-Del for a hair show? Is that what you do?"

"No, my best friend does and we didn't have anything to do so…"

"So you just up and leave B-more for Philly. Must be nice." I laughed. If only he knew the places I had just up and visited on a whim. "So what's your name Miss Baltimore?"

"Chelsea."

"Hmm, that sounds nice together, Chelsea and Charles. Look, I'm not sure if you know your way around Philly but I wanna get to know you. Maybe you'll let me take you to a nice spot downtown."

"I don't know. I'm here with my girls and we're bonding and everything."

I knew Chanel and Nikola wouldn't care if I left. They would probably see it as a business venture but I was feeling something different. I had no intentions on making Charles one of my wild flings. There was another kind of energy between us.

"Oh, I understand that, but I'm scared that I won't ever see you again. Come on, make my day and check wit' ya girls. I'ma sit here and wait for you. If you not back in five minutes I'm comin' inside."

They were asking me fifty questions before I could break free. When they found out about his ride they gave me the customary pep talk and told me they looked forward to seeing me the next morning.

I got to the car and Charles was rushing to open my door. He was really being a gentleman. In the truck he made me laugh so hard that my stomach was hurting. He didn't have a model face but his personality and charm were his best qualities. I felt like I could be myself. It was obvious that he had nice things but he wasn't arrogant like I knew some guys to be. And he didn't make it a point to talk about himself. The conversation was really focused on me, but if there was one thing I didn't want to discuss it was what I did for a living.

We ended up at a cozy sushi and sake restaurant on Walnut St. and instead of sitting across from me he took the seat to my left. The restaurant's lighting gave me a very warm feeling and with Charles seated next to me I felt even more comfortable. He was big but not sloppy, almost like a teddy bear. I looked down at the table where we were both holding our menus and admired our skin tones next to the other.

"Your skin is so beautiful," I said before I realized what had come out of my mouth.

He looked at me like I had said the craziest thing. "Beautiful? I've never heard that one before, but I was actually thinking the same thing about you."

"*Please.* Look at how pale I am right now. It's getting cold and my skin is only going to get lighter."

"But I love that, especially your red nose and pink lips. And the color of your sweater sets it off. What's this, cashmere?" he asked, rubbing my sleeve.

"Yeah, I love the way the material feels against my skin. At home I have this pink cashmere robe, but I'm still looking for a coat."

"Damn, you rollin' like that? Cashmere will set a nigga *back.* You must have a nice job."

I sat there for a moment, ready to tell him the truth and that I had slept with guys for the materialistic things I couldn't get from a normal job and the emotional attention my father had refused me. I don't know why I was ready to spill my guts to a stranger, but I liked Charles. I could tell he was really into me. But I knew that if I told him I had slept around in order to get the expensive clothes and jewelry I had on, he might have only wanted to do the same and turn our special moment into sex for payment.

Before I knew it, the words had slipped from my lips like it was the truth. "I'm a writer."

I picked up my glass of water and began squeezing the lemon so I wouldn't have to look at his eyes.

"A writer, huh? So, what, you write for newspapers and magazines?"

"No, I write online articles for different websites. Some of them are associated with magazines but I never know where they're going, I just write."

And just like that the lies were flowing. I felt uncomfortable so I shifted the conversation to him. "So Charles, I've been telling you a lot about me, but I want to know about you. What do *you* do?"

He looked away like I had done, like he had to think up an answer just as I had. His face got serious and he suddenly looked handsome in his black turtleneck that stopped at his chin. He put his right hand against his cheek and the gleam from the platinum pinky ring with diamonds bounced off the glass I was holding.

"Chelsea I just met you, but I don't want to start this friendship or whatever it might be with a lie, so I'll only tell you what I think you need to know."

"That's fine. I'm not asking you to tell me your life story or expose yourself," I said.

He took his hand away from his face and picked up his steaming cup of sake. "Well, I own two barbershops in North Philly and I'm tryna expand and open a spot in Jersey."

"You went to school to cut hair? I bet that took a lot of time and skill."

"Well, *actually,* I did some time in jail and taking up a trade guaranteed early parole," he said, scratching his ear.

"Really?"

Well then, I guess he had nothing *but* time. He had been locked up but it was good to know he had turned his life around. I didn't bother to ask him why. If he wanted to tell me he would.

We sat in the restaurant until the owner told us they were closing. I never thought I would enjoy sushi as much as I did that night and the sake was even better. I wasn't too fond of alcohol. Too many episodes with French Martinis had made me do some silly things. But the hot sake had me feeling warm and bubbly. Who knew that fermented rice could be turned into a delicacy.

After that night, Charles and me hung out all the time. If I was home in Baltimore he called and made arrangements for me to meet him wherever he was. It felt good to be away from "the life." That was the name we had given it. Giving up apart of our bodies and souls for a name brand wardrobe and I wasn't missing it at all.

As naïve as I seemed, I have always been fascinated with gangsters and anything associated with illegal activities. When I got a VCR in my room for my thirteenth birthday I must've watched *Scarface* at least once every week. His rise to the top with only a kilo of cocaine always seemed brilliant when I sat and analyzed the movie. As much as I loved it, I never liked to watch him die. To this day I stop the movie towards the end after he has blasted off all of Sosa's men, right before his demise.

So when I learned about Charles' stint in jail I knew there was something he wasn't telling me. In my mind it only added excitement to the relationship and heightened my attraction to him. Over time I got to see his barbershops and meet his closest friends. Believe me, there was no way he had the things he owned just by cutting hair.

By our fourth month together things had gotten hot and heavy. It went without saying that he wanted me to be his woman. I was visiting him in Philly almost every weekend and a few days before Valentine's Day he told me he had a surprise for me. I didn't think anything could top the other gifts he had given me so far.

After our first date that night in the sushi restaurant he had asked me to stay with him and the next day went out and got me that cashmere coat I told him I wanted. About three months after that he got me an even bigger surprise.

Charles met me at Philadelphia International Airport and we walked to the parking lot. He kept telling me how we were leaving for some place special as soon as we got in the car. He had this way of getting me excited without ever giving me a lot of details.

I knew something was wrong when we got to the A level of the garage and he had a confused look on his face. He said he knew he remembered parking by the elevator and automatically I thought someone had stolen his car. We stopped at each level just to make sure. By the time we got to level E he was furious since he had just bought the black 740i. The elevator doors opened. He hit the emergency stop button and told me to look for him. He said he just couldn't take it if somebody had stolen his week-old ride.

I stepped out and saw a baby pink Porsche parked to the left of the elevator with my nickname *Chelz* on the plate. I didn't even know they came in that color. I looked back at him in the elevator and he was looking at me like he hadn't planned the whole thing. He followed me to the car and gave me the keys. He knew I didn't know how to drive a stick but said cars like those were only meant to be driven in clutch mode. An hour of instruction later, we finally got out of the parking lot. He taught me how to get out of second gear and we were on our way to a weekend of spending time with one another.

Monetary surprises like that definitely made me fall for Charles more and more but there was something else to him. Him being thirty-one and experienced definitely intrigued me. And his sense of humor and knowledge about world issues allowed us to get to know one another on levels beyond anything sexual. Wherever we were on our travels, he made sure he started his day with a paper. Little things like that only made me love him stronger. So when he told me about another surprise, I didn't expect anything *but* a proposal. Nothing but a ring could get better than a pink Porsche.

We were sitting in his living room by the fireplace melting chocolate and marshmallows between cinnamon graham crackers. Earlier that morning we had spent Valentine's Day on a horse and carriage ride through downtown Philly talking about the first night we had met. Later that evening he fixed my favorite meal: steak with a side of broccoli, fried potatoes and onions. He knew how much I enjoyed Outback Steakhouse but his steak was by far the best I had ever tasted. I always asked him to cook for me but he said the time would come when he was ready to ask me something special.

Our stomachs were full and I was sitting in between his legs on the black plush rug that was made from thick ostrich feathers. I had on one of his blue Ralph Lauren sleep shirts. I loved wearing his 4X shirts around the house. There was always a trace of his cologne left on them.

I was leaning my head against his right shoulder when he took my left hand in his two large ones. "Can I tell you somethin'?" he asked.

I lifted my head and looked at him. "What baby?" I asked, ready for the proposal.

"Your skin is so beautiful," he said.

I remembered our first date and realized he was making fun of me. I threw my head back and went into a fit of giggles. He was rubbing my fingers while we laughed and I noticed that my left hand felt a little heavier. I looked down and a platinum band surrounded by intricately placed diamonds and one large solitaire in the middle engulfed my ring finger. I guessed that there were at least seven carats on my finger. You would think I was Jacob the Jeweler.

"Well, I'm still waiting for you to tell me something," I said, never taking my eyes off the ring.

"Oh, yeah I forgot," he said playfully, "will you be my Valentine's forever?"

If it meant having him hold me in his arms like that forever than I would scream *yes* for the whole world to hear. Instead I kissed him lightly and we finished off the rest of the Zinfandel we were drinking and fell asleep to the flickering fireplace.

Nikola and Chanel were happy about the proposal, but I think they were even happier that I was marrying someone who had unlimited bank. Nikola was ready to begin planning, and Charles wasn't complaining when I told him I wanted to get married the following month. He said it could've been the next day for all he cared. Just show him where and he would be standing there waiting.

We only had four weeks to take care of everything but Nikola said it didn't take four hours to spend the money we were about to. I think she did that better than any of us—spend other people's money that is. Charles was cash money and Nikola was ready to do her thing. The first thing she did was put together the list of invites. I couldn't understand why she was including the girls from high school she claimed to despise. I had never had anything against them so I had no problem with my fellow Westernites sharing in my day. Besides, I didn't have a lot of friends anyway.

My whole bridal party consisted of my cousins and most of them could be just as snobby as the girls we'd gone to school with. I don't have to say what my color was. I tried to put Charles in a pink bow tie and cummerbund but he wasn't having it. Nikola insisted that I add a touch of red to give the wedding some more flavor and romance. She didn't have to tell me twice. *Romance* was the only word I needed to hear.

While Nikola took care of the catering, decorations and every other major detail, Chanel took care of me. We started first with my dress. For some reason I still felt like the innocent girl I was back in the day. With all of our ventures involving sex in this state or that one, that innocence was something I still wanted to hold onto. Chanel looked at me like I had lost my mind when I told her I wanted a pure white Cinderella-type-of-dress.

"You can't be serious. Bitch, the only virgin was Mary," she said, literally laughing in my face.

Maybe so, but as far as Charles needed to know, he might as well have been changing his name to Joseph.

I had moved most of my things to Philly since that was where Charles and I spent most of our time before the wedding. I was driving his Escalade the day Chanel and me had our outing so we would have room to pack in my wedding gown and the bridesmaids' dresses. After stopping at Barnes & Noble and buying a couple of Bridal magazines I knew where I wanted to go for my dress.

The first and hopefully the last stop was in Fountainville. I saw the gown and affirmed we didn't have to look any further. It was beautiful just like the dresses I envisioned as a little girl. It was made by *eve of milady* and it was more than elegant. It fell over my bottle-shaped figure like a soft cloud. I wasn't too fond of trains, but I was happy with the big ballroom effect it gave the dress. It was outlined with small, beaded pink and red roses that glistened like diamonds, and the veil's crown was made out of dried pink and red roses. I pranced around the store while Chanel picked out the bridesmaids' dresses.

"Wait until everybody sees you," Chanel said, oohing. Her hand fell over her mouth as she whispered, "You look so beautiful."

I didn't want to start crying but it sounded like a comment that should've been coming from my parents. My mother was happy for me even though she felt twenty seemed too young to be getting married. My father wasn't quite as supportive. I had wanted to tell my parents in person about the wedding so I asked my mother if Charles and I could stop by for dinner so they could meet him.

Since I wasn't living at home anymore and they thought I was a college reject, I hadn't seen them in awhile. When I called home I kept up with the facade that I was an online writer just so I could cover my ass and please them at the same time.

Over dinner I could tell Daddy wasn't pleased with Charles. He was the first man I'd brought home since I'd moved out so Reginald was asking a bunch of questions to which the answers weren't what he wanted to hear. He heard the news and left the table.

"Chelsea," he said when I caught up with him in the den, "this hood you have brought home is nothing but a lowlife drug dealer. I see fools like him everyday at the shop with their fancy cars and jewelry and it makes me sick."

I looked at his disgusted frown and began to plead. "But Daddy, he isn't like that. True, he was in jail, but now he owns barbershops and a lot of other businesses," I said, almost crying.

He refused to believe me and told me I wouldn't have him to walk me down the aisle and that I had better not *ever* bring Charles to his home again. Well, then he wouldn't be seeing my face either. I was so tired of trying to please him that I felt like I didn't need him in my life ever if he couldn't accept me and the decisions I made.

I could never forget the look on his face when I told him exactly that. Despite the times I thought he didn't love me or didn't care about me, I watched as his face grew from one of a handsome man that I loved more than myself sometimes, to a crumbled heap of sadness and regret. I quickly left before I broke down and cried myself.

"Chelz, you listenin' to me?" Chanel asked, bringing me out of my daze.

"What did you say?" I asked, too wrapped in my own thoughts to see that she was at the counter ready to ring up the purchase.

"I *said*, give me some money. The total came to $20,340.58."

I gave her the credit card Charles had gotten in my name. All of the plastic he had was in my name and paid in advance since he didn't like me carrying around a lot of cash.

After we left, Chanel and I stopped to eat lunch and to get a massage at a nearby spa. She could tell I was stressin' over my family situation so to get my mind off of things, we laid on our stomachs and she got me excited with details about my bachelorette party two more days from then.

If the party was any sign of the extravagance I had to look forward to at the wedding, I was in for an eventful occasion. Nikola had rented a motorcoach to come to Philly with a few ladies from my family, their families and associates from school. I suppose seventy-five women was more than a few but who was counting? After the party, the bus was taking them all back to Baltimore where I had arranged for the out-of-towners to stay at the Hyatt across from the Inner Harbor.

That evening we had reservations at a steak and seafood restaurant where we ate lobster and steak until we couldn't move. At the end of the night my entourage went back to my new residence. Charles wasn't there of course. He was staying with his best friend Smalls whose huge frame made them look more like brothers. Who knew what they were getting into. He and his boys had flown to Miami to go to some club called *Rollexx*.

Everyone was telling me how nice the house was. It was in a neighborhood where vines grew up the sides of the house's brick front and around the windows. I wished my mother was there to see it, but she was staying with her mother. Grandma Cleo was old and her asthma was getting worse but I'm sure if she quit smoking two packs a day her lungs would be just fine.

The house hadn't needed a lot of decorating but I still added that woman's touch to change it from a bachelor's pad. *You know, a little pink here and there.* Above the fireplace was a huge picture we had taken on Valentine's Day standing beside the horse and carriage. It looked like it could've been sent out as a Christmas postcard. A light snow was falling behind us and we had on matching red mohair sweaters with black mink coats to keep us warm. My nose was red like the sweater and though our skin contrasted, the red sweaters complemented us both.

All of the ladies that walked through the living room kept staring at the picture and all of the other things that made the living room cozy and inviting, like the fireplace that reflected off the shiny hardwood floors and the plush couches that could put a person to sleep instantly.

Nikola was being such the perfect host. It was nothing more than a chance for her to show off for the so-called friends she had invited from high school. "Okay ladies, before we get into the real fun, we have to open up the bride-to-be's gifts," she said in a singsong voice.

Mr. Parker, the bus driver, had started bringing in the wrapped gifts and shopping bags and I was getting excited. It was better than a birthday party. After opening the boxes of dishware, lingerie and cards with gift certificates I wondered where my gifts from Nikola and Chanel were.

"Okay," Nikola said, "time for the party to begin!"

"Excuse you, but where are my gifts?" I asked, looking at them both blankly.

"Oh, I almost forgot," Nikola said with her finger to her cheek like my gift was an afterthought.

"Yeah, okay. Play games if you want," I told her, smiling.

She left the room and when she came back she had two bags. One was the signature blue bag from Tiffany & Co. and another was a long squared box. I knew who had given me what. I looked inside the bag first and there was a delicate platinum bangle resting on a tiny plate with my name engraved in script style. On the inside was another inscription: *Sisters Forever.*

And we really did look like sisters. We had on the same skintight brown leather pants and knitted halter-tops in different colors. Mine was camel like my boots, Chanel's black and Nikola's, a pumpkin orange. I slipped the bangle on my wrist and admired the way it matched my ring.

"Something new," she said.

"Aww, thank you Kola, it's so pretty," I said.

"See, now we all have one," she said, holding out her wrist. I never paid attention but now I saw that Chanel had on the same one when she handed me her gift.

The looks from Nikola's rivals said they were more than sick of her. Every chance she got she was throwing something in their face. When we took the tour of Philly she insisted that the bus follow her in her new convertible Lexus. Me and Chanel both knew she hadn't vacationed or stayed in Philly long enough to have somebody follow her but I guessed she was using her navigating system. She was too much. She even had all three televisions going inside the whip so they would see that she had it like that.

I couldn't help but shake my head in amusement at the thought of it. I pulled the pink crepe paper off my last gift. I started flailing my arms when I saw the picture we had taken the night of the Jay-Z concert two years ago. I thought I had lost my copy but there it sat in a large silver frame, which had the same *Sisters Forever* insignia emblazoned on it that was on our bracelets.

It was true that a picture was worth a thousand words because when I looked into our eyes it was obvious that we didn't know what we were getting into. I placed it back into its box and made a note to set it on my nightstand in the bedroom.

"Thank you so much Chanel. I was wondering what happened to my copy," I said through tears.

"You thought I was gettin' you some high-priced shit didn't you?" she asked teasingly.

"Well..." I started to say.

"You don't have to lie. Shit I can give you some exclusive stuff any day of the week. I just thought I'd show you my sentimental side," she whispered so sincerely that the tears kept coming.

Her and Nikola were sitting on opposite sides of me on the couch and I wouldn't have had it any other way. I reached for them and hugged them both. "Thank you so much, I'm having the best time."

"You know that's not it though," Chanel said, as Nikola stood up.

"What do you mean?" I asked her.

Moments later, Nikola returned to the living room and turned up the surround system. Missy's 'One Minute Man' belted out loud and full of bass. Men in every shade and color came from the basement and after they finished throwing me around like a rag doll, they gave everyone else the time of her life as well. The corks were popping and I forgot about my distaste for alcohol and had my own bottle.

Around two that morning everyone was boarding the bus staggering, not ready to return to Baltimore. We didn't know where Nikola had stepped off to. She had probably made plans with somebody in Philly that she'd met. I swear it was always about money with her. She could never hang things up and just enjoy the moment.

Chanel and I started cleaning up after the guests had left. We threw out all of the empty bottles and plastic cups that filled up four large trash bags. Chanel sat down on the couch and put her hands to her forehead. "Oh my goodness," she said.

"What's wrong Chanel?" I asked after I sat down beside her.

"I just been feelin' so dizzy lately."

"You sick?" I asked worriedly.

"I don't know what the hell is wrong wit' me. Might be the flu. I just started havin' dizzy spells but I've been tired for a while now, fevers and everything."

"Maybe it *is* the flu," I told her, trying to convince myself.

I looked at Chanel's face not knowing what I was searching for. She had been a little more crabby than usual, but she didn't look sick. *But*, her skin was glowing more than usual. She stared back at me with those slanted eyes of hers and I think we both knew she had something more serious—something called the nine-month flu.

Upon reaching the church I saw that there was a huge traffic jam. Police were directing cars that had created their own parking spaces. People in the neighborhood had come out to sit on their steps to watch the commotion.

I was sitting in the back of the white stretch Cadillac with Chanel and Nikola. She still hadn't told us where she had snuck off to at the last minute the night before. She would have been quick to grill Chanel or me with a bunch of questions if it had been one of us. But Kola could be private like that sometimes.

My four bridesmaids were sitting in front of us in the second row of seats. My cousins Mandi and Rachel were staring out the windows like they had never seen so many people at one time. The other two, Maria and Bianca were asleep. As stuck up as they pretended to be, they had had the most fun the night before. I knew a lot of them would still be tired or suffering from hangovers, so I had scheduled the wedding for three that afternoon.

The day that I had dreamed of had finally arrived and all I could think of was the trail of lies I had told Charles. I wasn't worried about my career fib. I was always typing on my Apple iBook so he never questioned me and assumed it was a new assignment I was working on. The other big lie was my virginity, and Charles thought mine was still intact. If only he knew.

I was so caught up in him being the romantic he was that I didn't want to even tell him I had been with one guy, let alone thirty or more. So when sex came up, that's what I told him. That I was waiting. He hadn't found it too far-fetched since I was only nineteen when we had met and was Catholic.

I thought about those things when I saw St. Bernardine's. This was the same place I had Holy Communion for the first time. The place where I made my first confession about letting David Martin kiss me on the neck in the seventh grade. I was so into my own world that I almost didn't see the black Land Rover parked across the street from the church. I knew that there were more than a few of those trucks riding around Baltimore City with those expensive 20-inch rims, but the chances were slim that any truck other than his would have the phrase, *MY SHT* on the tags.

Nikola

The time had finally come for us to run our shit. Everything had gone smoothly so far. The plan in Nordstrom *really* went well. I was surprised that no one was monitoring the dressing room and with Lila in the shoe department, I felt like we had struck gold again.

Back at Chanel's apartment we looked at all the things I had lifted and after adding all the price tags, we had over $8,000 in merchandise. The dress that I was wearing to the concert was $2,500 by itself. I had never owned a piece of clothing that cost that much. In fact, it cost more than the shit I had in my closet altogether.

As I was putting it in the bag I got real anxious because I knew I was going to get away with it. After I had removed all the sensors from our clothes I put them onto the other clothes I had brought into the room that I didn't want. There wasn't any way I was leaving them on the floor for an employee to find. I couldn't mess it up for the next girl who was as smart as me.

Chanel seemed a little nervous at first but when she saw that I had it under control, we were like two pros that had been stealing forever. Chelsea was all fidgety in the car when we left the mall, but she didn't have any regrets when she was trying on the dress and spinning around in the mirror. I had to tell little miss ballerina to sit the fuck down.

It was around six when we started getting ready for the concert and eight when we finally left out the door. Chanel had bought a car right around the time she moved out of my house. I think she used the money Petey gave her before he left. He just should have, considering he almost got her killed. We were pushin' a black '96 two-door BMW she had got at an auction in Delaware. It would do for our first night out, but I knew that I would have to get another phat whip soon because we had an image to uphold. It wasn't mine, but I was driving that night since Chanel was scared to maneuver in the bumper to bumper traffic.

We reached downtown Baltimore, and the area near Lexington Market and the Baltimore Arena was congested. I looked around and got excited when I saw the limousines, expensive cars and phat-ass trucks with the tight stereo systems. We had the windows halfway down when a new Mercedes truck pulled up beside us.

Chelsea was in the back applying powder to her shiny nose, Chanel was checking her purse for the tickets I had given her before we left, and I was taking in everything that was around me. That included the cherry red truck to my left that looked like it had just been driven off the lot.

Although I was looking straight ahead I saw the waxed hood out the corner of my eye. There was no way I was looking directly at the driver. That was a minor rule of mine: never make eye contact with the driver of a phat car unless they make the initiative.

We were still riding side by side when we stopped at the red light. I turned up the radio and lowered the windows since DJ Reggie Reg on 92Q was representin' with the club music. I still hadn't looked inside the truck but I was sure they saw us.

We were all moving our bodies to the music when Chanel tapped me. "Kola yo, that nigga in the truck is honkin'."

I finally made eye contact and when I saw him I was so disappointed. I was never attracted to red niggas and everything about him was red—his skin, his truck, and his goddamn outfit. He was really overdoing it. He even had the nerve to have a stack of golds in his mouth.

"Chanel he's a yuck mouth," I whispered.

"Shiit, those golds are lookin' good to me."

We certainly had different tastes.

"Hey ladies! W'sup wit' y'all tonight?" he yelled.

I looked back at the light and it was still red.

"Nothin'," we all said together.

"W'sup wit' you?" Chanel asked, leaning over me to get a better look.

"I'm Reds baby, what's your name?"

I couldn't believe it. How appropriate for him to have a nickname like that. He was making me sick. *Why couldn't he have given her his real name?* Reds was probably better anyway since his real name was probably Jaquan or some shit. People behind us were beginning to honk but Reds continued to talk. I guessed that was one of the bonuses of owning a phat whip—you could hold up traffic as long as you wanted.

"I'm Chanel, and I know I'll be seeing you inside, right?"

"No doubt ma, no doubt," he said.

After he pulled off I saw his tags and figured right that he was from New York. They were always bringing that *ma* shit to Baltimore. *Did I look like I was Hispanic bitch?* I circled the block once more and remembered a parking lot in one of the apartment buildings a block from the arena.

Before I turned off the car I gave "the talk." It was something I had thought about during the whole ride. "Alright tonight is the night!" I said, like we were getting ready to go out and meet our goal of selling girl scouts cookies or something.

"I know and I'm nervous," Chelsea said.

"It's no need to be. Tonight will determine everything else we do. When we get in here, we just have to remember who the fuck we are. You remember how you looked in the mirror before we left. Everything about us is tight and we won't even go there with the hair and makeup. Look, I don't know what kind of strategy you decided on, but the whole idea is to make these mutherfuckers *want us*. Before we leave from here they need to be beggin' us to do whateva it is we need them to. We all together on that shit?"

"No doubt ma," Chanel said, making fun of Reds.

"Oh, y'all forgot huh?" I asked. I had forgotten the coined saying myself.

"What you talkin' 'bout Kola?" Chanel asked, doing her Arnold impression.

I laughed. "What we gotta do tonight?"

They looked at me sideways and then it clicked. "We *gotta make shit liquid*!" we screamed in unison.

We all burst out laughing and then locked up. The screams and hollers started before we even walked a block. I think we were all used to it, so we ignored them and kept walking, *very slowly* since we wanted to avoid any falls or embarrassing trips. We all stopped when we heard the crash. I couldn't believe it, we had caused an accident with our outfits.

I knew mine was off the hinges. My shapely legs were setting off the dress even with my ass cheeks almost hanging out the shorts. But it wasn't nasty. Shit, with Prada written on my ass I dared anyone to call me out my name.

The guy with the J30 that had caused the accident slipped the guy in the truck some money and the altercation was over. That's what I was talking about, being able to handle shit with a few bills.

The front doors of the Arena were packed with so many people that we couldn't tell where the line began or ended. We finally made it to a line and I felt like we were the richest bitches in there. There was no denying how fly we were 'cause the crowds of people were separating to make room for us. Luckily, I had charged the tickets the first hour they went on sale so we had floor seats.

Once we had past the turnstile I felt the electric currents running through me. My insides were jumping but it was the good kind of butterflies. Before we found our seats we decided to take pictures while everything was in place.

We did three shots. The first was all smiles, the second was mugs, and the last was nothing but attitude. If the bitches from Western could see us, (and I knew a few would that night) they probably wouldn't even know it was us with our designer outfits and expensive shoes. When we were finished with the pictures and headed to our seats Chelsea suggested we stop and buy T-shirts.

"Chelsea, I know you ain't buyin' a T-shirt," I said.

"Why not? I love Jigga, that's my nigga."

If only she knew how corny she sounded. "Really, Chelz, please don't. You carryin' around a T-shirt will mess up your whole outfit."

"Just get it right before we leave," Chanel said, playing the peacemaker. "And if you say that Jigga my nigga bullshit out ya mouth one more time I'll hurt you. *For real*!"

We laughed again and walked past the vendor. On our way to the lower level all eyes were on us. Nastier looks came from the Rave and Lerner bitches who looked like they'd had to put their shit on layaway. I looked at our tickets and saw we were in row F. That was even better. It would give us a chance to walk the runway.

It was too bad we had arrived a little late because as soon as I began the catwalk, the lights went out. DJ Clue took the stage and we stood up with everybody else. We were all caught up in the moment, dancing and everything, but I made sure I didn't move around too much. I had to be cute without sweating out my hair or clothes.

The pounding of the music in my chest only made me want to be in a club atmosphere after the concert. An afterparty was definitely in order. I was feeling the performance and the audience participation but I was happiest when intermission arrived. This was our chance to work the place. The lower level was the best place to sit since it gave us a chance to be seen by everybody else, but the second and third levels was where the ballers would be hanging around and mingling.

We went to the second level first and stood in line for drinks. I got a medium coke and stood to the side to wait for Chelsea and Chanel. I couldn't believe they were ordering food. Not me, I knew there was no way the night was ending without someone buying me dinner. I was looking around at all the prospects when I felt someone tapping my shoulder.

"Excuse me but I think you owe me somethin'."

I almost broke my neck turning around. *Who the fuck was this nigga telling me I owed him some shit?* "Yes, excuse you is right. Who the hell are you and I don't owe nobody a damn thing."

"Calm down hottie, I was just about to tell you I had to pay a nigga off since you made me hit his shit."

Then I recognized him. It was the guy with the silver Infiniti who had slipped the other driver the money. I liked the way his sideburns connected to his beard. He was real sexy and the fact that he was laced in Moschino didn't hurt either. I had to remember what kind of mission I was on before I let his looks sidetrack me. But I didn't hide my attraction to him. We shared the same caramel complexion, only his had a tanned hue to it. His dark eyes were blatantly undressing me. I could tell the chase was about to be on.

"Oh, *I* made you, huh?" I playfully asked, joining in on the flirting game.

"Come on now, look at you. Your outfit is fly and you are pretty as hell. But if I had to, I would crash somebody else's shit again just to get a longer look at you."

I found out his name was Justin and after I programmed his number in my phone we made plans to hook up. He told me he had two friends who might want to meet my friends anyway. I didn't know what Chelsea or Chanel wanted to do and I really wasn't for the bullshit of friends meeting friends. Hooking up for dinner was one thing but I wanted to get paid and get to the point.

"Look Justin, I'm not for a bunch of people taggin' along. If it's gon' be about me and you, that's what we need to be doin'."

"Oh word, it's like that?" he asked while opening his hands.

I noticed all the diamonds on his wrist and my pussy started jumping. *"Oh yeah*, it's like that," I said, running my fingertips over his cheek.

The concert ended at 12:30 and we were standing outside with everybody else who wanted to be seen, or who was trying to decide what to do that night. There was plenty to get into. I had the volume on my cell turned up high since me and Justin planned on hookin' up at two that morning. I was checking my messages when a group of guys walked towards us. I immediately put on my player face.

The one guy Terry said he owned a club not far from where we were and was throwing an afterparty. He gave us the flyers with the address, pulled me to the side and asked if we could hook up when I got to the club. He wasn't ugly and a club meant money, so of course I had no problem with that.

We stood around for another twenty minutes before we walked to the car. There were some girls from DC who said they wanted to follow us since they didn't know their way around the city. When I pulled out of the parking lot I saw them sitting in their Volvo. I flashed them and we were on our way and in tight traffic again. Guys and girls were hanging out of car windows and drinking straight from champagne bottles. The excitement had only heightened after I peeped this particular scene.

"The concert was live, huh?" I asked Chanel and Chelsea.

"*Yes*, especially Jay with those sexy-ass lips. All they were sayin' to me was, '*Chanel let me eat your pussy*'."

"Eww Chanel, why you gotta use that word," Chelsea said.

"What? *Pussy*? It's nothin' wrong wit' that word. That just shows I'm comfortable with myself and if I want to say it three times, guess what? Pussy, pussy, pussy!"

"I just gotta ask a question. You call him Jay like you know him. How is it that you communicated all that from a rapper. Did he even see you?" I asked, fucking with her.

"It doesn't matter. Wit' lips like those that's what they're good for, eatin' pussy."

"I can't believe we're having a conversation about pussy," I said.

"Me either, so can you just turn up the radio and get us to this afterparty or whatever it is," Chelsea said.

"Whateva, but I bet both of you will be looking out for pussy lips from now on," she said as she messed with the radio.

The scene ahead of us on Charles St. was a repeat of the traffic jam we were in minutes ago. I saw the club and the parking lot across the street and checked for signs of towing. Once again we locked up and headed out.

Waiting for a chance to cross the street, I saw the bouncers flashing their lights over ID's. *Oh shit*. I forgot that we might be carded, but I had to keep my cool. I couldn't let Chelsea or Chanel see that I hadn't covered all aspects. Instead of waiting in line I walked straight to the door, ignoring the girls who were sucking their teeth. "Can you let Terry know that Nikola is here?" I said to the bouncers.

The one with the shiny bald head called him on the walkie-talkie and I heard Terry tell him to let us in. The pounding music was a combination of house and old school. And though we were only eighteen, the old beats sounded good enough to make us move our bodies.

I was asking the bartender for a coke with grenadine when Terry came up behind me. He was holding onto my waist like we had known each other for years. "You smell so good," he said, burying his face into my hair.

I almost lost my footing trying to turn around since I had caught my heel in the stool's silver footrest where I had propped my foot. "Well, I got something that smells even better," I said, quickly gaining my composure.

I didn't mean to sound so straightforward but he was hugging on me like he was my man. I started to tell him that even my affection wasn't for free, but I knew that I had to give away something before I got what I really wanted. My comment had him all ears because he was leading me upstairs to his office.

I looked back and Chanel was ordering another Hennessy and sweet tea and Chelsea had some big nigga hemmed up by the DJ booth. She had to be tipsy because she was being a little too bold and so was her dancing. I laughed and followed Terry into his office.

The inside of the room reminded me of this Italian guy I had given my virginity to. I had just turned sixteen and was walking through Mondawmin Mall. It was the mall where all the ballers shopped if they wanted to get laced in Versace or any other over-priced shit. It was also a ghetto girl's heaven. She could find an outfit for ten dollars and rock it at the club that same night like she had paid top dollar for it.

I had seen his red Corvette parked out front with *CARLITO* on the tags. He owned one of the main stores that sold expensive Italian leather, gator boots and anything else that had been imported from Italy.

That was the first time I had ever contemplated sex or sexual favors for money, and what was crazy is that I knew what I was doing. That day I had gone the extra mile with my hair and clothes. It was the middle of July and I had on a dress I had bought from Express when they'd had their spring sale. The wrap around was red and tied on the side. My titties weren't that big but the dress made them look full and the curves could be seen if someone was looking down on me.

I'm not sure why I had never had sex before. Maybe it was because I had been sheltered in Catholic school until I was thirteen and right after that I was in an all girls high school. I just had this feeling that I was holding out for something big.

Now, I had seen Carlito before when I pretended to browse through the store a month ago. I had even wasted $150 that I didn't have on some sandals just so I could have some kind of conversation with him.

He had to be the sexiest man I had ever seen. Carlito had dark curly hair, big dark eyes and the scar on his left cheek made him look dangerous. He always wore expensive shirts that showed off the curly hair on his chest and his gold and diamond chains. That day I walked in the store like I was on a mission, yet when I saw him my heart stopped. I knew I was there to do something but I didn't quite know how to initiate it.

He greeted me like always—barely concealing the nasty thoughts just beyond his eyes. I asked him if I could talk to him in the back. He locked the door like he didn't want any interruptions. I sat down at the chair facing his desk and took in my surroundings. He had four large TVs monitoring the store and a mini bar beside a large file cabinet. I wondered if he had any incriminating evidence locked away like I had seen in the mobster movies.

"You like my office?" he asked in his thick Italian accent, hands folded on top of the intricately carved desk.

"Umm, yeah," I said nervously.

"So what do I owe your pretty face?"

I searched for the words but I had to tell my heart to calm down first. "I came to you because I need a favor," I said.

He nodded his head a little like he was waiting for me to continue. "Did I tell you how beautiful you are?" he asked.

I think he interrupted with similar *pretty* remarks throughout the whole conversation. He was really making me nervous and it was difficult for me to get the words out. The dark beauty mark below my left eye started pulsating and I pretended to move my hair to the side to touch the spot.

I smiled and continued. "Well, I ran into some money problems and I was wondering if you could help me." *There I had said it.*

"Sure I can. What? You want job at my store?"

*Okay, so he didn't understand what I was trying to say.*

"No, that's not enough money. I need *a lot* of money. Like what you have."

"*Oh*, like so you can pay for expensive clothes and shit?"

It was funny to hear him curse.

"Yes," I said, giving him my sexy smile.

"Oh, well I can do something about that."

He came from behind his desk and motioned for me to stand up. My back was against the TVs but I didn't know where else to stand.

"Your name Nikola right? Well, I like you. I think you hot, you face, you body," he said, moving my hair behind my ears. "Ever since I see you that day, I say, 'she be mine one day.' And I think we can do something about the, umm, money thing. You have boyfriend?"

"No," I barely whispered.

"Oh, too bad no boyfriend. Well, I think that your problem. You need someone like Carlito, older, experienced. These guys, they can no do for you what I can."

"And what's that?" I asked nervously.

I had tried to prepare myself as much as possible but I never thought that I would actually go through with it.

"You like sex?" he asked, running his tongue over his lips.

"I don't know."

"You don't know? What, you don't have sex, you don't like it the first time?"

"I never had sex," I said.

His eyes got all big like he couldn't believe what he was hearing and he was close enough for me to feel his dick bulging in his linen pants. "Oh, that's good. You see, Carlito is good with that. I teach you what I know. You know, show you what it feel like, how it supposed to feel like and after, I give you those things, money and stuff."

I didn't say anything else. I let him kiss me and rub on my titties. After he untied my dress he laid me on his desk and unbuckled his belt. I had never seen a dick but when he pulled his out, I knew I couldn't call it anything but perfect. It was a nice color, like his skin, only I saw large veins bulging down the sides as if it was about to bust. I wondered then if it would hurt like I had heard girls talk about.

He began sucking on my neck and when I felt him bite me I felt another sharp pain between my legs. I think he did that to distract me from feeling it. Once he was inside me he laid his head on my shoulder. "Oh, you feel like heaven," he said.

After he was in me for awhile he lifted me up and began fuckin' me in the air. I had gotten used to the feeling so by then I was good to go. When he was almost finished he put me back on the desk and told me to lay back. He spread my legs apart and started jerking his dick up and down. In an instant his face had turned red and he was spraying my stomach and face with his cum.

I was floored. I had walked in there a virgin and was about to leave as a completely different person. He laid over me for a long time while he played in my hair. I think that was the only thing I enjoyed—the warmth of his body and him touching my face and hair.

We got dressed and then he opened a small door I hadn't seen by the file cabinet. Carlito pulled the stack of money out for me. He told me he looked forward to seeing me again and I left out, pulling my damp hair into a ponytail with a blue rubberband I had picked up from his desk.

I looked at one of the girls on the floor that was helping a customer and felt my ears turn red. I hoped I had removed all the stuff from my face. I knew she was aware of what went on and I prayed I'd never see her again.

When I got on the bus to go home I secretly looked in my purse and saw that he had given me $700. That was more than I made doing two months of hairdos. About a week later, I went to visit Carlito but he was too busy to see me. When I called the store he said he would call me back. I went on like that for another two months, hoping I would get another "visit" in his office. I got over it and realized that I had been fucked and forgotten about.

As I stood in the middle of Terry's office that night after the concert, I noticed all the similarities to Carlito's spot. There was the extra artwork, an expensive couch, but no visible money hideaways. Terry poured himself a drink and asked if I wanted another coke. I told him I wasn't thirsty. He directed me to the black and white couch and started asking me questions about myself. I looked at the clock on the wall and saw that I had a little over an hour before I hooked up with Justin.

I told him the things I thought he wanted to hear: his club was bangin' (when it was really bootie), how much of a businessman he was (when I really didn't give a fuck and was the one about her business), and asked him how he came to open the club (when all I wanted was the money he made from that fucker). He said he had owned the club for about three years and that he was looking into opening a strip joint. He was just looking for the right place to put it. That told me he had money to spend.

After twenty minutes he had poured his third drink and had started getting touchy feely. He was rubbing my thigh when I had to set things straight. "What are you doin'?" I asked.

"Gettin' to know you. You *did* tell me you had somethin' that smelled good."

"Yes, I did but I don't fuck for free."

I was surprised at how nice it came out but proud at the same time. He set his drink beside the couch and looked at me for a long time. When he got up I just knew he was going to tell me to get the fuck out his office with my talk about *fuckin' for free*.

I saw him hit a button and everything got dim. He went behind his desk and came back with a stack of bills. I tried not to seem too interested in what he had, but it was hard not to notice the bands with $1,000 written on them. The money looked like it was fresh out the bank.

*A thousand dollars. What did a nigga deserve for a G?* Not much, I told myself. If he was throwing that around, there was no telling what else he had to give away. Thinking was worthless so I prepared to deliver.

I slid off my shorts. Next I moved to my end and propped one of my legs on the back of the couch. I started rubbing my pussy real slow and lickin' my lips, making them wet every time my tongue went around. He was looking good to me so it didn't take long for me to get wet.

He saw that and leaned down and started lickin' my thighs and the hair around my clit. After minutes of him down there it didn't feel like he was tryna lick my pussy. It felt like he was playing around. So I shoved his head to the spot where it was supposed to be. *Was there something wrong with his damn tongue?* Terry finally found the spot. The fool was sucking on my shit so hard that I had the feeling he thought it was a dick. I couldn't take it so I faked it and started shaking and clamping his head between my legs. He sat up and looked at me like he deserved a trophy. I was so ready to get up but he touched my leg.

"Nikola, before you leave can you do something for me?"

I knew he didn't want me to suck his dick. I could get down when it came to the headpiece but his wasn't shit. He didn't deserve my soft lips around his dick, and if that's what he wanted I was prepared to tell him about his shitty performance. "*What?*" I said like I was doing him a favor.

"Can you *please* wrap your pretty little hand around my dick and make me feel good?"

*Oh, that was it.* I looked down at my American manicure. Yeah, they were pretty and I had no problem with a hand job so I leaned over and began kissing his neck. I loosened his pants and reached inside his briefs to pull out his dick. It was dim but when I looked down while I was kissing him, I saw how little he was. His head was trash and he had the nerve to have a little dick to go with it. He would definitely have to pay extra to even *attempt* to poke me with his little man.

By the time I finished my hand hurt. He wasn't working with much and had the nerve to be longwinded. I couldn't believe it. When I sat up I was a little embarrassed to look at him. The TV screens made me remember Chelsea and Chanel downstairs and I got up from the couch.

Little Man followed me to the door and kissed my cheek. "I hope I can see you again on some real shit," he said.

If the real shit meant actual sex he had better come up with some *real* money. On the other side of the door, I checked my bag for the money again and went to the bathroom to wash my hands. I looked in the mirror and couldn't believe that I had just pulled it off. My eyes were lit up like I just got a bike for Christmas. Again, I couldn't believe that I had pulled it off.

$1,000 wasn't bad for my first time *makin' shit liquid*. In fact it was more than I expected. I wondered what else I would get into that night and reached into my purse for my phone. It read 1:50am and I searched for Justin's number. I tried calling but my cell was out of range and wasn't getting a signal. I checked the mirror a last time and went downstairs.

I saw Chanel at the bar and gave her the car keys and a quick rundown of Terry. She laughed and told me she would tell me her story later. I asked her where Chelsea was and she pointed to her dancing with yet another big guy.

"Her and her big boys," I said.

"I know, and they seem so happy to be wit' somebody so pretty."

"Listen, I'm about to call that guy Justin and have him meet me here. Come stand outside wit' me until he comes and get his license plate info just in case."

"Aight, let me tell Chelz where we're going."

Justin called me at exactly 2:00 and I told him where to meet me. By the time he pulled up, Chelsea had come outside with us and hadn't stopped talking about the guy she had met at the concert. "He's not cute," she said, "but he dresses nice and is cuddly like a bear."

63

I hoped she wasn't taking these niggas seriously 'cause she was all psyched up like it was her first date or something. I would have to get her mind straight *later* because I too had a date and didn't have time for coach class.

"Aight Kola, see you in the morning. You got ya key right?" Chanel asked.

"Yeah," I said after fishing around in my purse. "You aight?" I asked, looking at her relaxed face. Her slanted eyes were dilated from the Hennessy and teas she had been throwing back all night.

"Yeah yeah, just feeling good," she said a little louder than normal.

"*Okay*. Chelz you watch out for her anyway."

Chelsea nodded and looked at Chanel's face like she couldn't tell the difference between a sober or drunk countenance. We had all planned to meet at Chanel's place when we were through for the night. It was going to be like a slumber party, only with more detailed stories and better gossip.

When I saw Justin I noticed he had changed cars and was driving a green Lexus GS. He had also changed clothes. He had on jeans, a navy Polo sweater and fresh Timbs. Summer was around the corner, but since it hadn't arrived just yet the nights were still chilly. I got in and the seat warmer had me feeling good.

I had never sat inside of a Lexus and was impressed with the interior. I couldn't wait to buy my whip. Despite the sexual shit I had done just minutes ago I was nervous sitting next to Justin. He seemed like he was more of a thug and I didn't quite know what to expect. I did know that I was hungry. I hadn't eaten anything since lunch when I got the cheese steak from the sub shop near Chanel, so my stomach was talking to me.

"You hungry boo?" he asked.

*Boo*? I would rather him call me *ma* if anything. But that was beside the point. I wanted to eat and finish up for the night. "Yeah, you know what's open at two in the morning?" I asked.

"Mos def. I'm a night person."

In the car we didn't talk much since DMX's 'It's All Good' was drowning out anything I would have wanted to say. But it was fine with me since all I wanted to do was get my eat on. Fifteen minutes later we were in *Mo's Seafood and Pasta* ordering lobster, crab imperial and oysters. They were open later than usual since so many money niggas were still seated at the bar, poppin' bottles.

Justin turned out to be a hard one to figure out. I felt like he could see right through me, like he knew I was out to get his pockets. But it wasn't like I was trying to get him for everything, I just wanted some of it.

After he ordered his fourth Dewar's and gingerale he loosened up. "So Nikola, you like to fuck?"

I almost choked on my lobster tail. Before I could answer him he went on to respond to his own damn question. "You see a nigga like me likes to get down. I mean nasty off-the-hook shit. I like fuckin' in the ass, the pussy, the mouth. I don't give a *fuck*."

I couldn't believe how rough and raunchy he sounded. Was he serious or was it the liquor talking? "Are you for real?" I finally asked him.

"Hell yeah. Oh, what you sayin' you don't like sex?"

"It's not that, I love anything that's gon' make me feel good, but that ass fuckin', now, you can keep that."

"See, you only say that because you haven't tried it. That shit'll have you cummin' from all directions."

"No, that's okay. I would like to hold onto my rectum."

He let out a long laugh and from then on, the mood lightened and we were trippin' like two old friends. We finally left at three, and in the car he had switched the CD to R. Kelly's *12 Play.* It was cool that he was trying to set the mood and I couldn't find a better way to end the night than listening to some old school from the nasty man himself. We were riding around the city and I had my head tilted towards the sunroof. The liquor had mellowed out my serious mood and my stomach was full.

"So, you never did tell me what it is you like," he said.

"You mean as far as sex?"

"Yeah, what you think?"

"Well, depending on the mood, I can go for slow sex or rough sex against the wall," I said.

He raised his eyebrows like he was picturing me against the wall. "Yeah, that sounds good. So what's your favorite way to get down? You already told me you don't like it in the ass, so what *do* you like?"

"I like head."

"Givin' it?" he asked with his eyebrow raised.

"No doubt."

*There I went again.* Saying shit before I thought about it. But like earlier, I was ready to get down and get home since the night was coming to an end.

We were still riding around downtown when he drove to Federal Hill. That's where the nice historic-looking houses sat on streets that overlooked the harbor. They were nice as hell. Everything about them was original and rich looking. It was like Harlem's brownstones meet the waterfront.

When my parents were together we used to come and park on the hill for the fourth of July and watch the fireworks in the distance, instead of competing with the crowds of people at the Inner Harbor.

Justin stopped the car and we sat there and looked at the lights from the boats on the docks. He reached behind his seat and pulled out a bag of weed. After he rolled it he offered me the first puff.

"No thank you," I said.

I needed to keep a clear mind and stay focused. He didn't have a problem getting his smoke on by himself because he hit a switch beside his seat and reclined back. I looked over and he had lifted his shirt and undid his jeans. "So I'm sayin' boo,

I'm feelin' you, everything about you. And I want you to show me what you're workin' wit'."

"What?" I said.

"Come on, I bet you could make a nigga feel like no other. Slide on down here and show me somethin'."

"Justin I don't know you and I don't do shit like that for niggas I don't know," I lied. "Besides, I don't see no cash."

"Come on, I got that. I'll take care of you. Just make me feel good and I'll take care of you later." His speech had suddenly become slower and softer.

I looked at him and could tell he was flying high. His eyes were halfway shut, but I figured he was good for the money. I unzipped his pants and saw his dick sticking out of his boxers. I leaned down and hoped he wouldn't take forever. While going up and down, I opened the hole in his boxers wider and felt something smooth and hard with my left hand. I was still sucking when I saw the black handle of a gun.

My first instinct was to stop and grab it, but I didn't know if he would want more from me and use the gun to get it, so I continued. My jaws were just getting tight when he grabbed my hair and moved my head with extra force. It felt like a huge headache was coming on.

I was so ready for him to finish so I gave him three hard deep throats and felt his lower body begin to tighten and shake. I moved my face away from his dick but he was still holding onto my hair and when it was over I felt all of him in my hair. I just sat up and tried to relax my cheeks and jawbones. I couldn't wait to get to Chanel's to take a shower.

"Whoo! That shit was so good," he said and started up the car. He didn't even bother to fix his seat. I never could understand how guys drove like that. And he was high so I really thought we would crash.

When we finally got to the apartment I didn't move. He hadn't said anything about the money the entire ride and I was ready to get paid. I had put in more work than expected.

"Aight Nikola boo, that shit was live. I be calling you tomorrow."

I knew he wasn't getting ready to fuck me over! Suddenly I felt so stupid. I should have demanded my money before I did any fuckin' thing. If I could have, I would have used my own foot to kick myself in the ass. "Nigga, where is my money?" I asked.

"Oh."

*Oh* was right. I knew he hadn't forgotten. He sat up to dig in his pockets. After he pulled out the money he practically threw it in my lap. The two bills were easily visible.

"Two hundred dollars? Nigga you better come again."

"What you mean *two hundred dollars*?" he said, making fun of me. "That's what the fuck you gettin'."

"You better start diggin' deeper 'cause two hundred dollars ain't gon' do shit for me."

"Girl you better take ya high-priced ass to bed wit' all that. I'm not the one."

There was no way I was beggin' for shit and it wasn't like *I* had a gun to make him give me anything else. *He had the burner*, and I wasn't trying to catch anything that night. I grabbed my bag and slammed the door.

"The fucker won't be hearing from me again," I mumbled as I walked inside the building.

Chanel wasn't home yet but I had seen her car so I assumed Chelsea had driven home. I looked in the second room and there she was, laid out on the bed like she was getting paid to sleep. I wondered if she had run into any luck. *Where the hell had Chanel gone?*

I called her phone and she said she was cool. She was on her way to New York so I figured she had hooked up with Reds after all. That was the only thing that could make me laugh at that moment because my night certainly hadn't ended the way I expected. She gave me the number to where she was and I got in the shower.

The first thing I did was wash that shit out of my hair. I just wanted to get clean and wipe the remnants of my last episode away. When I dried off I got in Chanel's queen-sized bed and turned on the cable. I was glad she had changed the sheets. I had never heard of anybody ironing their sheets, but the starchy feeling made me feel a little better and made me forget that I had been fucked over. Outside, the sun was rising and I was about to rest my head, but angry thoughts about my loss only propelled me to plot at the next opportunity to *take no shorts*.

# Road Trip/ 5

## Chanel

I couldn't have asked for a better first-time experience. The night of the concert I was looking fly just like I said I would. Earlier that day Nikola had relaxed my hair and thinned it out. When she finished I was sportin' a flat wrap and a fresh black rinse. I loved to get it dyed black. It made my hair look shiny and healthy. I wanted a couple of copper red streaks to set off my outfit but she said she didn't want my hair to fall out from the bleach she'd have to use.

Downtown traffic was crazy as usual but it was fine with me since I got to sit back and relax while Nikola handled all that stop and go bullshit. My first run in for the night was with this New York nigga named Reds. He was worth flirting with but he was too flashy for me. I mean come on now, how obvious can you get than centering your life around a fuckin' nickname. He was sexy in his own little way but I liked dudes who moved quietly. I had a feeling he was going to end up being a big hemorrhoid on my ass that night.

The Baltimore Arena was packed and all I could think about was how many niggas were strapped that night. Security wasn't as tight as I would have liked so there was bound to be a few gunslingers who got past the detectors. Shit, the bitch that was checking me only glanced in my bag. She didn't know what I had on me, and my hot pants were so tight she didn't even try to feel on my ass.

After we took pictures I ran into this dude from around my old neighborhood, Raheim. My, how time changes people. When I would see him standing on the corner all I could give him was a hi and bye. He wasn't ugly, in fact he always looked more presentable than the other niggas out there slingin' who just threw on whatever. His light brown skin always made him look nice in natural colors, but having a boyfriend wasn't on my mind at that time. Plus he was like eighteen when I was twelve and my mother would've killed me.

"Damn Chanel, is that you?" he asked, breaking away from his group of friends.

"Yeah, it's me. W'sup Raheim?"

"Ain't shit, maintainin'. You look good," he said, gazing at my titties. "What happened to lil' Chanel with the ponytail?" he asked, opening his arms for a hug.

"I guess she grew up."

"You ain't lyin'," he said.

68

I could still smell his cologne on my nose after he pulled away from me. It was my favorite, Issey Miyake. Raheim had definitely changed. He was still quiet, I could tell, but that's one of the things that made him so attractive. I knew he was probably doing big boy things. But I was grown as well and ready to show him.

"So, how are things goin' for you?" I asked.

"Ain't shit changed. Just tryna survive, you know how it is."

"You know I do," I said, letting my eyes hold their gaze on his strong cheekbones.

"So, who you here wit'?" he asked, looking at Nikola and Chelsea. I introduced them and we exchanged numbers. "I'm for real Chanel, I'm tryna see you tonight," he said before he walked away. Raheim didn't have to worry 'cause I was definitely tryna see him too.

I looked back at him one more time. From behind I looked at his shoulders and legs. They were so muscular and he was tall of course. I could never get into short niggas. They seemed to fall short in all other areas: money and common sense.

When we started walking to our seats I noticed a group of girls looking our way. At first I thought they were just checking out our gear but then I realized that the one girl with the weave and the blue contacts was staring straight at me and so were her other three friends.

"What the fuck are they lookin' at?" I said loud enough for them to hear and slow enough just in case they had to read my lips.

"Chanel, please don't start anything. The concert hasn't even began yet," Chelsea pleaded.

"I'm not startin' shit. I'm just wondering what the fuck is the problem."

I looked back and the bitches had looked in the other direction. There was still something strange about the one with the weave, though. She had looked at me for a long time like she knew me, but I couldn't place her face for anything. It would come to me, but in the meantime, I was preoccupied by Jay-Z's sexy ass taking the stage. I hoped I could enjoy myself without having to fuck a bitch up. I wasn't scared to mess up any of that Gucci shit, it could be replaced.

The concert was live. I hadn't been to the Baltimore Arena since I was about seven when my mother took me and Rico to the circus. I think that was the last time we were together and happy. I wondered then what my mother would say if she saw me with my expensive clothes and my apartment. *Did she even know I had graduated?*

I had called Aunt Charlene to let her know about graduation but I didn't see her in the bleachers either. My mother probably didn't even care if I was okay or not. I hadn't seen or heard from her since I tried to return home that day after the incident with Petey. But she had no excuse. Aunt Charlene had every one of my numbers, even to my apartment. Shit, if she couldn't be proud of me, I was. I had moved into my own place during the summer before senior year and was really taking care of things.

I had been living at Ms. Diane's house for about six months when I knew I had to get the fuck out. At first things were fine between me and Nikola but by the third month she started trippin'. I think it was because she had started hangin' with this group of girls at Western who were only into keeping themselves in name brand shit and were just plain ol' snobby bitches.

She was doing hair and had learned how to do weaves so she was charging more. With the extra change in her pockets she could afford to buy the things she had always wanted. But I knew it was all a front, because in the end she was still broke.

Nikola was doing so much to fit in and her attitude reflected it. But I wasn't crying over her though, 'cause I knew she would be crawling back later when those bitches showed their true colors. We were living in the same house and she was treating me like I was beneath her. That bitch didn't know I was holding more money than she had ever seen at one time. Instead of fussing with her I made plans to move out.

I liked the neighborhood so I found a nice apartment building on Madison Ave. where the rent was only $400. I saw the inside and knew it could look even better when I finished decorating. The hardwood floors and large windows gave it an old-fashioned kind of look that made it feel warm and peaceful—like a home.

Ms. Diane cried when I told her I was moving. "Chanel baby, you know you don't have to leave. I like having you here."

"I know Ms. Diane, and I appreciate everything you've done for me, but things are just so different."

"Look, I know Nikola has gotten above herself but it's only because we've had to struggle to get what we have now. You understand right?"

"Yeah, I do, but she's like a sister to me and it's like she forgot about that."

"I understand. I guess you have to do what's best for you. But I don't want you to be a stranger," she said after patting her eyes with a tissue.

"Ms. Diane I'm moving right there on Madison."

"Oh good, I have to come by after you're settled."

She told me she had something for me and went to her room. While she was gone I sat there and held back my own tears. I was going to miss her so much. There were nights I had laid at the foot of her bed because I just wanted to be under her and feel some kind of love. She never bothered me or told me to leave and she would always cover me up and kiss my cheek before she turned out the light beside her bed.

"Now, Chanel I know what you're going to say but I want you to have this," she said when she had returned to the living room.

I looked inside the envelope she had given me and it was the same $600 I had given her when I first came to stay with them. In the back I saw a piece of folded paper.

"Aww, Ms. Diane," was all I could say.

"I held on to it 'cause I never knew when you would need it again. Use it to buy a nice plant for your window and the rest for savings. Always save Chanel. You never know when rainy days are coming."

All I could do was hug her and cry on her shoulder. I was leaving again, only this time it was from a house that felt like a home.

I was moving one of the last boxes from the trunk of the BMW I had bought for only $3000 at this auction. The envelope between the driver's seat caught my attention. I removed the money and stuffed it in my pocket. I planned on opening a savings account as soon as I was settled. I sat on the front steps and opened it:

*Chanel,*

*By the time you read this you would have probably accepted your diploma and walked gracefully in your pretty white dress. If not at graduation perhaps at another momentous journey in your life. I've watched you even before you came to stay with us and it's amazing to see so much strength in such a young lady like yourself. I know that life can bring heartache but it brings sunshine as well. The day you came to me I knew the pain you were feeling. My mother cut off our relationship too. She wanted me to go off to school and become a nurse like we had discussed but when I decided on a husband and a family she was disappointed that I had given up my dreams. When I had my marriage and family I decided to reconcile but it was too late. She was dying and I had waited too long to come around. What I'm saying is that, no it's not right to let arguments push the ones we love away, but in the end all that's left is love. And nothing will ever change a mother's love. No matter how many mistakes you or your mother have made. Chanel, I'm proud of you and I admire all of your strength and courage. No matter what you do, keep a place in your heart for love. That's the one thing we can never push away.*

*With Love Always...*

She didn't have to sign her name. We both knew she was more of a mother than I would ever have. Just the thought of my mother's behavior and her void in so much of my young life made my eyes sting. I hated to feel tears form in my eyes. I stood there at the concert and blocked out everything around me.

There was the battle going on between the left and the right to see who was the loudest. The groupies were there just to get a chance at sucking somebody's dick on the stage and the niggas had come out just to feel on and look at some ass.

In my mind everything was silent and I knew that I had to put my issues aside and see my mother. I had to make plans to see Rico as well. I didn't even know if he had been transferred to another jail. He had so many big dreams of being this big-time lyricist. That's what he called himself even at the age of ten. He said "rapper" wasn't good enough a word and he wanted to be as big as Rakim. Him acting out his own concerts with his Kangol, Adidas sweatsuits and matching tennis made me smile wide.

"You comin' or you gon' stand and stare at Jay?" Nikola asked jokingly.

"Oh," I said unaware that intermission had arrived.

My mind suddenly went blank and the memories faded as quickly as they had come. I was back in the scene I had tried to block out. I was upstairs in line ordering french fries when I saw this nigga who fit the description of the type I had laid in bed and dreamed I'd meet. He wasn't exactly red like the ones I was used to but he would do. His complexion was closer to Nikola's, like hot caramel.

He was standing against the wall with two of his friends but he could have held his own. His chiseled face had this real serious look like he was about handling his and didn't have time for games. And his clothes, I could tell they were expensive, but he didn't have to have Versace written on his sleeve to show it. His phone rang and when he flipped it open he got this look in his eyes like whoever was on the other end would have been dealt with had they been standing in his face. I had to find out who he was before I left from there.

There were three of them and three of us but Nikola was talking to some dude, and looked like she was fussin' instead of getting his number. I don't think he would've cared if she called him a million mafuckas. Her outfit had been getting stares all night and Nikola the exhibitionist was eating up all of the attention. Chelsea was still in line waiting for her nachos. I was on my own but I didn't have a problem with that. I trashed my fries, bent over a little to tug on my boots and strolled over with a walk that let niggas know I had that "I'm the baddest bitch" attitude.

I didn't get far before you know who stepped in front of me. "Damn ma, I didn't realize how good you looked when I saw you in the car."

"Hey Reds," I said with no real interest.

"Yo, you know I been lookin' everywhere for you?"

"Is that right? Well I'm kind of in a hurry. I gotta use the bathroom real bad," I lied, looking over his shoulder. *Damn that nigga looked good.*

"Oh, okay. Well let me get that number so we can hook up the next time I'm in town."

I didn't want him to see me giving out my number so I moved over to the left. Reds was tall and thick so hiding was no problem. I gave him my cell number and hoped he wouldn't be a nuisance. When Reds walked away I wanted to call him back so I could slap him. *Dude was gone that quick.*

"Fuck," I said to myself.

I assumed it wasn't meant for us to talk. The concert would be ending soon and I knew Chelsea would forget to buy her shirt so I went to the stand and got her a navy fitted tee with "Hard Knock Life Tour" written on the front. They were so cute that I bought us all one. My bag was large enough so I folded them and stuffed them in. As I was zipping my bag I felt someone looking over my shoulder.

"Damn, can you back up?" I asked without turning around.

"Yeah, I can do that," the deep voice said.

It was the cutie and he looked even better up close. I gave the cashier the fifty and waited for my change. I never get nervous when it comes to meeting somebody but he had my heart doing cartwheels.

He touched me lightly where the mink trim of the coat met my shoulder. "You look nice tonight."

I didn't expect him to tell me that. He said it so calmly, like he was choosing his words carefully. "Thank you. You do too."

"I see you're popular tonight," he said.

"Popular? Who me?" I said coyly.

"Yeah I see the way these cats are breakin' they necks to say somethin' to you."

"I guess, but I already see what I want," I said.

I could see that he wanted to smile but he only opened his mouth wide enough to show me he was enjoying my comment.

"So you got a name?"

"Chanel."

I took my change and we started walking away from the booth. I wished there was a mirror so I could see how we looked standing next to each other. His cornrows were neat like everything else on him, although his hair was so curly that they looked like they would unravel at any time.

I was tall but he towered over my 5'8" frame and his walk matched his voice. It was real smooth but not pimped out. "So, Chanel you have plans tonight?"

"I'm not sure what I'm gettin' into tonight. Why, you got plans?"

"My plan is to hook up wit' you."

I did the number thing and he was about to walk away when I remembered I didn't know his name. But I really didn't care what it was, I just hoped it wasn't a bogus-ass nickname. I had had enough of those for the night.

"You never told me your name," I said after I caught up with him.

"Does it matter?" he said.

"Well yeah, I want to put a name with your face."

"Oh, I *forgot*, you got so many you gotta have a way to keep up wit' 'em. But it's cool. Quentin."

"Whateva Quentin, I'll be talking to you soon," I said with much attitude.

"Yeah, aight," he said before he walked away.

Later, when me and Chelsea finally left the club I ran into a problem. Nikola had gone off with her second victim for the night and we were in the parking lot across from the club. I was about to open my door when I heard someone mention Petey's name.

"Yeah, that's that bitch Petey was fuckin' wit'," the one female voice said.

"I think her name is Chanel. My friend told me her motha is a junkie," the other one said maliciously.

My heart started beating faster and I felt my ears getting hot. *Who the hell knew that much about me to mention Petey and my mother in a conversation? And if what they had said was true, why didn't I know?* I turned around slowly and when I saw them I knew why the bitches I'd seen at the concert couldn't stop lookin' at me.

The one with the contacts was one of the many girls who used to call the house for Petey. Her name was Kimia and I had called her back myself. After she said she was fuckin' him and would continue to do so, I told her I would be seeing her ass, and I did.

I wore my tennis to school the next day and left early to go wait for her at Forest Park High. My friend Nika went there so she knew what she looked like. When Kimia came outside, Nika pointed her out and I gave her the worst ass beating she'd ever felt.

I noticed how different she looked from then. I guessed she was doin' all right for herself 'cause she was driving a red CLK, but then I remembered her outfit. It was the same unoriginal shit that any bitch could have put together. The ride *had* to be somebody else's shit, typical chickenhead tactic.

Her and her girlfriend were sitting in the car waiting for the club to let out along with a couple hundred other people. I was so angry but I decided to wait. If I went over to the car she might pull off so I opened my door and sat behind the wheel.

I looked over at Chelsea who didn't have a clue about what was going on. "Chelz, don't look right away but you remember those bitches from the concert?"

"Yeah, why?" she asked.

"Well, they're sitting in that red Benz to our left. The one driving is this girl I fought a long time ago and I might have to tonight."

"For what? You lost the last time?"

I looked at her like she was crazy. "You jokin,' right?"

"Well if you beat her up before, why again tonight?"

Chelsea could be a fuckin' airhead at times. "'Cause she's being real cute, tryna front for her bitch-ass friends."

"Well I only see one right now," she said, looking into the car.

"I know, but I don't know if the other two are hangin' around somewhere so when I pull off, you watch my back."

Chelsea looked scared as shit. She probably had never been in a fight before but she needed to get it together if she was going to be in "the life." Putting bitches in their place was going to be a crucial part to us making a name for ourselves.

I pulled off and blocked in the front of her car, not bothering to cut mine off. Her friend was talking to some dude leaning in the window with half-braided hair and Kimia was looking in the mirror, fixing her nasty-ass weave.

"Bitch you must've forgot about the last ass whipping," I said before spitting in her face.

Before she could roll up her window I was pulling her hair and landing blows in her face. I got this rush, knowing I had caught her off guard. I was still punching her in the face when I saw her friend getting out the car to help her. I was ready for her ass too, especially after she had said those things about my mother. There was no way my mother was using drugs. She wasn't perfect, but she had put Rico out for the same thing.

When I finished with Kimia I met the other bitch with a blow in the nose. I felt her holding my hair and grabbed her by the shirt to pull her to the ground. I was stomping her with my stiletto boots when one of the bouncers lifted me off her. I was livid and it felt good seeing her on the ground wiping her bloody nose.

"Bitch when I see you I'm gon' kill you!" her friend screamed.

I watched Kimia finally leave the car. She was trying to cover her bald head and help her friend off the ground at the same time. I had pulled her weave out and all she had left was a short haircut that was flying out from every direction.

The bouncer held me long enough for them to get in the car and Chelsea had moved my car so they could get out, but if he hadn't pulled me off her and held my arms tight I would have been ready for round two.

When they were gone the bouncer gave me this speech about conducting myself as a young lady or I would be in jail. I didn't fuss with him but everything he was telling me went in one ear and out the other. It had been that way since I was younger. When anger came over me like that I never thought about the repercussions. I felt like I had to do what I had to, and shuttin' two bitches down was the thing to do at the moment. But that was small shit. I wasn't letting it fuck with my night.

I got in the car on the passenger side 'cause I was too fired up to drive. After I straightened out my hair, I fished in my bag for my phone and dialed Quentin. While I waited for him to pick up I noticed the crowd that had gathered in the parking lot. Niggas was laughing and acting out the whole fight scene. I hoped they didn't think it was over one of their dumb asses. That shit was about respect and nobody was disrespecting me.

"Yeah," his sexy voice said into the phone.

"W'sup Quentin it's Chanel."

"I know. Where you at?" he asked.

"On Charles St."

"Is that right? Well look don't be mad, but I got somethin' I need to take care of tonight so we gotta hook up tomorrow."

I tried to listen for other voices, particularly female. "If you got plans wit' ya girl that's cool. Just don't give me no stupid-ass excuses, aight?"

"Yeah, aight Chanel. It's not even like that. And besides I don't have a reason to lie or give you any explanation. Later."

And just like that, he was gone. I wasn't used to no nigga puttin' me in my place like that but I was turned the fuck on. Fuck all that money shit. That's a nigga I wanted on the side 'cause with a strong and demanding voice like that he probably controlled the bedroom and that's all I wanted in mine, a nigga who knew how to handle me.

I was about to tell Chelsea to drive to the IHOP on Loch Raven when I heard someone screaming my name. I looked out the window and saw Raheim in a dark blue Tahoe. *Okay, so the night wasn't over.* He was blocked in so I got out and walked over to him.

"Yo w'sup? Why you out here whippin' bitches asses and shit?" he laughed.

"Just some bitches who were askin' for it since earlier that's all."

"Oh, so you just block them in and beat 'em up?"

I told him the story and he shook his head.

"What the fuck are you shakin' your head for?" I asked. "Like you embarrassed for me."

"It's not that 'cause I would've done the same shit if I heard somebody say that, bitch or a nigga. So that's you?" he asked, pointing to my car.

"Yeah that's mine."

"Well, how 'bout you drop your girl off and you and me hang."

I looked in his eyes for any signs of sneakiness. True, I knew him from around the way but I knew a lot of niggas who thought a ride in their shit or free dinner entitled them to some head or free pussy. He seemed like it was all a friendship thing so I was down, plus I had a blade for his ass if he tried to crack slick.

"We can go now," I said. "She can take my car. That's my girl."

"Oh well, do you. I'll be waitin' here."

Chelsea was cool with taking the car. She said she was hookin' up with somebody anyway. I kind of wanted to stay with her 'cause she seemed so gullible at times. I just hoped she wouldn't fall for any dumb shit and forget about gettin' her paper.

"Chelz you gon' be alright?"

"Yeah, and if somebody tries something I'll just give 'em the ass kicking I just saw you give," she laughed.

"You be careful aight, my phone'll be on all night."

"All right mom," she said in a valley girl voice.

I got my bag out the car and walked back to his truck. Raheim reached over and opened my door and I almost broke my neck tryna hop into the seat.

"So you gotta curfew tonight Ms. Chanel?"

"Nigga, I'ma grown-ass woman."

"No denying that," he said, looking at my legs hungrily. "Well I need to stop and get some gas. You hungry?"

"Hell yeah," I said.

We drove to W. Franklin Ave. and stopped at the gas station. After the pump stopped at forty dollars we pulled into the McDonald's across the street.

He looked over at me and must've seen the "no he didn't" look on my face. "I know it's Mickey D's but we'll eat a real meal when we get to our final destination. This is just for the road."

*For the road?* I didn't ask any questions, I was anxious to be going somewhere outside of the city. While we waited for our food I turned on the TV in the dashboard.

"What's on at three in the mornin'?" he asked.

"Good Times."

After he paid for the food we headed back downtown to get on I-95. We were going north to New York so I repositioned my seat and stretched my legs. When I had finished off my fries I closed my eyes and went to sleep. About three hours later I woke up to my phone ringing. It was Chelsea asking me questions and I told her I would call her later.

I noticed that we had stopped at the New Jersey Turnpike. I looked around for Raheim and when I saw him behind the truck talking with two Spanish-looking dudes, I pulled down my mirror to see what was going on. The one with the shiny head had a snake tattooed on his neck that wrapped around and stopped at his ear. The other one had hair but it was cut close and he had tattooed teardrops under each eye. These niggas looked like they were straight out of jail with big arms and chests. The one with the snake handed Raheim a small black bag and they gave each other pounds. I put the mirror back in its place and sat back.

"You finally up sleepyhead?" he asked after he got behind the wheel.

"Yeah."

"I hope you all rested up 'cause we about to put in work."

"Put in work? Doin' what?"

"It's a surprise."

"Well, I think I'm still tired," I yawned.

"Shiit! Not the way you snored during the whole ride."

"Whateva," I said, laughing and feeling very comfortable with him.

"Oh, it's whateva? I had to scream your name like three times, '*Chanel yo can you stop snoring?*' You was 'bout to wake the dead."

All I could do was laugh. I wanted to ask him about the two killers but if there was anything I knew about his lifestyle, it was to avoid asking questions. If it couldn't be figured out it was better left alone. We joked each other the rest of the way. I saw we were in New York and headed for the Lincoln Tunnel.

I was pumped as hell on the inside since I had never been to the big city. All I could see happening was a shopping spree. After we checked into the Marriott in downtown Manhattan we went and had breakfast at the hotel's restaurant. I forgot all about wanting to lay down and get some sleep. Everything about the city said excitement and nightlife, but after the pancakes were settled in my stomach I wanted a nap.

Raheim must've been thinking the same thing. "Chanel I think we need to go back to the hotel and sleep this food off before we head into the city or we'll be too tired to do anything."

"I bet you *do* wanna go back to the hotel," I joked.

"Girl please, you think I want that coochie? It ain't all that."

"Whateva nigga. After you taste this pussy you'll be beggin' for more."

"Oh, so just like that, you think I'll be tastin' it? Ha!"

Our joking back and forth made it feel less like work or even a date for that matter. When we got to the room I stripped down to my panties and bra and laid down. It didn't take me long to fall asleep. Minutes later I felt Raheim slide in behind me. Turned out that he was the one with the snoring problem.

At around five that evening we were dressed and ready to go somewhere else. Raheim had woke me around 3:30. I felt somebody staring at me and when I turned over he was in the chair watching me sleep. He was dressed in clean clothes and when I asked him about a change of clothes for me, he pointed to the shopping bag in the windowsill. I looked to my right and it was from Nordstrom. I laughed, remembering the shopping adventure two weeks ago.

I got up from the bed and felt him gazing at my titties sitting in my bra. I didn't try to cover up since I was practically naked the day before. Inside the bag was a pair of Azzure' jeans and a matching half of T-shirt that would spread across my titties like a sports bra. Underneath the jeans was a pair of denim thong Jimmy Choo's and a denim Coach handbag. He even had all my sizes correct. Oh, this nigga was definitely on point and he had on almost identical jeans and a white T-shirt with his fresh buttas. Another small bag from Victoria's Secret had some scented powder, lotion and a pair of red thongs. I wondered when he had left the room.

"Nigga you don't know if I want to wear bloomers or not," I told him.

"You can save bloomers for your own bedroom. Besides, when you see how those jeans fit you might not even want to wear the panties I got you."

He was right. After I showered and dressed I kept looking in the mirror at the way the jeans stopped at the crevice of my ass. My tattoo of the moon goddess hanging from a crescent-shaped swing on the small of my back had me looking real sexy. New York City wasn't ready for a bitch like me.

We got the truck from the second floor parking lot. Raheim cruised the streets like he had drawn a map himself and I found out he was originally from Jamaica Queens. He told me he had come to live in Baltimore with his grandmother while his mother was in school in New York. I wanted to meet her since he said she could throw down in the kitchen, but instead we stopped at a corner restaurant owned by his friend.

While he went in the back I took a seat by the window and counted the cars with the Jamaican flag. There were so many of the exotic looking inhabitants walking around and all of the stores seemed to be owned by them. I was impressed. I never saw Black people owning shit back home. There might've been one or two stores here and there, but guaranteed, their shit was closed down before it had a chance to profit.

Raheim came back with his friend Tahir who introduced me to his wife Mikala. They were both tall and had dreadlocks. Only hers were wrapped in a black crocheted head garment. Tahir was dark like me and Mikala was the opposite. She said she was from Nicaragua and got her color from her mother. She kept telling me how beautiful my skin was and gave me some shea butter before we left. She said it would maintain my already natural glow.

I hoped that I wasn't obvious when I was looking at their hair. It just amazed me that they could get their hair to wrap into what looked like silk worms. Before Petey I always thought the locs were matted balls of nappiness. Their hair made them seem taller like they possessed some secret power. I smiled to myself at the thought of my first love, and how he used to beg me to grow my hair in natural. I touched my own permed hair and quickly erased any thoughts of going natural. I wasn't about to forego my straight chic style.

Heaps of oxtails, callaloo, jerk chicken and steamed cabbage were eaten before we said our good-byes. Tahir and Mikala had really made me feel like family. I expected them to speak with accents, but they spoke slang just like I did.

Before we left Queens, Raheim took me to a few shops where I got a variety of incense, smoke bottles and natural skin and hair products. I knew I wasn't letting my hair go natural but the shampoos smelled so good. They even had shit to use when smoking weed. I got this cute little tin to hold my weed and of course one for my girls. They were going to flip when I told them about all the drug paraphernalia they carried in the stores.

I would've been happy if we left and went back to Baltimore then, but he told me we were going to Greenwich Village. I had no idea where that was so I just laid back and rubbed my full stomach while I finished my Red Stripe beer. I never liked the taste of beer but that Jamaican soda pop shit went down nice and smooth.

I was kind of missing Jamaica Queens. I felt like I belonged to the groups of people with skin like me. Though I was never ashamed of my complexion, when I was younger, it always seemed like the lighter girls got more attention. I was so used to people defining their self-worth by the lightness and darkness of their skin. Back home the women and men seemed to think lesser of themselves depending on their complexions. I had even continued to believe the same thing as I got older since the light-skinned girls still got all the preferential treatment.

Petey had made me see the beauty of my skin. It wasn't until he was gone that I appreciated the things he filled my head with. I touched the spot on my left arm where I had his name tattooed. If I ever missed his presence—which was most of the time—I had a habit of rubbing the tattoo and reflecting.

The change of scenery brought me out of my daze. The different boutiques in the Village made me forget about any homesickness I was feeling. The mannequins in the window were wearing shit I had only seen in exclusive magazines and catalogs I received in the mail. I was so anxious to get in the stores and do damage.

"Remember I told you we were 'bout to put in work?" he asked.

"Yeah," I said, becoming excited.

"Well this is it. I know you used to shit like this Chanel, so I figured we could come here and do some shopping, hang out. You know?"

I was smiling so wide on the inside but my face maintained its composure. I couldn't let him know that I wasn't used to spur-of-the-moment shit like that. Well, actually I was, I just hadn't done it since Petey, and Raheim seemed to be ready to go all out.

The theme colors were black and white in the first store. It was just right for me. Those were my colors so I didn't bother to try on anything. I was just picking up clothes and handing them to him.

After the fourth boutique he started getting restless. "Chanel, you don't need me here wit' you so I'm gon' to this spot I like down the street. You know, so I can pick up some things for me."

"That's cool," I said without looking up.

I didn't need his ass to hold my hand. Shit, I could shop with me eyes closed. Before he left I gave him the shopping bags of clothes I was carrying and he handed me a wad of dough.

Now that I was alone I had more time to pick and choose. I noticed a store on the opposite corner with a fall sale. Spring was almost over but no season could fuck with the fall fashions. I was impressed with the colorful sweaters, jackets and knitted dresses. They had a vintage look but it was obvious that that they were made from the best materials.

After the two smiling cashiers bagged up all of my things my total was about $3,300. *Damn, that was their idea of a sale?* I pulled the money Raheim had given me from my bag and saw that there were rows of hundreds and fifties. He must've gotten the money when we made the stop in Jersey. I knew he had money but I didn't know he was rollin' like that.

I paid for my stuff and had about $3,000 left. I did the math and couldn't believe he had given me almost seven G's. Walking out, I looked up and down the street for him but figured he was still shopping.

My feet were getting tired and I remembered that I hadn't bought any shoes. I wanted to put the rest of the bags in the truck but didn't want to interrupt his spree so I made my way to a shoe store that specialized in imported shoes and bags.

Outside, the sun had my titties sweating and feeling extra heavy, so before I went inside the shop I stopped at a café and bought a raspberry slush drink. I loved the look on those white bitches faces when they peeped my bags. They weren't the only ones who could rock that exclusive shit.

The sign inside the shoe store said *No Drinks Allowed* but I was sure they wouldn't mind when they found out I was gonna be spendin' a grip. I didn't have to look any further. Before I sat down, I had already seen ten pairs of shoes I wanted. I was so busy trying on every shade and style that was calling my name that I didn't realize two hours had gone by.

I heard my phone ringing and thought it was Raheim looking for me. "I'm in the imported shoe spot across from you," I said, without screening the call.

"Is that right?" the voice asked.

*Shit, it was Quentin.* I should have looked at the caller ID, but I was glad I hadn't used any first names. I was in New York with somebody else but just that quick I wanted to be with him. I was glad to hear his voice despite my slip up and my heart started jumping again.

"Hey, w'sup wit' you?" I asked.

"Nothin' much. Tryna see you. Where you at?"

"Umm, kinda far from the city."

"Where, you need me to come and meet you?"

"Well, it's New York," I said.

I hoped he wouldn't ask me who I was there with. I had no problem lying, but Quentin wasn't stupid, and as soon as I told him where I was I knew he was already thinking I was with a dude.

"NY, huh?" he asked and got real quiet. "Well, just holla at me when you get in, aight? And tell that funny lookin' New York nigga I said w'sup."

Like before, he hung up without a goodbye. I was getting tired of that hanging up bullshit. *That New York nigga, was he talking about Reds? I laughed to myself. How the hell did he know him?* I was amused at the circle of hustlers. They knew one another just like they were competing on the floor of Wall Street. I shrugged it off, but for some reason I was a little disappointed after he hung up 'cause I really wanted to be with Quentin. But shit, he blew it the night before when he hooked up with his bitch, so there was no need to cry over spilt milk.

I looked at all of the boxes of shoes and asked the Puerto-Rican girl that was helping me to get me the matching bags. The bags were one of a kind and I knew nobody would have them back at home. I spent another $1,200 and was happy with the extra cash I had left over.

I had too many bags to carry so I called Raheim and he said he was finishing up too and would meet me in front of the store in ten minutes. By the time everything was packed away in the back of his truck it was getting dark again. We stopped and ate at a Szechuan restaurant in Chinatown.

Over dinner I got to know Raheim better. He told me about his reasons for hustling and how he and his mother were poor when they came to the states. I asked him where his accent had gone, and he said he had tried to fit in so much that he had learned how to speak without it by listening to hip-hop and R&B.

It seemed like the drug game called for a mean streak but I couldn't sense any signs of cruelty or anger in him. Maybe that was why I felt like me and him weren't anything more than friends. When I saw him at the concert I was attracted to him but being in his company showed me that I wasn't feelin' him sexually.

And I also couldn't get Quentin out my mind. He was the type of thug nigga that could fuck up my mental without warning. I guess I was never too big on nice guys, and Raheim had definitely thrown me a curve ball. I just knew he was going to want to fuck, but after we ate we were on the road again going home. I didn't know it then but that would be the last time I got a free ride.

# Foot Fetish/ 6

## Chelsea

Marco was the last person I wanted to see at my wedding. He was my first target the night of the concert. And of all the men I had been with, he was definitely the most memorable. After that night we had hooked up two more times before I found out what kind of person he was. To this day I don't think I have ever broken my mode when it comes to guys fitting a certain description and that night was no different.

I had never been so dolled up in my life with the exception of prom. Unlike Nikola and Chanel my outfit left something to the imagination. And although I enjoyed looking down at my newfound cleavage accented by the bodice, I knew how to wear innocence on my sleeve. True enough, I wasn't too experienced in the areas of sex, but I knew that men were drawn to a girl who was a lady in public and a freak in the bedroom.

I was tired of being in Chanel and Nikola's shadow, and to prove that I could "make shit liquid," I was willing to go to the extremes with whomever I hooked up with. More than anything though, I wanted to prove to myself that I could do what they did with less the effort.

I felt so inadequate when it came to sex. Especially giving head. Whenever that became one of our conversational pieces I would always pretend like I knew what I was doing, or that I enjoyed it as much as they did when the truth was, I had never done it. After Derrick I had only had sex with one other guy and it wasn't anything to brag about.

During the concert I told them I was going to use the bathroom when all I really wanted to do was be by myself for a minute. I wanted to test my own sensuality and see what I could get into. While I was in the bathroom I stared at myself in the mirror for a long time. There was no denying that I had it going on. My hair was its natural jet black and before we had left Chanel's, Nikola had ran the straightening comb through (since I didn't perm it but once every year) to give it a nice shine.

I was glad no one was in the bathroom with me because I was playing all in it. I loved to watch it grow and since I hadn't had a haircut since I was twelve, it hung freely to the center of my back. I loved my dress as well but my shoes made the outfit. They strapped around my ankle with a five-inch heel, and since I had gotten a French pedicure earlier my feet were flawless. I wanted them to look as natural as possible since I liked for them to look clean and simple.

I hated to see women with purple and blue polish caked on their big toes along with a hundred rhinestones. The word ghetto wasn't strong enough a word. I was so happy to be blessed with ten perfect toes, and I didn't have the biggest breasts, but I knew that most women would've been happier with my feet than a double-lettered bra size any day.

After I checked myself in the mirror once more I stepped out to roam the floor. I was enjoying all of the attention from the men who were commenting on my outfit and hair when I saw Marco. He was built, black and ugly, but I wasn't a fool. I could tell he had money, and from the way he was looking at me, I knew he was about to be my first victim. A lot of females would've passed up a guy like him based simply on his untraditionally handsome face but I knew that if he lacked in the looks area he would make up for it in some other way.

Instead of going back to my seat and counting on seeing him later I decided to buy time so I got in line to get lemonade. While the girl shook up my drink I looked over to where he was standing. I made sure that we had some kind of eye contact. I wanted him to know I was interested. After I got my change he extended his index finger and motioned for me to come over.

Now I knew that I was supposed to have him come to me, but I wanted him to feel like it was all about him so I took a sip of the drink and walked over. When I got closer I saw that he had moved his eyes from my face to my feet. *So he was a foot man.*

"Hello," I said, touching his arm softly. I knew that guys liked a lot of attention and subtle body contact was important.

"Hello to you too," he said. "You are gorgeous."

I was glad he wasn't nervous around me. Nor was he overbearing. Just my type. I know my cheeks could've turned red had I allowed them to, but instead I told myself to calm down. "Thank you. You look nice too."

And he really did look nice, so that part wasn't a lie, but there was no way I was telling him he was handsome. He had on a white linen shirt and khaki-colored linen pants. I was glad the brown leather Kenneth Coles weren't sandals that exposed his toes. I would've thought he had a little sugar in him.

He would not stop looking at my feet and while I knew they were perfect in every way, I was surprised that he wasn't looking in my face. Most guys and even females couldn't stop gazing into my money greens. That was usually the first thing that got people's attention after the dimples.

"I think your feet are the prettiest I've ever seen. What's your name?"

"Chelsea," I said.

"Chelsea huh? Well, Chelsea I really want to take you out tonight if that's okay."

"Yeah, that's fine," I said.

I gave him my number. To my surprise he pulled me to him and swallowed me with his two large arms. If somebody saw us they would say we were total opposites.

I was small and petite and he was just huge. I was kind of disappointed that he lacked that thug quality I was looking for, but Marco would serve his purpose for the night.

After Chanel got into a little catfight later at the club I was on my own. I had made plans to meet Marco at his house since it was too late to go anywhere else. At first I was leery until he told me he was having a card party. Well, by the time I got there, there was no doubt that there had been a card party, however all of the people were leaving when I pulled up.

I told him that I didn't go into strange houses when I didn't know the person, so he gave me his wallet with all of his info and the keys to his house and his truck. That was good enough for me so I joined him in his living room. Everything about him was clean and in place. While I sat on his cranberry, Italian leather couch he finished cleaning up the mess his previous guests had made, *if you could call it that*.

"I'm sorry you have to see my place like this. It's usually so much cleaner," he said.

"Oh, I understand," I said.

But I really didn't know what he was talking about. I could see my reflection in his floors and the walls looked like they had just been painted the refreshing taupe and sienna colors. All that wasn't immaculate was the card table, and all he had to do was fold it up and put it away. On the chrome table in front of the couch was every hardback edition of the season's newest collections. I picked up Versace's spring 1999 and pretended to be occupied.

While Marco finished cleaning up the imaginary mess in his house, I had to really wonder if he was gay. I hadn't dated a lot of guys, but the ones I did date never put as much effort into themselves as he did. His manicure and shape up was perfect and I had never seen such crispness in a pair of khakis.

"Hey Marco, can I take a tour of your house?" I yelled from the couch.

What I really wanted to do was take a look in his closet because it would definitely give me the answer I was looking for. If his things were color coordinated I knew we had a problem.

"Sure sweetheart, make yourself at home."

I had entered another color scheme as I ascended the slanted stairs and walked around the corner. The three walls in his room were painted three different shades and hues of blue. The king-sized bed was made up and all of the corners were tucked in as if he had maid service. The Victorian chairs matched the sheets and the walls. I couldn't believe that I was standing in the middle of my dream room minus the color scheme. I just needed to do one more thing before I left.

I opened his closet and walked in. Everything was separated into its own family. It was like looking at a color wheel. Half of the stuff still had tags and the boxes of shoes could've had their own closet. But what shocked me more than anything was a few pair of expensive shoes I had spotted. They favored ones I had in my own closet. *No he wasn't a cross dresser!* I was too through and prepared to call it a night when I heard him calling me.

I walked downstairs into the living room and saw that he had lit candles everywhere. I hoped Mr. Sensitivity wasn't trying to seduce me. He looked at me and patted the seat beside him. Suddenly I didn't want to hurt his feelings so I sat down and swallowed.

"So, why all the candles?" I asked.

"Well I think you're a special lady and I want to show you how you should be treated."

He didn't have to tell me how special I was. I was just wondering what he wanted to show me in the brief time that I had known him. We hadn't even had a real conversation yet, and there was no way we were having sex without him giving me something.

Before I could express that, he was in front of me on his knees. He picked up the remote and moments later I heard Maxwell's *Unplugged* fill the room. He took his hands (that were too soft to belong to man if you asked me), and grabbed the calf of my right leg while he unstrapped my shoe. After he did the same with the other, he took them both in his hands and poured some kind of oil that was sitting on the floor by the couch.

His expensive sound system gave off a sound so crisp and clear that it was like Maxwell was there giving us the concert live. I had never had the manicurist give me a massage like that before. I laid my head back into the soft cushion and let him work all of my pressure points.

My eyes were closed and I wanted to ask him if he had done that for a living, but I quickly sat up when I felt something prickly touching the bottoms of my feet.

I couldn't believe that he was rubbing them over his face. His eyes were closed and it seemed like he was enjoying it more than I was. I wanted to stop him but I was interested in what was going to happen next. Marco looked like he had experienced a mental orgasm. I saw him reach for a can of whipped cream. He had made a human sundae out of my toes and topped it off with a few cherries.

I waited to see what other kind of surprises he had on the floor. Marco was in pure bliss but I had to stop him before things went too far. I had already broken the code by not asking for my money beforehand.

"Umm, Marco," I interrupted.

He was licking off the last of the whipped cream so I touched his shoulder.

"What's wrong? Is there a problem, gorgeous?" he asked.

"Well, yeah. I mean this is great but I just can't go and do these kinds of things with you on a first night. I don't even know you," I said.

He looked like I had slapped him in the face. "So you don't like what I just did for you?" he asked.

"Oh, I'm not saying that, it's just that…"

"This is kind of strange to you," he said, completing my sentence.

*Try bizarre,* I wanted to say. "Well, yes," I said instead.

"Chelsea, I wasn't lying when I told you I've never seen feet so beautiful, and I guess I just wanted to enjoy them."

*Enjoy them, was he serious? What about me?* "Look, Marco you're really nice, but I need to be going."

I was so ready to get the hell outta there. There was something creepy about him. He wasn't gay, he was just a freak.

"Please don't go," he said and touched my knee. "Chelsea listen, I know what you're probably thinking about me, but don't. There's just something about feet that turns me on and you have the whole package. A pretty face, a perfect body…"

"Can you get me a warm washcloth," I said, cutting him off. I didn't care what his fetish was, I just wasn't going to be used. We hadn't had sex but he was still using my time to indulge in his little fantasy.

I heard him coming down the steps. "Listen, if I make it worth your time will you stick around?" he asked while he handed me the royal blue washcloth.

I didn't know what he had in mind, but I had told myself that I was willing to do whatever and I wasn't planning on leaving empty-handed.

"Stick around? Marco I should've told you this before, but my time isn't free," I said with a serious face.

He returned the look and stared at me like he knew exactly what I was talking about. "Well then. That's fine. We both have things we want. You want money in exchange for my pleasure. Am I right?" he asked, raising an eyebrow.

"Yes," I said embarrassed to look at him.

"I wish we had taken care of this earlier so there would be no interruptions," he said with an agitated tone.

That was my cue to get up and leave. I picked up my shoes and was prepared to walk out of there barefooted.

"Wait, where are you going?" he asked.

"I'm leaving. We *are* through right?" I asked.

"Oh no, I want to work out something. Chelsea, please make my night and stay for awhile."

"Well let's start talking," I said.

"How much?" he asked.

I thought about Nikola's question in her basement and she was right. No amount could make up for the pain I had been through with the abortion. I had eradicated something that was a part of me and the memory of Derrick's abrupt attitude change suddenly made me bitter.

"Two thousand," I said, looking around at his expensively furnished condo and back into his eyes to let him know I was serious. I knew the price went beyond far-fetched but I wanted to see how far I could go with him.

"That's fine," he said. "But…"

There was that *but*. If he couldn't come through I was leaving. I didn't have time for Mr. Freaky to think he was getting off for free. "*But* nothing. I'm leaving," I said.

"I was just going to say that I don't have that kind of money sitting around the house, *but* I can write you a check." He must've seen the way I was looking at him. "You can listen to my account balance over the phone to see that the funds are there," he said quickly.

I was ecstatic. I didn't think he would go for it. He had to be desperate because if I was him there was no way I was letting anyone hear my information. I figured then that he was probably used to paying for his sexual acts.

"Okay, well how much do you have on you now?"

"About a thousand. You want me to give you that and I write a check for the rest?"

*What do you think?* "Sure."

He handed me the phone and I heard the computerized voice say, *your existing balance is $350,052.00.* I should've gone higher, but satisfied, I placed the cordless on the charger. I sat there while he left the room and prayed that he didn't get carried away with whatever it was he wanted to do with me.

"Here you are," he said, handing me the check.

I looked at it before I folded it and put it in my purse. The check was for $2,000 instead of the remaining $1,000 he owed me. I hoped he didn't think he was getting anything extra.

"Thank you," I said.

"No, you can thank me later Miss Chelsea."

*Miss Chelsea?* I brushed it off and waited for the evening to end. He started the CD again and took a seat in the corner of the couch.

"Have you ever modeled before?" he asked.

"When I was younger," I said.

"Well put on your shoes but do it nice and slow."

I did as I was told and listened for the next instruction. After I had both shoes strapped up, he sank back into the couch and started rubbing between his legs.

"Now cross and uncross your legs slowly."

Again, I followed his command. I felt like I was playing a game of Simon Says.

"Now, Miss Chelsea I want you to get up slowly and walk across the floor. When you stop at the window throw your right leg back into the air and arch your foot."

He talked to me like that for another hour and a half. The bottoms of my feet were burning since my heels were five inches and squared.

"Come and sit in front of me on the table," he said.

I quickly sat down, glad that I had a chance to rest.

"Put your feet between my legs," he said, patting the leather cushion.

I hoped that whatever he was getting from the experience would be over soon. Just as I was thinking that, he pulled his dick out of his pants and squirted on my feet. I didn't want him to see that I was grossed out so I turned my face towards the ceiling and kept it there until he was finished.

"Oh, oh Miss Chelsea that was sooo good. Damn! You make me feel good," he kept repeating.

I let him clean off my feet with the by then cold washcloth, and me and my $3,000 were out the door fast. I rolled all of the windows down to bring the normal temperature to my flushed face, and quickly drove to Chanel's to bathe the memory away.

After that, we went out two more times and each time Marco took me shoe shopping. Since he was paying I let him pick out the shoes. I admit that he had great taste, but after spending real time with him I realized that Marco the freak was arrogant and so full of himself. And just like his tag said, everything was his shit. Even the shoes he bought for me! He said he wanted them to stay at his place so he could look at them when I wasn't there. I inspected them a few times and I knew I wasn't crazy when I saw cum on a couple of the solid-colored shoes.

The second time we went out, we ate at *Phillips* after I had tried on fifty pairs of shoes. We agreed that we would start out with the Alaskan crab legs as an appetizer. When the waitress set them on the table I reached for one and he had the nerve to grab my wrist.

"Don't *ever* reach for anything I'm paying for until you see that I'm ready." And then he looked at me dead in the eyes and released me.

"Is that right?" I asked.

He sat back in his chair and crossed his legs. I looked at him for a long time with his legs crossed and his hands folded on the table. He really had issues and it didn't help that he dressed better than I did.

"Well you know what you freaky fucker, kiss my ass," I said. I took the napkin from my lap and threw it in his face. I hardly ever cursed but he deserved it.

Later he called my phone and left messages like nothing was wrong and made plans to go out as if I had agreed to it. I didn't care how much money he had. His arrogance and every other sick thing about him were unbearable.

Almost three years later, Nikola and Chanel didn't remember him from the concert so when I told them I had seen his car in front of the church, they begged me to tell them the foot story again. I definitely didn't expect to see him again, and there was no telling who else was going to be at the wedding. I calmed down by telling myself that Marco was just in the neighborhood visiting someone and got ready to marry the man I really wanted.

When I walked into the church it was breathtaking. Nikola had really outdone herself with the decorations. The pink and red rose arrangements were spread across the church and sat on the end of each pew. Everything was beautiful but I felt like I was the prettiest thing in there.

Both sides of the church balanced out in the amount of people present and there were even people standing against the walls, most of them people I didn't know. I assumed they were friends of Charles. While I looked into the crowds of people, I searched for Marco and any other familiar faces, but it was pointless. I walked slowly down the aisle and the last years of my lifestyle flashed before me. *Did I really know what I was getting into?* I wanted to turn around and leave everything behind and realized that the long walk was leaving me too much room for regrets.

At the front of the church Father Kearns asked who "giveth me away" and Chanel and Nikola both replied, "We do." We had practiced it during the ride when I told them I wasn't sure if my parents would be there. My mother was there in the front pew but she never opened her mouth, and my Grandma Cleo sat there looking mean as ever. Reginald and Michael were both away at football training camp. My father was no where to be found. I held back my tears and focused on the colorful, stained window towards the back of the church.

As Chanel and Nikola straightened out my train I looked at Charles. I didn't see any signs that he had found out anything about my past thus far, so I took his hand in mine.

"Your skin is so beautiful," he mouthed.

I laughed quietly at our private joke. Father Kearns said his peace and we said our impromptu vows that ended up being very touching. When Smalls handed him the rings, my eyes were as wide as everyone else's when he slid the connecting band on my finger.

In the words of Chanel, *it was off the hinges.* I saw that he wasn't disappointed with the matching six-carat band I slipped on his finger either. I had used $16,000 of my own money to buy it, and that was the hookup price Nikola's *private* jeweler had given me.

After the rings, I was surprised at Chanel's solo. I knew she had a book of songs she had written and a voice as pretty as a dove, but she had rarely let us hear anything. Like Kola that would be too much like her showing her soft side. When the song was over I was so anxious to get past the *I do's* and when we kissed, I felt like I could finally exhale.

Charles and me walked to the back of the church as husband and wife. While his boys gave him hugs, I accepted kisses from my side of the church. We had almost made our exit when a familiar face stepped out of the last pew and embraced me. It was Marco and I was too startled to say anything.

"Hey Miss Chelsea, lookin' good. Nice shoes, I hope you'll let me get a peek under that dress," he whispered in my ear.

I held onto Charles' hand tighter as we kept moving through the crowd. I turned to him to see if he had heard Marco's comment but he was too busy with his boys to notice anything. On the way out I dipped my free hand into the bowl of holy water. After I made the sign of the cross on my forehead, I said a silent prayer that my day wouldn't end in chaos.

Chanel

There was no doubt that things had changed for us. We were all "makin' shit liquid" and had the things to prove it. I was able to buy out the three-story apartment building I was living in and my savings were phat. Nikola on the other hand, didn't know what saving was. Every dime she got went into clothes, jewelry and cars. Whenever a new ride came out she was at the dealer trading her shit in. I told her to slow down but she wasn't tryna hear it. I didn't know about her but I wasn't fuckin' for dollars forever. It was cool in the beginning but the money didn't come as easy as we had planned.

I had done a lot of things I wasn't proud of to get what I wanted, like the three-way I had done with the two dudes who played for the 76-ers. Yeah, we were big time after six months, and had started doing niggas in the music industry, the fuckin' NFL, NBA... all of them. Shit, I had even fucked a white hockey star and fuck the stories about them and their little dicks. That mafucka could've given Petey a run for his money.

I was happy for Chelsea though. She had found love and everything else we had worked for. When she showed me her house in Philly it was like some black soap opera shit. In the master bedroom they had a flat screen that spread across the wall, expensive-ass aquariums in almost every corner of the house with indigo lighting and exotic fish. They even had baby octopus.

Charles' love for Chelsea seemed genuine. That's one of the reasons I put so much into the song I had written for their wedding. I'd started writing to simply fill the void in my heart. Nikola and Chelsea were the only people with whom I had any familial love, and after Petey, I hadn't felt love from or for a man.

Months after I got into that fight at the club I went to see Rochelle. At my mother's dilapidated house I didn't have to try to use my key again. The door was wide open. I walked in the living room, and the glass table was cracked. Large scuffmarks covered the walls, beer cans were scattered across the floor, and it smelled like piss.

I called out her name but I didn't get a response. I opened the door to my room and the memories came rushing back. It was just like I left it, except she had set the trash bags I thought had been stolen beside my bed. I walked over and sat down, and at the foot of the bed was a stack of letters from Rico. Excited, I shuffled them like a deck of cards and put them in my purse. I opened one of the trash bags and on top was the picture I had taken with Petey. A smile came to my face as I remembered my first love. I wondered what he was doing with himself or if he was even alive.

I peeked into the bag and looked at all of the brand new clothes that had long gone out of style. When I heard a cough from the other room I grabbed the picture and closed the door. I walked across the hall afraid of what I would find. Rightly so, I saw my mother spread out with her face down and I didn't know what to think. Her room's appearance was worst than the living room. Her thick hair was matted and her clothes looked like they had been worn all week.

"Rochelle," I called out to her.

She lifted her head to speak but let it fall back down after she realized it took too much effort. I had never seen her like that before. She always put so much into how she looked. In fact the last time we got into our brawl she had on a nightie and her hair and makeup was done. As I got closer to her I could smell the piss and liquor.

"It's me, Chanel," I said as I shook her shoulder.

"Oh, hey. I been lookin' for you," I barely heard her say.

I looked at her arms, and just like I suspected, I saw the needle marks. As dirty as it felt in the room I sat on the stained sheets and stared at her for a long time. I thought about Ms. Diane's letter and started cleaning up. I ran some water and pulled her into the tub. Her body was so thin and frail so it wasn't hard to move her. After I washed her hair I let her soak and went to the bedroom and changed the sheets.

When she was dressed and looking decent I tried to have a coherent conversation with her. She still seemed out of it but at least she was walking on her own. Since the stench of the smell wasn't completely gone I asked her if she wanted to go somewhere and eat.

"Ooh Chanel, this is nice," she said after she had sat down in my car.

"What you call this?"

"A Benz," I said.

"I know that much. What kind?"

"CLK 430," I said, suddenly uncomfortable in her company. My newly acquired wealth didn't help either.

I saw her looking at me from the corner of my eye, and I knew she was wondering how I could afford a car like that. I couldn't afford it when I first got it, but monthly payments of hour-long head service ensured that it was mine after six months.

I remembered that she liked crab imperial so I took her to the Windsor Inn where all of the seafood was fresh. Our food came and I decided that I had had enough of the small talk. I wanted some answers.

"Rochelle, what's wrong wit' you? Why you usin' drugs now?"

"Chanel, I told you about calling me anything besides your mother. *I'm still your mother*," she said.

It was the first time I had seen her show any kind of emotion in a long time. "Oh really? Well, you really know how to show me," I said.

"I know what I did wasn't right," she started to say.

"What? Putting me out or keeping me up every night wit' ya fuckin'?"

"Both," she said after looking down at her untouched food. "Chanel, I love you. I know it doesn't seem like it, but I do. And all of the stuff I put you through, it wasn't me. Well, it was but... I had a lot of nasty things happen to me when I was younger."

She finally looked up and I knew that she had been raped as well. I didn't want to hurt her anymore than what she was already feeling so I reached out for her frail hand. "I understand, but you can't escape through drugs. It's not that simple. Don't you realize that gettin' our people strung out is the plan? That's how the system is able to get over on us." I stopped myself and realized how much I was sounding like Petey.

Surprisingly, my mother looked at me like a reprimanded child who understood completely. "I know," was all she said and we ate our food in silence.

Back in the car, I broke the silence by asking about Rico. She told me he was up for parole at the end of the year. I couldn't wait to open all of his letters. In front of her house I wondered how our relationship would be after that day. Before she got out the car she leaned over and gave me half of a hug. "Chanel, I'll always be your mother," she whispered.

After that I only saw her when she needed something, and soon I regretted giving her my address. She was always knocking on the door and asking for a G here and there. It was always some excuse about the gas and electric getting cut off or the landlord threatening to put her out. And I never asked questions. I knew what the money was for, but who was I to tell my mother no and have her get it anyway she knew how.

It was just too much for me and I didn't want to talk about it so I wrote. The phrases that turned out to be poetry were too repetitive so I turned them into songs and when they were complete, I sang them aloud and came up with a chorus for each one.

At the reception I was sitting at the table reserved for the bridal party when Charles' best man Smalls asked if he could hear my pretty voice again. I was so mad that he put me on the spot so I told him that I would sing for him later. *Anything to shut him up.* Smalls was already big and his voice drowned out everybody else. He was built like a big-ass bouncer and so were the rest of Charles' boys sitting at our table and his other friends spread around the Bay Lady. I noticed that when everyone was boarding the boat for the three-hour cruise around the Chesapeake Bay.

As they were coming over to the table to show him love I noticed that a lot of them were the same ballers I had seen at exclusive fashion shows, album release parties and any other event where we had all been to trying to get money.

I looked at Chelsea and thought that I should've been the one sitting there instead of her. I wasn't attracted to Charles, but I did know that his lifestyle was made for a bitch like me. He was one of the biggest hustlers in Philly and even had shit on lock as far as Connecticut.

Things had gotten serious between me and Quentin and he was running shit in B-more and VA, but I didn't expect to hear wedding bells anytime soon. After we met that night of the concert we didn't go out until two months later. He was always out of town or hemmed up. We finally went out and he took me to *Jillian's* on one of his runs.

That was my first time stopping in Philly and from the first road trip with Raheim and then the second with Quentin I knew that I would be moving soon. Baltimore would always be home but there was so much other shit to see.

Just like I thought, Quentin was quiet and always serious. Jillian's was a grownup version of Chuck E. Cheese's and I expected us to have fun. I thought he would loosen up but he remained tight faced. We played virtual bowling and when he beat me four of the six games he never got excited. It wasn't until we played pool that he showed me the part of him I had been feenin' for.

He was teaching me how to hold the stick when I felt his dick against my butt. That night I had on a Pucci-inspired wrap dress with swirls of black, white and gray. I knew I had surprised him by leaving my underwear at home 'cause when he reached under my dress to get his feel on, he quickly pulled his hand away.

"Chanel, where ya panties at?"

"At home," I said.

He shook his head. "Girl, you off the hook."

I had finally learned how to knock some balls in the pockets and could tell he was getting irritated. He was obviously tired of the missing competition. "Aight, let's hang this up and get somethin' to eat," he said.

"Oh, you can't handle my game?" I flirted.

"It's not that. I'm just tired of whippin' that ass," he said and smacked my ass cheek.

When we sat down to eat, Quentin turned back into the same distant person he was before we had started our game of pool. It was bad enough that both of his cell phones *and* his two-way were blowing up, but what was worse was him talking to whoever was on the other end and looking me in the face at the same. I felt like I was alone. I looked down at my mozzarella sticks and pushed them to the side. I had lost my appetite.

"What's wrong wit' you?" he asked, closing his phone.

"I'm ready to go," I said.

And I was serious. I didn't care how fine he was or how good he looked in his gray and white Akademiks hookup. I was out with him on a whim. If I wanted to put up with bullshit I could've been spending my time with a nigga who was going to pay me and then get the fuck outta my face.

I thought that my comment would at least make him say something to me, but he was serious and instead slid my plate in front of him and began eating my food. "Aight, I can take you home, but not until I do what I gotta do while we here."

"Fuck you nigga," I said before leaving the table.

I was so upset while I stood in the entrance. I had Nikola on the other end of my phone ready to tell her to make the two-hour drive to pick me up when I heard him talking to me.

"Hang up the phone I said."

I turned around and he was standing there looking pissed. Even with his discolored lips from the weed smoke I still wanted to shove my tongue down his throat. "Kola, I'll call you back in a few," I said.

"No you won't," he said.

"Excuse the fuck outta you nigga but you the one who thinks it's all about him. I don't need that shit! I could be out wit' somebody else rather than put up wit' ya bullshit."

"No you couldn't 'cause ya ass wouldn't be standin' here now lookin' at me like you wanna get fucked."

"Whateva nigga," I said and turned around.

I looked at my reflection in the door and tried not to smile.

"Chanel, bring ya phat ass in here and finish eating this good food they cooked in that hot-ass kitchen."

It was hard not to laugh. I turned around to walk back into the restaurant and he grabbed me by the hair and smacked my ass again. I was ready to take him to the nearest bathroom and get down. I hadn't had enjoyable sex in a long time.

We finished our food and started drinking. I dared our goofy-ass waitress to card me. I ordered a Kahlúa and Cream and he got a Corona with a lime wedge. As the drinks started to settle he opened up a little. "Chanel, if anything is gon' come from this you can't get mad when I'm doin' my thing. Whether it's on the phone or whateva. If I don't take care of business, I can't eat."

"I never said I had a problem with that, but don't act like I'm not here. I don't like to be ignored," I told him.

"How the fuck can I ignore you?" he asked like I had said something stupid. "You know you sexy as a mutherfucker."

I didn't want him to see that he had me wide open at that point so I changed the subject. "So, Quentin where's ya girlfriend tonight?"

"I don't know. Probably fuckin' the bitch she supposedly left alone," he said with ease.

I didn't care about his girlfriend being bi, I was more surprised at his honesty. He must've seen the look on my face. "What? You surprised that my girl likes pleasure from another bitch?" he asked.

"No. She's not here now so it's not my problem."

95

I tried not to let his comment bother me, but *his girl*? I instantly wondered how she looked and what kind of powers she had to make him stick around. *What the fuck could another woman do for her that his sexy ass couldn't?* Fuck her, I was there with him and ready to make up for the neglect.

We finished our last round of drinks and he asked if I wanted to play a real game of pool. I was determined to beat him at his own game and when it looked like I was going to win, he came around and leaned over me like he had done earlier.

"Can you back up off me?" I asked playfully.

"Yeah, after I do this."

He lifted my dress and I felt him fumbling with his pants. I couldn't believe he was about to fuck me in the open like that. I looked around and there was only one other couple at the end of the room. The guy was too busy teaching his girlfriend the game so I knew they weren't paying us any attention.

"You real smart, right?" he whispered.

"Yeah, I'm smart," I said.

"Well bend that ass over and feel this dick."

I felt him inside of me and let out a long gush of air. I forgot how good it felt to have a nigga fuck me and know exactly what to do. To prevent myself from making any noise I laid my face in the crevice of my arm while Quentin moved my hair to the side and pressed his dick deeper into my body.

"You ready for it?" he asked.

I couldn't open my mouth to answer him.

"Take this shit," he said.

Feeling my thighs get wet, I gave him time to put his dick away and slowly moved from under him to go to the bathroom. I cleaned up at the sink and combed my hair into place.

He was waiting for me outside in his black Q45 and on the phone again. Since he was in the passenger seat I assumed he wanted me to drive. I hoped he didn't think I knew my way around the city so I asked him, "What, am I driving home?"

"Nah, I'll show you where," he said.

We got off the exit and he had me driving through back streets that were more rundown than the trashiest alleys I had ever seen in Baltimore. Driving through two narrow alleys, he reached over and turned off the lights.

"Pull up right here," he told me.

I pulled up to the curb slowly and wondered where he had brought me.

"Aight, listen up Chanel. When I get out you keep these fuckin' doors locked. I got a piece in between your seat and the door. Anybody come near you lookin' or actin' out the ordinary, use that shit and don't hesitate."

I was never the one to ask questions but I needed to know why I was preparing myself to shoot or even worst kill some stranger I didn't know. "Quentin, I know you can't tell me too much right now but I need to know something."

"Look, I'm going in here to pick up this shit from my new connect. Don't go nowhere 'til you see me come out this mutherfucker. As soon as I come out you need to be startin' this shit up, matter fact don't cut it off."

He slammed the door and I saw him walk into the abandoned building. I locked the door and reached for the gun. I found it where he said it would be and let it sit in my lap. This was the second time I had come that close to a gun. I picked it up and laid it in my left hand. It was so little, yet so heavy. I slipped my finger around the trigger and felt so many things. How powerful niggas must feel to actually shoot someone or point a gun in somebody's face. I remembered that I had to be on point and tightened my grip around the smooth black handle.

I looked at the clock and it was 1:36am. It seemed like I had been sitting there forever. At 2:00 I started shifting in my seat. I was tempted to get out but I didn't know how long something like that took. I felt like I was on a stakeout and the waiting was nerve-wracking. I kept looking into the mirrors at images that weren't there.

Going out with Petey was never like that. He was always picking up money so it never took that long. Finally at 2:15 I saw him walking down the steps. His hands were empty so I figured he had the stuff hidden on him. He had to cross the alley to get to the car so when I saw him step off the curb I put the car in drive.

Even though he was only a few feet away I wanted to tell him to hurry the fuck up. My heart started racing uncontrollably when I saw a guy come from nowhere. I couldn't scream, but I think he saw my mouth open wide. The only thing I could do was honk the horn.

Quentin turned around and I saw him reach in his pants. I couldn't believe how fast everything was happening. The guy fell and the gun left his hand. What got my attention was the blood leaking from his pants. I heard another gunshot and saw Quentin rushing to the car. Before he could sit down I pulled off. My heel had gotten caught in the pedal and we ran the red light at the corner of Jefferson and Broad St.

"Chanel, slow ya ass down!" he shouted.

"Stop fuckin' screamin' at me! My shoe got caught and I couldn't brake."

"Just keep going straight. 95 is ten minutes from here," he said in a calmer tone.

We took the back streets again and I sniffed the air and smelled the smoke from the gun.

"You alright?" I finally asked him when we got on the highway.

"Yeah, I'm cool," he said and leaned his seat back. He touched my thigh where my dress had opened. "Chanel listen to me."

I was tired of him saying that shit. *Who the fuck else was I listening to?* "I'm listenin'," I said.

"After that shit from back there I don't have to say that it's between you and me. Whatever thoughts you have, I want you to leave 'em back in that alley." He looked at me and I took my eyes off the road for a moment to show him that I was just as serious as he was. "We bonded for life now and I don't give a fuck who you got dealings wit,' that shit is secondary when I'm in the picture."

And after that things were just like he said. If I had plans to *make shit liquid* and he called, it went out the window. I knew he was still dealing with that girl or whoever, so I didn't stop what I was doing completely.

Quentin laced me with a lot of things but I regarded him more as a boyfriend and a nigga who could throw down the dick. If he decided to turn what we had into something more serious than him staying with me one or two nights out of the week I could've given up the things I was doing. But street life was holding onto him and having a relationship was the last thing on his mind.

I had known him for a minute and still I didn't know where he lived. He told me he didn't want anyone to know we were together and that it was his way of protecting me. Only I knew different. The real reason was a girl who wanted her cake, him and another chick too.

I was ready for the party to get jumpin' after Charles' boys gave their ghetto-ass toasts. One of them had the nerve to say, "Man, me and Charles go way back. When I was on lockdown in '90, this was the only nigga who looked out for me." And then he stopped to actually wipe his eyes. "I got mad love for him after that shit. Cheers!" I wasn't mad at his love for his boy. I was just upset that we had to sit through thirty minutes of that shit. I looked at Nikola and she rolled her eyes and quickly took the mic.

That was just like her to be in control of everything. It was Chelsea's wedding but it should've been called Nikola's party because she was keeping track of everything, and every event that went on was timed. I had to give it to her though, the boat looked like a scene from a fairytale.

Each table was covered with miniature Gilda-imported dried-rose arrangements in silver-plated julep cups. She even had a slide show with pictures of Chelsea and Charles, but I swear there were more pictures with us three partying in places like Hawaii and Jamaica. If she was out to make bitches envious, she had succeeded.

After the first dance everyone was ready to get down and eat. The caterers Nikola had hired were serving our table. We had the choice of soul food or seafood from the huge selection of lobster, shrimp and salmon. When we all had our food, the guests started getting up by tables to get their own.

While I ate I had a better chance at seeing any unexpected visitors I had missed earlier. I was getting ready to stuff my mouth with the salmon when I saw Quentin. I hadn't invited him so I looked over at Chelsea. She shrugged her shoulders and I decided to ask Charles if he knew Quentin, but instead placed my fork back on the plate.

Maybe Charles *hadn't* invited him either and he had come as a guest with the pretty bitch who was grinning in his face. She was everything I didn't want her to be,

beautiful and likable. At least she looked that way since all eyes were on her at their table. Her lips were pouty and dramatic and her hair was lightened to the same color as her skin. It was all glazed and vibrant. That bitch!

I looked at Quentin and he was into her as much as she was into him. I couldn't believe he was disregarding my presence. I *know* he was aware that Chelsea was my best friend and if he had forgotten, I was sure he had seen my tonsils earlier at the church. I saw this as the perfect time to give him and his part-time girlfriend the news. I had been throwing up all week and every time I called him to talk he was out of town or too busy. I now saw why he was so preoccupied, but he was about to acknowledge me and this time the bastard didn't have a choice.

Elvita Horace

# That Bitch/ 8

Not many women can carry the title of being *that bitch*. You got the ones that think they're the *baddest* bitches when they throw on a mink or rock a few pieces of ice, but very few can say I was, or I am *that bitch*. I can.

I was fifteen when I met Violet. She looked like she was straight from *Vogue* or *Cosmopolitan*. I had never seen a black woman in person who dressed the way she did or even came close in looks. Each time I saw her she had on a different designer outfit. I knew it was designer because her clothes fit her like they were made especially for her body. Her hair was always covered with a new wig or a large hat that hid her doe-like, oval-shaped eyes.

From the time I was eleven I had been moved from home to home, ever since my mother overdosed on heroine when I was ten. That Orphan Annie shit wasn't for me. Each home that I went to had a husband or teenage boys who made me the opportunity for some free pussy every chance they got. I couldn't understand what I had done to make them want to treat me like that.

The last lady I was staying with was really into church. I mean, the only time Ms. Gloria wasn't at the altar was when she was sleeping. Everything revolved around the Lord and if she saved a dollar at the grocery store she would say shit like, "Oh yes, I feel the spirit. The Lord 'den blessed me with a little extra this time around." It was ridiculous. Ironically she was a Jesus fanatic and her husband was Satan.

I was staying with them for about two months and almost every night he was in my room asking me to do some nasty shit for him. I knew she knew what was going on 'cause she would come in the house after worshiping all evening and beat my ass. "I feel the devil all in this home of mine Lord. Help me!" she would say as the wooden paddle with cutting splinters came down on my back. I got so tired of that shit.

She should've been beating her husband, but instead would go in the kitchen and fix his slimy ass something to eat. When I decided to leave, the only thing I took with me was the $300 she had hidden in her sewing kit.

For about four days I slept on subways and walked the downtown streets. At night I would go to Baltimore St. which was also known as *the strip*. While the rest of the city slept the night away, that was the one street that remained alive until the sun came up.

It was about three in the morning when I first saw her. The strip clubs like *Eldorado's* and *Pussycat* were letting out and the streets seemed to be filled with at least a hundred erotic-looking women dressed in nearly nothing with glistening faces from hours dancing. Violet came outside of the club she was working in and she didn't stand around like everyone else. She got inside of her sleek, red, two-door Mercedes and sped off.

The night that I met her was by chance. I had stopped into one of the twenty-four hour eating spots and went into the bathroom to wash up, use the toilet, and keep warm from the January winter that went beyond being brick. It was good that I had used some of Ms. Gloria's money to buy another outfit because embarrassing as it is to admit, I was smelly.

I walked out of the bathroom and Violet was in line waiting for her order of fries and a shrimp cheese steak sub. I had to say something to her but didn't want to risk sounding silly to a woman as beautiful as she was. I straightened out my clothes, pulled the too small jacket down over my wrists and moved over to the line to order.

While I searched the menu board over the grill, I couldn't stop looking at her out the corner of my eye. She hadn't had a chance to change so I could see the hot pink halter outfit under her gray mink jacket she must've worn on stage. I badly wanted to reach out and touch the velvety material.

"What you havin' honey?" the Italian cook asked, breaking me away from my thoughts.

"Umm, a slice of pepperoni," I said quickly.

I gave him the two dollars and she reached for her food. I hoped she wasn't leaving. She opened the aluminum foil that covered her sub and frowned her face. "This is *not* what I asked for," she told him.

"Well what did you ask for?" he replied in a cutting tone.

"You're the fuckin' cook, you should've been paying attention when I told you *no hots*," she said.

He turned sideways and looked at what I thought was the manager. "She say she don't want no hots," he said, talking to the man with the newspaper and a long cigarette hanging from his lips.

They both laughed like they were dismissing her complaint and he turned around and got my pizza from the oven. After he put a second plate under the first, he threw my food on the counter. I went to reach for it and she grabbed my wrist gently.

"Did you hear me the first time?" she asked him.

"Hear what? That a fuckin' stripper bitch wants no hots. I tell you what, you don't want no hots, you take 'em off 'cause I'm not making that shit over again," he said and looked her over like she was cheap and dirty.

"And what about her pizza?" she asked calmly.

"What about it? She don't like hers either?" he asked, smiling in my face.

"Not served to her like that. Give her her food the way she gave you the money. In her hand," she said.

I couldn't believe she was being so calm about him calling her a bitch, and I didn't know what the big deal was with my pizza. I was used to him and his nasty attitude.

"You like it your way, huh?" he asked, waiting for a response. When she didn't say anything, he continued. "Well in order for you to have it your way," he said, leaning closer to her, "I need you to come back here and suck my dick or get the fuck outta my face." The spit left his mouth and landed on her forehead.

I looked around and by then more people had walked in and were standing in line. I saw her reach for her food off the counter and thought she had given up on making him see things her way. I was ready to leave when I saw her other hand grab the large Mistic bottle that had also been apart of her order.

Her heels had given her extra height so she was able to tower over the counter. My mouth hung wide open as I watched her break the bottle over his thinning hair. While he held his hand over his bleeding head, the manager was reaching for the phone to call the police. She grabbed my hand and we ran to her car.

Once inside, she sped off the same way I had seen her do all week. I didn't know what to say so I sat there and waited for her to speak first but she didn't talk. She just reached for a box of red hots from her glove compartment and drove in silence. I smiled to myself at her choice in candy, especially since the episode in the sub shop involved hots on her sandwich.

She had an apartment not too far away on Calvert St. I followed her inside and was scared to touch anything, let alone sit on the white couch. She turned on Anita Baker and disappeared into another room. I looked at the high ceilings, matching white rug and the chiffon curtains hanging over the windows. Her apartment was as stylish as she was.

The slender, beautiful woman had changed clothes to a black silk lounge outfit. She had removed her bob-shaped wig and I finally got a chance to see her hair. The soft, lightened brown curls that fell around her forehead and shoulders only bounced back in place when she raked her fingers through them. I had always wanted hair like hers. Instead, I had to endure a perm every other month to even try to achieve her hair texture.

"What's your name?" she finally asked me.

"Elvita," I said, starting to feel uncomfortable.

"That sounds like a dancer's name. You work on the strip?"

"No, I'm only fifteen."

"So," she said, rolling her eyes. "What does that have to do with anything?"

I shrugged my shoulders. "I don't know."

"*Anyway*, you look older than that. I figured you to be at least nineteen. Why you walkin' the streets this time of night Vita?" she asked.

I liked the way she had shortened my name. She said it like I was one of her girlfriends. "'Cause I don't have anywhere else to go," I said.

"Everybody got somewhere to go. It's just a matter of you claiming that place as your home."

"Well, I claim this as my home," I said, suddenly feeling like I had known her for a long time.

"Girl, I'm only twenty-eight. What I look like havin' a fifteen-year old stayin' wit' me?"

"What does my age have to do with anything?" I shot back, using her same words. She smiled and sat up from the couch to open a silver box on her black marble table. On the lid was *Violet* in script. I guessed that was her name. Inside were rows of Montecristos. I had never seen a woman smoke a cigar. She grabbed one and clipped off the end. Beside the box was a silver lighter that she flicked open to produce a spark.

"You smoke those?" I asked, intrigued and transfixed at her ease with the cigar.

"Well, yeah. What? You think a woman is only supposed to smoke Newports or something?" she asked.

"No," I said, feeling dumb.

"Don't look like that. It's cool that you aren't used to it. This is all I smoke, and well, a little weed here and there, but these make me feel so sophisticated. You want one?"

She didn't wait for me to answer. She lit it and showed me how to puff in to get the spark burning. I listened to the crackling sound and tried to hold it the way I had seen her, with it almost dangling between my first two fingers. I practically let it burn away before she held out the ashtray for me and asked about my family.

I told her the truth. I didn't have any. She must've felt sorry for me 'cause she showed me the bathroom and got me identical silk pajamas and brand new panties. I showered and put them on. I felt like a princess and the power jets from her shower had cleaned the grimy feeling from my skin. The silk fabric was lightweight and the heat circulating throughout her apartment made me feel more comfortable.

Violet told me that was her real name and said she didn't have any family either. She had a father who lived in New Jersey but had never met him. Her grandmother had raised her and died when Violet was sixteen. After that she was on her own. We sat there in her living room while she told me her stories about being on her own. As enthralling as her life was, I was exhausted and sleep within minutes.

A week passed and I had officially moved myself in. Violet never told me to leave after that first night and I didn't question it. I think she saw a lot of herself in me. Soon she had switched to clubs in DC and it was exciting to hear her stories when she came home from working at the different strip clubs.

February came and I turned sixteen. Violet told me it was time to learn some things. She asked me if I knew how to dance. I didn't so she took me into the living room and turned on some music. She had me stand beside her so that we were looking into the long mirror covering her wall.

We were dressed in our bras and panties and I couldn't wait to get some of those lace thongs she wore. I was instructed to grab my titties and bend over. The music was pumping slow and then fast. According to her, all of a woman's power was in her legs and Violet instructed me to use my legs and thighs to move my ass cheeks.

Soon I had the idea of things and was moving them up and down. I didn't know how she did it but I heard her make a clapping noise. Slightly shocked I stood up and looked at her like I knew I wasn't hearing her slap her ass cheeks together. She smiled and made me continue with the ass-jiggling exercises until I had it. I started out slow and then picked up the pace.

Violet guided me and showed me how to arch my back to gyrate my pussy. There was a song with Diana King on Biggie's first CD that always made me want to move my body so I picked that as my favorite song. She put it on and told me to show her what I had learned. I was never nervous around her so for the next five minutes I made her proud.

The next day she took me with her to the salon and I got a haircut. Her hairdresser Jewel couldn't believe what she had to work with. I had never been to a real salon so my hair was split and growing out in different lengths. With two hours, a perm, and a large bristle brush attached to the blow dryer, I had a full and healthy-looking head of hair. It had never felt so soft.

"I want you to always keep your hair up," Voilet told me when I got out the chair. "Even with only a dollar to your name, a well-kept hairdo can get you five hundred."

Our feet and nails were next. That was the first time I had treatment like that. I couldn't stop looking down at my full set. I wanted a few designs but Violet told me that French or American was the only way to go. With drying nails, we went to this boutique where she knew the owner.

"Pick out an outfit," she said.

"Outfit for what?" I asked her.

"'Cause Vita, this is your night. We gon' see what you workin' wit'."

I followed her around while he held up various g-strings and half pairs of shorts. "Vita you gotta favorite color?" she asked.

"No, but I like red," I said, thinking about how much I liked her car.

She laughed. "Red, huh? Yeah, I knew you were made to do this. Mutherfuckers," she said, referring to men, "say you should never trust a bitch in red. They say she's the devil in disguise. You believe that shit?"

"No," I said, unsure of what to believe.

"You shouldn't 'cause if it was true I would've been in hell by now," she said, laughing at her own joke. "Besides, when they see a bitch in red they already know what they workin' wit'. They know we don't take no bullshit and that they better come correct."

I loved to hear her reasoning behind everything. It was always on some well thought out shit. We decided on a red bikini top with shingles in the form of rhinestones and a matching g-string and left the store to get ready. I never considered if it was the right or wrong thing to do. Unconsciously I was allowing Violet to take on the role of my mother.

It was 10:00 when we finally left. We had spent one hour getting dressed and another with her doing our makeup. She said that we didn't need a lot, but still took extra care applying the foundation and small beauty marks we hadn't inherited.

"You nervous?" she asked in the car.

"A little," I said, tapping my nails against my teeth.

She quickly cut off this old couple who were in the left lane moving like snails and stopped at a liquor store. When she came back she poured me a cup of Southern Comfort and Vodka.

"Drink this," she said while she rolled a blunt.

I took a few sips. She handed me the blunt and told me to inhale like I had done with the cigar. A cup of the liquor and a few puffs later and I felt my shoulders drop from the stiff position they had been in all day.

"You like that don't you? Not too strong, but good enough to make you feel relaxed?" she asked.

I didn't answer her. I just poured another cup and added more Grey Goose than I had before and enjoyed the ride. I expected us to be going to a club but it ended up being her friend Cindy's house out in Woodlawn. Cindy was real cute. She had this baby face with a woman's body and giggled a lot like she had some invisible friend whispering private jokes in her ear.

We went through the basement and I met the other girls who were there changing into their outfits. I had never seen Violet around anyone else except her male friends so I was surprised at the way she treated them. She had quickly turned into a pimpstress. She was cold, but you couldn't tell they didn't mind from the way they broke their necks to speak to her. It was Cindy's house but Violet was giving her orders.

"I thought these were your friends," I said to her when we went into the backroom to take off our coats.

"Vita, listen to what I'm about to tell you and take it with you wherever you go." I opened my ears and listened to her like what she was about to say would decide my fate. "The relationship you and me have is different from what you see. True, you're young and haven't experienced what I have, but you'll learn that niggas and bitches are two completely different species. A nigga will always be predictable. His main concern is getting his dick sucked or fucked, however you want to put it. And he'll let you know that if you don't do it, somebody else will. A bitch, now her shit changes everyday. You never know which way she's coming. One day she's your best friend, and the next day she'll spit in your face *or* on your man's dick. You be the one to decide which one you want around you."

I just stood there and suddenly needed another drink. I looked out into Cindy's spacious basement and thought about what Violet had said. I had never had a real girlfriend or best friend because the girls I had for friends always wanted to fight me when they saw the clothes I wore repeatedly. I couldn't afford anything else since my mother was always supporting her habit. The guys I had met, well, they just wanted pussy. They didn't care what it had on. Violet was right, I said to myself, as I watched the girls practice their different moves.

Cindy had her downstairs set up like a real club. She had a small stage with the infamous gold pole in the center and the girls who were already dressed were taking turns.

"Violet," I said, "you never showed me how to slide down the pole."

"I know. If you want, get up there and ask the girl with the turquoise g-string to show you." She looked away and quickly turned around to stop me. "Vita never mind, don't ask that bitch for shit. I'll tell her. I can't stand her ass anyway. She's one of them bitches who can't keep they mouth shut, and if you let her she'll swallow two at a time." She walked out of the room with ease in her six inches and called out to the girl. "Hey Mia, won't ya' freak-ass show Vita how to use the twelve-inch."

They called it that since niggas always claimed to be working with twelve inches. I walked to the stage and tried not to look at Mia. I wondered if she was offended at what Violet had said, but when I got there she smiled and grabbed both of my hands and wrapped them around the pole, one above the other.

"Now, propel your body like you want to spin around and when you come around once or twice, throw your legs around it," she said.

I practiced until I heard Violet calling me. The guys had started showing up. "Yeah, these mutherfuckers look like they got the dollars," she said.

The guests sat on the couches and the extra chairs that had been set up. Cindy started the music. Her and Mia began dancing around the groom-to-be while he sat in the center chair. Some of his friends had stood up and were cheering Cindy on as she sat on his lap and bounced her titties in his face.

When she was finished, one of his boys came over and blindfolded him. He slipped what looked like two hundred-dollar bills into Mia's g-string. My eyes got wide as I watched her suck his dick like it was her last meal. I guessed that a STD was an afterthought. The niggas were going crazy. Cindy finished and Violet walked from where we were standing to get on the stage.

This would be the first time I saw her dance for a real crowd. I knew she liked Jodeci so I wasn't surprised when I heard the 'Freak 'n You' remix with Ghostface. Violet looked like she had been dancing forever. She was sucking up dollars in her pussy and still moving her body. That was something else I hadn't caught onto just yet but she made it look so easy.

She removed her zebra print bikini top with one hand, exposing her D cup and the money started flying out of pockets. They were standing by the stage throwing twenties everywhere even when the song ended and Cindy's brother Cory was helping Violet off the platform.

"Vita, you up next," she said when she came back breathing hard.

"Violet I can't go up there after you did all that. They'll probably boo me."

"Girl, please. Them niggas like it when they see amateur pussy, and with your honeydew skin and those big brown eyes you'll clean up."

She had made me feel better. I tightened up the straps on my outfit even though I knew half of it would be coming off. I heard Cindy introduce me as *Vita, the honey from the beehive*, and when I walked out in my glass platforms, I transformed myself.

The drinks and weed from earlier were still working so I took the stage and pretended I was back in Violet's living room. When I heard D'Angelo's 'Brown Sugar' I stood there for a moment and waited for the tempo. I felt my body moving to the pace of his voice and undid the top and turned towards them while I slowly moved my ass. Soon I was clapping my ass as loud as I could.

I knew they were happy with my routine 'cause I looked down and saw more twenties than anything. The song would be ending soon so I decided to use the pole. I was feeling bolder. I gave myself a hard push and some kind of way I was upside down with my legs crossed over the other. One nigga tried to jump on the stage and Cory grabbed him by the collar and yanked him to the floor. It was okay for them to touch us but when we were on stage doing our thing nobody else was allowed unless we pulled them up. I knew then that my time was up. I got down and gathered up all of my money.

Violet was smiling when I got to her. "Vita, that shit was all that," she said like a proud mother.

"Really?" I asked with a fast-pacing heart.

"Girl, yes, and after those bitches do their thing up there and we all go out on the floor you gon' see some real money."

She was right. I left there with about $1,500. After that first night, stripping was all I wanted to do and there was always a party to give. Nothing that went on at those private parties surprised me. The guys could get crazy, but I had gone to see male strippers as well and the women got more carried away than men did with the female strippers. I had seen women suck off one dancer while they let another fuck 'em and all of this was at the age of sixteen.

I went to Edmondson High School for a minute but after the tenth grade I said *fuck school*. The best teacher for me was experience and I was getting a lot of it from being with Violet. Stripping wasn't the only thing she taught me to do. She kept a mutherfucker with money and told me to never have a nigga sittin' in my face that couldn't do shit for me. Everyday with her brought something new but one of the biggest lessons was one I learned on my own.

She had been seeing Kasaan for about two years and he was her main nigga. If there was going to be something serious between her and any one of the ten dudes she was messin' with, it was him. One week in early June things got real crazy between them. He knew he wasn't the only one, but had started catching feelings. I was at the kitchen counter pouring a bowl of Cinnamon Toast Crunch when I heard him fussing in the living room.

"Violet I told you before I wanted you to stop fuckin' wit' 'dem other niggas," he said. "So why is that mutherfucker still calling here?"

"Kasaan, I'm my own woman and you already know shit ain't changin'. I told you how shit was goin' down in the beginning. You can't change the game boo boo," she said, further irritating him with the pet name she used for all of the men in her life.

"Whateva, but know that if I even *think* you fuckin' another nigga, they won't be able to recognize your face."

They being the morgue I guessed. I emptied my bowl of cereal into the sink. I had lost my appetite. Moving closer to the living room, I heard her laugh at him mockingly and then him get up and walk to the door.

"You think I'm fuckin' playin' wit' yo ass," he said before he opened the door to leave. "That pussy is *mine* and that's for real."

I guessed she thought he was joking 'cause when I asked her if she wanted to do a party that night she said she had plans with somebody new.

"Violet, you heard what he said. That nigga is *really* crazy."

"Vita, you must've forgot the shit I told you about takin' these niggas serious. What the fuck is he gon' do but come back over this bitch tomorrow, lick this pussy and give me some more dough to go shopping. Kasaan knows better than to pull some crazy shit and besides, you know niggas start talkin' shit when it gets hot outside."

"When it gets hot?" I asked with a raised eyebrow.

"You'll see. When the weather changes, *girl!* They mutherfuckin' mind go crazy. I don't know, maybe their brain starts releasing some extra dopamine and they feel like superman and shit, wantin' to own what ain't there's."

I laughed nervously and thought about Kasaan's tone. If words were any indication of a person's feelings, his were crazy—and Violet's flippant attitude had made him irate.

Before I left I tried to plead with her again. "Violet, go with me tonight."

"Stop givin' me those sad eyes. You know I'm a sucker when you look at me like that."

"Then come with me," I said again, blinking my eyelashes.

"Vita get outta here and make that money," she said, throwing me her car keys. She must have really trusted me with her car being as though I only had a provisional.

"You sure?" I asked her again.

"I love you too," she said and her and her silky hair disappeared around the corner to get ready for her date.

It was about three in the morning when I pulled up to our street. I saw the fire trucks and police cars were out front and knew she was gone. I felt that same emptiness in the pit of my stomach the day my mother died. I sat behind the wheel and finished off the red hots she had sitting on her dashboard before I drove down the street and prepared myself for what I would hear.

I looked at our building and the two connecting houses. They were so burnt that I couldn't recognize where they had joined. A police officer asked me if I knew who lived there as he watched me gazing at the remains. I nodded my head as he told me the story.

I couldn't even cry when he said she had been set on fire. My legs got weak and I felt him pulling me up. They gave me oxygen and a cup of water. A neighbor said she had given the police Kasaan's tag number and description of the car. Her mention of his reddish brown hair only further confirmed my initial assumption that it was him.

She said Violet had left out around eleven with some guy and across the street Kasaan sat in his car. When she came back home three hours later, he was still sitting there and had followed her into the house. I shook the thought of him pouring gasoline on her out of my head and tried to remember the last image I had of her saying *I love you.*

It took a long time for her death to sink in but there was still a part of me that was missing. Nothing could fill the big-ass crater in my heart, *nothing*. Love wasn't even in my vocabulary anymore. She had schooled me about the lack of trust in females but at that point I didn't trust or give a fuck about anybody but myself.

I found out about the wedding from Michelle, a booster who always looked out for me when she knew I was coming through. Since I had moved to New York I only came to Baltimore when necessary. April, my stylist in Manhattan had gone to Jamaica for two weeks so I came back home to let Jewel do her thing. It had been five years since Violet's death and me and Jewel still kept in touch.

I was sitting under the dryer looking through the bags of clothes Michelle had lifted. She always had so much good shit that she could never go broke. More than half of my clothes that came from her was straight from the magazines.

"I know Jewel told you about the wedding," she said.

"What wedding? Somebody I know?" I asked, looking at the Graffiti Moschino bodysuit.

"I don't know, but I think you know a lot of the niggas that'll be there like Q and his boys. I heard that it's supposed to be *like that*, at least four hundred people."

My ears shot up when I heard her mention Quentin. "Where at?" I asked.

"Not sure, but the reception is on the Bay Lady," she said, holding up the Louis Vuitton bag I was on the waiting list for.

"Michelle, how the fuck did you get that shit already?" I asked, eyes wide open.

"Come on now, who you talkin' to?"

I gave her the $1,500 for the bag and another G for the fifteen outfits I knew very few bitches would own. I laughed when I put the extra stacks away. Watching Quentin handle his money for years had me facing all of my bills in the same direction. The dryer cut off and I waited for Jewel to finish eating her grilled chicken sub before I sat in her chair. *Damn she was making me hungry.*

I didn't tell my business but it was inevitable to get into some kind of conversation with the person who had been doing my hair since I was fifteen. Plus, there was an unspoken connection with us both having known Violet. Jewel would definitely know about the wedding. Bitches that sat in her chair couldn't wait to tell her their life story. My thoughts quickly returned to Quentin. Michelle had mentioned him and a reception with four hundred people. That could only mean one thing: a meeting of ballers. And there was no way Quentin wasn't going to something like that without money being his main agenda.

"Jewel," I said when I finally sat in her chair, "w'sup wit' a wedding on the Bay Lady?"

"Oh yeah! I knew I had to tell you somethin'. Ricky was tellin' me about that shit. Nothin' but high rollers on that mutherfucker tomorrow."

Ricky was Jewel's husband. He was big-time a while back but pulled out after doing five years. He was still doing a lil' somethin' here and there though, 'cause he had just bought Jewel her shop six months ago.

"Tomorrow? Damn I was leaving later on tonight. I just came home to get my wig done and smell Baltimore's pissy air."

"So, what you gon' do? You stayin' wit' Q tonight or ya girl ain't havin' that?" she laughed.

She never surprised me with her straightforwardness. Besides Violet, that was the main reason I got along with her—that and her contagious laughter. I looked at her in the mirror and watched the infusions fall over her left eye. The six hundred-dollar hair weave was so fly I wanted to get the wax and go to work.

"Jewel don't be a smart bitch, you know I haven't talked to Quentin in like… Shit a long time," I said.

"Cause you know KC ain't havin' that. That's why."

"No, because he ain't no different from all them other niggas, and I don't need to stay with him. I can take my pretty ass right to the Wyndham downtown. It's only for one night."

"Yeah, okay," Jewel said, throwing the cape around my neck.

Quentin was to me what Kasaan was to Violet, only I was smart enough to cover all aspects of our so-called relationship in order to prevent some crazy shit from poppin' off. I met him shortly after I had been on my own again. I was still sixteen, and by then, word had gotten out that I was the shit when it came to entertainment and giving niggas what they paid for. It was a few months after Violet's death and dancing had become my escape.

Quentin paged me and I thought he was just having a small get-together with his boys 'cause he didn't ask about bringing any of the other strippers I knew. I was cool with going there by myself though. He already knew that I needed $2,500 at the door. I set it up that way 'cause I knew that a small group of niggas meant they would want to run a train before the night was over. And if there were at least five of them, that meant at least $500 per nigga. Anything else they wanted to do while I was there was fine as long as they kept the money coming.

I liked doing small parties where I was the center of attention. I also liked the fact that I was controlling all of the money. If niggas wanted a two-girl show I usually brought along this girl Tammy, but I hated splitting what we made 'cause after awhile she would start complaining about suckin' dick. She said her jaws starting locking up after the fourth one.

It was already hard enough to make the kind of money I was asking for and she was trippin' off some lockjaw. After she told me that shit I never asked her to do another party with me. I felt like this. If I was doing most of the work I kept most of the money so it was just too bad if I only let her keep $500 of the three G's or so we made. It was funny. I was only sixteen but no one would ever know. I controlled every situation like Violet had taught me. Every girl I did parties with was at least eighteen but my mature face and overly developed breasts left no room for questioning.

I pulled up to the house and looked down at the address Quentin had given me. They matched. I took the small Beretta out of my purse and made sure it was loaded. I was glad that it was cold outside. I would be able to stick it in the side of my red leather knee boot instead of leaving it in my purse. I always brought my shit with me. I could never be sure about what would go down.

Quentin said he didn't want me to have on the regular costumes I wore. He preferred a sexy outfit like a leather skirt with an expensive shirt and a black thong. He was paying so that's what he got. Shit, I would've worn a clown costume if he asked me to.

I grabbed my bag that contained another outfit in case he and his friends wanted to see me in something different later on, stepped out and set the alarm on my new red two-door Jag. I still had Violet's car but it was so special to me that I could only sit behind the wheel when I was missing her. I vowed that I would always keep a red car in memory of her, and I hadn't broken my promise yet.

Quentin answered the door and I was surprised at my own reaction to him. I had been around enough mutherfuckers to know what turned me on and there had only been two or three. He had on a plain white T-shirt and I could see the outlines of his tattoos on his muscular chest. He had on some navy Phat Farm loungewear pants and was barefooted. I saw his dick bulging in his pants and could feel the string in my ass warming up already.

He didn't say anything. He just handed me a thick envelope and opened the door for me. Things were too quiet for him to be there with friends so I figured right away that he wanted a one on one.

"You thirsty?" he asked.

"Yeah, what you got?" I asked, wondering why he was acting like we were on a date or something.

"What you want?"

"You got any Grey Goose?" I asked while looking into his dark eyes.

"That's all you want is the Goose on rocks?"

"Nah, give it to me wit' some Southern Comfort."

"I don't think I got none of that."

*Then why the fuck did he ask me if I was thirsty?* "Well, what about some Peach Schnapps?" I asked, ready to settle for some damn tap water. He must've had it 'cause he left and went into the kitchen.

I could tell he was into sports 'cause his walls were covered with framed posters of Michael Jordan and encased cards with MJ's signature. There was also a signed Allen Iverson jersey from his college days at Georgetown. *Now that's a mutherfucker I wouldn't mind knowing.* I assumed he had also played basketball at one time since there were plenty of trophies lined up against the wall above his fireplace.

He came back into the living room with my drink and it was clear that he liked what he saw in me as well. He couldn't stop eyeing my skirt and how it stopped at the beginning of my thighs. After he got his peeks into the black shirt that exposed my nipples, he sat down and turned on ESPN.

I wasn't one to hold my tongue. Shit, I was ready to get down. "Quentin, w'sup?"

"Chillin'. W'sup wit' you?"

I looked at him for a long time. *Why was he acting like we were the closest of friends?* "W'sup wit' me? You paged me to do something for you, right?" I asked.

"Vita, what we doin' now is cool. I paged you and told you I was havin' somethin' 'cause I knew that was the only way I could get you here." *What was he talking about?* I didn't know Quentin's face from anywhere, yet he was talking like he knew me. He must've seen how confused I looked. "Yeah, that's right," he said. "I wanted you here 'cause I wanted to see you for myself. Remember that party you and ya crew did for Sean's twenty-fifth?"

Of course I remembered. Sean's party was packed with so many hustlers that night that I could've cleaned up. It wasn't like those parties with a few big spenders and the rest, lil' niggas wit' a fifty, some ones and the misconception that it guaranteed them a lap dance.

I was mad that I had had to leave early. My period came on in the middle of my act and I was so disappointed. I could've slipped in a tampon but I bleed so heavily that only two thick overnight pads can protect me from leaking when I come on, and they only last up to four hours.

I would usually stay in the house 'cause my cramps always feel like I'm being kicked in the stomach, but it was so unexpected. Following that incident I tried to schedule shit around my unwanted friend, 'cause that was one party that could've brought me mad dough.

"Yeah, I remember," I answered him, hoping he hadn't seen anything embarrassing that night.

"Well I saw you gettin' into your car when I was pullin' up."

"And," I prompted.

"I figured you were there to do ya thing for the niggas, and I wondered why you were leavin'."

"Oh, 'cause something else came up," I quickly said.

"But, yeah, I felt somethin' when I saw you. This vibe like we came from the same dark place."

*What kind of dark place?* I turned away. I didn't like the way he was looking at me and I wasn't feeling that soft shit so I ignored him and got up from the couch to cut the TV off.

"Quentin," I said when I walked back to him, "I don't know if you know, but time is money so let's do this."

"I feel the same way," he said. "I don't like nobody fuckin' wit me and my paper either. You like Sade?" he asked.

"She's cool but after awhile I feel like I'm 'bout to slit my fuckin' wrists. Why?"

He laughed and got up to cut off the lights. He came back and I could see that he had taken off his shirt. I was definitely through with the small talk. *The Best of Sade* was filling the room when he told me to stand up and take my clothes off. *Finally, a nigga who knew what he wanted.* I was so tired of doing all the work whenever I made house calls. I had my shirt off and was about to remove my skirt but he told me to leave it on. I saw his eyes in the dark and it was obvious that he was more turned on than I was.

He sat back down in the navy chair he had in the corner and laid his head back. I walked over to where he was and moved my body to the music. I could tell he didn't want a raunchy ass-clap-type-of-dance so I slowly bent over and let my hands glide over my ass while I played with the string between my cheeks.

I turned and saw his dick standing up in his pants. I had seen the look in his eyes plenty of times before in other mutherfuckers to know what he wanted. I walked between his legs and played with my titties for him. He had his arms resting on the chair so I put my hands over his and placed them over my titties while he squeezed harder and harder until my nipples were calling out to him.

With him fingering my nipples with his thumbs, I bent over and reached into the slit of his pants. I loved to see dicks like his. It was the same caramel color as his skin and it was circumcised. I couldn't stand to see a nigga with his shit still intact. Them mutherfuckers got charged extra for even pulling that alien-looking shit out.

"You like that don't you?" he asked after seeing the way I was licking my top lip.

I didn't answer him. I pulled a throw pillow off the couch and kneeled between his legs. I got comfortable and proceeded to retrieve a piece of ice from my chilled drink. I waited until it had melted and slowly covered the head of his dick with my full lips. I knew the sudden coldness shocked him but excited him at the same time. Quentin took my hair in his hand and began massaging my scalp.

I quickly swallowed him whole and started taking his dick in and out, never letting it leave my mouth. Him pulling my hair only made me want to suck him harder as I took him to the beginning of my tonsils.

"Take it all," he said.

I felt his lower body jerk and tasted the chocolate that he must've been eating earlier that day. And I did something that I would never do. I swallowed. I'm not sure why, but maybe I was starting to feel that shit he was talking. He pulled me to him and I knew then that he was feeling something more for me when he kissed me with his warm tongue. Hustler niggas like him never kissed girls after they sucked their dicks. Surprised and uncomfortable, I pulled away from him.

He quickly grabbed my wrist. "You thought I was finished wit' ya sexy ass," he said and pulled my thong to the side. I couldn't believe his dick was rock hard again.

I had a feeling that he was a nigga that liked to fuck a bitch in the ass, but I was ready for him. He had paid me my money and I wasn't like those cryin' bitches who can't take long-dick fuckin'. I helped him and began to work his dick in my ass. I felt the latex on his dick and took back my regrets about swallowing. His initiative to rap it up got mad respect from me. He was the only nigga I had encountered who I didn't have to strap up myself.

Soon he was turning me on with the noises he was making. It wasn't like the moans I heard some weak-ass niggas make. His were all thug and every time he called me a nasty bitch I bounced on his shit harder and faster. The CD ended and we moved to the floor and were laying there sweating and out of breath.

"Damn Vita," he finally said. "I have *never* had a bitch take the dick like you just did."

"Is that right?" I asked him, knowing damn well that he was telling the truth.

Sex to me was mental more than a physical thing and I knew how to use my mental to get the same pleasure that niggas did. My heart returned to its normal pace and I slowly got up so my knees wouldn't buckle.

"Where you goin'?" he asked.

"What you mean? I'm goin' home."

"Leave tomorrow," he said.

I would have usually laughed in a nigga's face but instead I grabbed my bags and went to his huge bathroom. Shit, he *had* paid me a grip for the short two hours I had given him. After I had showered I went into his room with my towel wrapped around me. He was laid out in his large sleigh bed with a blunt in one hand and the remote in the other.

"Vita, can I talk to you for a minute?" he asked when I came back into the room.

"Yeah, w'sup?" I asked, sitting on the edge of the bed.

He offered me a puff of the weed and I shook my head. "I know what you do and I'm not knockin' that shit at all. You usin' what you got to make that dough but I got somethin' better."

*What the fuck could be better than making mutherfuckers pay to experience a piece of Vita?* I knew he wasn't talking about drugs 'cause I saw what they did to my mother and there was no way I was even going near that shit.

"I doubt it," I said.

"Just listen to me for a sec. You know that things kind of fell off for me when I got knocked by the O five months ago."

*Why did he assume I was a groupie who knew the hustler's stats?* "No, I didn't know," I said. "We just meetin' remember?"

I knew that Quentin was doing something by the looks of his phat house and the Range and Lex parked outside, but I didn't know that shit had dropped off for him.

"Well yeah, somebody leaked some shit to them crackers when I was traveling out to Cali. Them mutherfuckers took the five hundred grand I had on me, gave me a pat on the back and told me to go the fuck home. Yo, I never made it pass the gates at BWI."

Damn, that was a lot of money. I was sixteen at the time and knew I had made at least 50 G's since my first time dancing, but I had never seen that much dough at *one time*. I didn't even ask what he was doing with it. The shit was obvious.

"So, how do I fit into this?" I asked. "I don't fuck around wit' that shit. I know that all money is dirty money, but that drug shit has affected me too much."

He leaned against the huge pillows behind him and turned up the volume on the TV. "I never said anything about you touching or seeing the shit. I just got somethin' that's gon' set you and me. You won't have to do this anymore. You trust me?" he asked.

*Trust after a few hours?* I didn't know about that, but the genuine concern in his eyes touched something in me. I didn't answer him. I dropped my towel and got on top of him. After I let him suck on my titties and get me wet, I sat on his dick and rode him until we both fell asleep.

Two months later it was time for us to do what he had been talking about. It was a week before Christmas. That was the best time to travel so shit wouldn't be obvious. We took a cab to the airport 'cause we were the only ones who knew anything about our trip. He kept asking me if I was all right, if I had my ID on me, was I nervous. We had gone over the shit enough times for me to dream about it. *Of course I was okay.*

Pulling up to the curb, I stepped out to straighten out my floor-length, tan leather trench coat. He told the driver to circle around the airport again so the cameras wouldn't know we were together if someone was watching, which we knew they were. Behind my brown Fendi shades I saw two men rushing towards me to see if I needed help with my bags. All I was carrying were two large shopping bags, one from

Macy's and the other from Hecht's. Inside there were real gifts wrapped in expensive paper with huge bows.

"No thank you," I said as I watched their eyes fall over my titties that were pushed outside of my coat and my thick legs that glistened underneath the burnt orange leather skirt.

Inside of the airport I knew Quentin wasn't far behind while I waited in line to confirm my ticket.

"Next in line," the black clerk said.

*Damn, I was hoping for the bald white man to call on me.* If he got a glance at my titties I knew shit was going to flow smoothly. Instead I would have to rely on the black bitch and hope she didn't give me any unneeded attitude.

"How are you today?" I asked, trying to give her the sweetest voice I could.

"Fine," she said abruptly. "Has anyone given you any foreign packages since you entered BWI?"

*Oh shit* I wanted to say. Why the hell was she asking me that? It must've been a part of a new procedure. "No," I said.

"Fine, now can I see your ID?"

I reached into the matching tan leather purse and gave her the MD Driver's License. She looked at the name on my roundtrip ticket then back at the ID. "Miss, can you please remove your glasses?"

I hated black bitches like her who took their jobs too seriously. The lady in the side view picture had her hair pulled back into a ponytail and her complexion was the same as mine. I was glad my hair fell over my shoulders and hid most of my face. There was no way she could tell us apart. I told my heart to stop racing and pulled them off. She looked at the picture again and handed it back to me along with my ticket.

"Do you have any bags to check?"

"No," I said with a smile.

"Okay Ms. Barnes, you have a safe flight to Texas and a happy holiday. Your gate number is D25," she said and handed over my ticket.

I put my glasses back on and picked up the bags I had between my legs. I was so glad the lines were hectic with crying babies and stressed out mothers with one too many bags and strollers. There were two black dudes sitting behind the camera monitoring the contents of the packages flowing through the conveyer.

I had gotten past the first major part and the detectors were going to be the only thing left that could fuck us up. I purposely let a mother with three small children go in front of me. She had two car seats, a large stroller and three baby bags. Her two children that could walk ran off and she had to rush through and chase after them.

One of the niggas looking at the camera got up from his seat to grab the smallest one who kept running. While the other nigga had his head turned to see what his boy was doing I placed my purse and bags on the conveyer belt and walked through.

Before I left I made sure there was no kind of metal on me. My hair was free of bobby pins and my gun was in a shoebox in the back of my closet. I held my breath as I walked through and relaxed when I didn't hear any beeping.

I saw my bags waiting for me and when I went to pick them up, one of those mutherfuckers touched my hand. "Excuse me miss," he said.

"Yes," I said, praying that he hadn't noticed anything.

"You gotta man?" he asked me.

I couldn't believe he had left his chair to ask me that. There was no telling what kind of shit people were strolling through BWI with, and his silly ass was smiling in my face.

"Umm, yeah I got somebody," I said. "But you're a cutie," I lied.

He wasn't cute. His cornrows looked like little stitches and his teeth looked like they hadn't been brushed in weeks. "Well why you walkin' away if I'm so cute," he hollered after me.

"'Cause I gotta plane to catch."

I got to the gate and they were boarding. I didn't see Quentin anywhere and started getting nervous. I couldn't seem suspicious so I got in line to board the plane. Finding my seat in first class, I sat the bags under the seat near my tan leather stiletto boots. The plane was filling up and still no Quentin. The last time I saw him was in line when he stood about ten people behind me at the check-in counter.

After the last couple of people were taking their seats, the red-haired stewardess grabbed the mic off the wall. "Good afternoon and thank you for choosing Delta as your airline across the friendly skies. According to the pilot our 8:35 flight to San Antonio will be on time. In five minutes we'll prepare for takeoff."

I was ready to panic but remembered that I had instructions to go to Texas no matter what. As I began to bite at the acrylic on my nails I saw Quentin rush onto the plane with his navy pea coat and matching carry on bag. He looked at me real intense and then took his seat two rows behind me. When I heard them lock the doors and pull away from the gate I felt like I could finally relax. I pulled the premier issue of XXL from one of the bags and turned to the article on Faith Evans.

Four magazines later, a nap and we were landing in San Antonio. I hailed a cab to the Radisson since me and Quentin were still pretending to be single passengers. We would meet later on after things went down.

Around eleven I went to a Spanish restaurant, La Mariposa where I spotted a man with the previously described mole on his right cheek. By then I had changed clothes. It was December but it was sixty degrees there compared to the fifteen degree-weather I had just left. I had on a lavender Chloé wrapped shirt and fitted, tan leather pants, and still had my coat draped over my arm since the nights were extra chilly.

I asked the host if I could be seated at the bar and he placed me at one of the stools while I went to the bathroom. Checking to make sure the stalls were empty, I went into the last one and called Quentin on his phone.

"Yeah," he said.

"He's still here," I told him.

"Aight, don't forget what I told you. Cerezo thinks wit' his dick most of the time so handle yours. I won't be far behind so when you finally get back to his room page me wit' his room number. I'm givin' you thirty minutes to do what you gotta do."

I hung up and looked myself over one time before returning to the bar. Cerezo was still sitting there finishing off his drink. I figured that Quentin had just called him with the lie about trouble at the airport with customs and that he would have to catch up with him the following month.

Cerezo was laying the bartender's tip on the bar, ready to leave when I purposely bumped into him. "I'm sorry," I said, making sure I rubbed my titties against his arm.

"Oh it's alright," he said, looking at my lips and back down to my titties.

I smiled at him and started to walk away. Just like I thought he called after me. "You here alone?" he asked.

"Only if you are," I said.

"Well then let us get a table," he said and looked at the waiter.

We were quickly seated at a table in the back of the restaurant.

"So, what is your name?" he asked, rolling over the *r* in *your* with his Spanish tongue.

"Lissette," I said.

"Pretty Spanish name. You from here?"

"No, Arizona," I said, feeling like he was asking too many questions.

"What are you doing here?"

"Visiting a friend of mine," I thought quickly.

"Nice here, nice weather. Maybe not as good as Arizona but same, you know?"

I nodded my head and took a sip of the peach margarita he had ordered. "So why are you here tonight?" I asked.

"Like you, I want to get out and see the city."

He was lying. Quentin told me his Spanish ass ate there often and I knew he was supposed to be meeting with him later so they could go back to his room and make the exchange like they had done before.

"What's your name?" I asked, wanting to see if he would give me his real name.

"Miguel," he said, never blinking.

I had to pinch my leg so I wouldn't laugh. He knew damn well that wasn't his name. Our food came and I slowly sipped my drink while I watched him finish three margaritas and four shots of tequila. It felt strange knowing he would be dead in the next two hours.

I didn't have to flirt with Cerezo. The alcohol had turned him into a man with many hands. He wouldn't stop squeezing my thighs and at one point he even started sucking on my fingers.

"Miguel let's get outta here and go to your house."

"That sounds good. I have a room at the Hilton since I'm here like you visiting the city."

I had caught a cab to the restaurant so I got in the car with him. Cerezo had a black Corvette and I laughed to myself as I thought about him telling me he worked in a factory. He was really a funny nigga. I was surprised that he was able to drive after getting liquored up but we pulled up to the hotel safely. Valet parked his car and we took the elevator to the eighth floor. He opened the door to room 828 and I walked past him.

"You get comfortable while I go to the bathroom," I said.

"Sure sexy baby. I can do that," he said while he started taking his clothes off.

I rushed into the bathroom and locked the door. I hit Quentin's number on my speed dial and pushed in 828 after I heard the beep. When I came out I stood in the doorway and asked him to turn out the lights.

"Anything for you," he said in his alcohol-induced voice. "You got surprise for me, huh?"

"Sure do," I said, noticing the leather duffel bag in the back of the closet.

I took off my jacket and threw it over the chair near the door.

"Your body is so hot," he said, pulling his dick out of his pants. I couldn't believe he was already naked and getting started without me even touching him.

"So what do you like?" I asked.

"Oh I like it all, everything you can do," he said.

With that I climbed on the bed and started biting on his neck while I rubbed on his chest. He was still jerking on his dick so I moved his hand and started doing it for him. I looked at the clock and saw that I only had fifteen minutes left. I grabbed the blindfold I had under my left foot and tied it around his head.

"Oh yeah, I like the nasty stuff. I'm glad I see you tonight," he said as his breathing got faster.

I got up and dug in my purse. Feeling the cold metal, I pulled out both pairs of handcuffs and walked back to the bed. There wasn't a space for me to clamp the cuffs so I used one pair to cuff his wrists together behind his head.

I had ten minutes left so I sat between his legs and worked my magic. While he made his crazy noises I listened for Quentin at the door. He said I would only hear a soft knock so I had to keep my ears opened. It was hard when Cerezo was wailing like a wounded dog.

"I'll be right back," I told him when I finally heard the tap.

"Where are you going?" he asked, trying to peek under the blindfold.

"It's a surprise. Something real special," I said as I rushed to put on my jacket. I grabbed the other pair of handcuffs on the bed, ran to the closet and unzipped the bag. As scared as I was I picked it up. "Oh, you are going to like what I have for you," I said to him.

"And I can't wait baby," he said, squeezing his balls together with his thighs.

I tiptoed past the bed and grabbed the handle on the door. He was still telling me how bad he wanted me when I opened the door. Quentin brushed by me like we were strangers and slipped the keys into my hand.

Walking onto the streets I saw the black Mercury he had parked at the corner. I sat behind the wheel and waited for him. Ten minutes later he was at the passenger side knocking on the window. He was always quiet but his mood went beyond that while we drove back to the hotel. Later I asked him if anything was wrong.

"Nah, the shit went better than I thought," he said.

"Then why do you look so angry?" I asked.

"'Cause I'm just in another state of mind after I take care of some shit like that."

That meant having to use a gun. Before he told me what we were going to be doing he said he had found out that Cerezo had leaked info on him when he made the trip to Cali. He had used the money to pay off the mutherfuckers in customs. In exchange for them stopping Quentin at BWI, Cerezo was able to go untouched whenever he came through with shit. Cerezo took the other half and pretended like he was sorry for Quentin's fallback.

I asked Quentin if he thought anybody else knew he was meeting with Cerezo. He said Cerezo's supplier in California didn't know about his plans to branch off on his own and thought that Cerezo just had dealings with a small-time nigga from Baltimore named Chauncey.

I sat on the bed while he counted the packs of powder and watched as he concealed them in the hidden pockets sewn into the lining of my coat along with the $150,000. Quentin told me he had wanted me to hold onto the money in case things went wrong in the hotel room and he really needed to flash some kind of dough for Cerezo.

"We don't have time now, but when we get back, you best believe I'm takin' care of that ass," he said, looking over at me the same way he did the first night I met him.

We had roundtrip tickets but that was only done so we wouldn't alert customs. They paid extra attention to people going one way so instead of flying back to Baltimore, we took the Amtrak.

The almost two-day ride gave us time to talk and play plenty games of checkers and Scrabble. I had to keep pulling out the dictionary on his ass when he made words like *gybe* and *kyat*. Before I turned to the word he had a definition. I was surprised at his intelligence. Maybe it was wrong for me to assume that a hustler couldn't know words beside *kilo* and *consignment*. Scrabble would later become the only game we played on the other out-of-town "trips" and rainy days when all we wanted to do was lay up.

My heart had hardened so badly that I forgot what it felt like to enjoy being in somebody's company besides my own and actually have fun. Besides the bundle of drugs in my coat, I felt at ease with Quentin.

"You know how much shit you had on you?" he asked later when we got to his house.

"Nah," I said.

"After that shit is cut, about $700,000 worth."

"Then why did we only take one fifty?"

"'Cause that's yours," he said, and spread my legs apart to take care of my ass the way he promised me.

When I finally fell asleep that night I thought about the risks I had taken. Quentin did say that I would never have to work for money again, but I knew that even with me as his "ride or die chick," I would come across tougher shit than I did when I was just shakin' my ass.

Within two years of us doing our thing I had caught a bullet in my left thigh, watched him get shot in his shoulder and back, and had lost three babies. The doctor said my womb was too weak or some shit, but I knew the real reason was my worrying. I kept a bottle of Mylanta on me and was always watching my back.

The end of me and Quentin came after I lost the third baby. I was more attached to this baby since I had carried it the longest. The first two I lost after a month. This one was with me for almost four months. My stomach had even formed itself into a cute little pouch. Quentin would rub oil on my belly after we got out the shower and talk to it. It was something we both wanted.

Arriving at the hospital, I already knew I had lost it. Quentin was in Virginia when I called him. I knew not to put any extra stress on his plate when he went out of state but it was just too much for me to handle by myself. He said he would be there within the next two hours and was flying in. A few turned into a day.

I came home from the hospital that first day and it was hard enough just to make it out the cab. I had to ask the driver to help me into bed. He was even nice enough to fix me some tea and soup. I was curled up in bed high off the codeine they had given me for my cramps that felt more like contractions. I couldn't even get up from bed to use the bathroom.

"Your boyfriend is a fool to leave you here alone," he said before he left.

I gave him a fake smile and turned over. Hours later I woke up and Quentin still wasn't there. On the third day I started gaining some strength and I packed my shit. I had enough money to be on my own and I needed a new start.

When Quentin finally came home he saw the boxes and got this shook look on his face. "Vita what's goin' on?"

"I'm leavin' nigga, that's what's goin' on. Quentin, I called ya mutherfuckin' ass on Tuesday. Today is Thursday and you just bringin' ya ass through the door. Do you know what I had to go through? I had to order a new fuckin' mattress since I couldn't make it to the toilet. Blood, piss and shit… I didn't make this mutherfucker on my own," I said, pointing to my empty stomach.

I turned around to look away so he couldn't see the tears welling up in the corners of my eyes. I knew in the beginning that shit wasn't going to come easy but me having to go through that alone wasn't cool and besides, I wasn't stupid. Quentin had been to Virginia so many times before and it never took him three days to do his thing. I would usually go with him, but suddenly he wanted to go alone. That could only mean another bitch, and I wasn't coming second to no fuckin' body. Not when I was carrying his child.

He was standing there trying to talk me into staying. I had never seen him cry, but that day when I pulled away from the house, I saw the tears running down his face like raindrops.

A year later I was nineteen and living in New York on my own. Violet had always filled my head with her big city stories and I always envisioned myself living the same life she had talked about—VIP passes to exclusive shit, partying with the money makers and just living life.

A year of being there and I was doing all of that. I still kept in touch with Quentin and after I left I could tell from his voice that things were real thick for him. He said that I would always be in his heart and hoped I would come back to him one day.

"Vita, I don't give a fuck who you wit' after me or who I'm wit' you will always be my heart."

I didn't know what would happen with us, but for the moment he was doing his thing and so was I. I thought I was through with ever having a relationship or feeling anything. That is, until I met KC. I swear that I had never looked at another female in any kind of sexual way. I used to gag at the thought of dyke love, but I was at a Sean John fashion show when I met her.

It was the winter collection and I was representin' with my powder blue mink vest, black leather pants and powder blue armadillo boots. Like always, I was rollin' solo and when I left my seat to get my favorite drink she was standing behind me.

I had seen her earlier and had to look twice to make sure it was a girl I was looking at. She was thick and her hair was cut close. Her skin was this toffee color and she had these oriental-type of eyes only they were slightly rounded. She had on a black motorcycle jacket with matching pants and boots, and if it was a nigga I would have been slipped the number for a private party.

"You drink that stuff?" she asked when she heard me order Southern Comfort.

"Yeah, it's sweet and it gives the Grey Goose a smooth taste," I said.

"Yeah, I like that sweet stuff too," she said, trying to seduce me with her light brown eyes.

"You take care," I said before I walked back to my seat.

I ran into her again at the afterparty where she asked if I was seeing somebody. What's strange is that I actually told her no. Yet, had it been a nigga I would've given him a smart-ass reply with a little attitude.

"Well, can I take you out later?" she asked.

"I don't know…"

"Come on. I can even have a car pick you up," she said.

"Oh, I do fine drivin' my own shit."

"I didn't say you couldn't," she laughed.

Later we went to *Justin's* where she knew everybody and went all out to make sure I was having a good time. After that I went out with her a couple more times before she took me to her house. She had a phat-ass place in Long Island with a three-car garage.

We rode in her silver A8L most of the time but she owned a Lexus truck and a Lamborghini. Her house was huge and everything was black, white or silver. The floors were either covered in white carpet or gray and black marble.

One night at her house, she had me sit in one of her white Artesian chairs and then disappeared into the kitchen. Davina's *Best of Both Worlds* was playing and when she came back was holding a bowl of sugar-covered strawberries and raspberries.

"You like berries with sugar?" she asked in her New York accent.

"Yeah," I said suddenly feeling like I wasn't in control.

"Well, can I show you the right way to eat them?"

I nodded my head like I was in a daze while I watched her kneel in front of me. It was still brick outside but I had on cream leather boots that stopped at my thighs with no panties.

She sat the bowl beside the chair and grabbed my inner thighs. I had only let her kiss me on the cheek and her massaging my thighs made my head drop. She tilted her head towards my face and kissed my lips, passing me a raspberry with her tongue. I told myself that it had to be the money, but quickly thought otherwise after I felt her tongue working my clit. She was taking her time and had reached my spot where gentle tongue action only took a little effort.

Feeling like I was 'bout to bust, she took a strawberry and ran the tip between the lips of my pussy. I couldn't believe how good she was making me feel. I knew there was no way I could fall for another bitch, but Katrina, who was better known as KC made that shit hard.

From that point on when I would turn down her dates that were sometimes trips to Vegas and the Bahamas, she had shit like rare flowers that priced at $350 a bouquet sent to my penthouse and jewelry with cards that read, *Just because I can't be with you this weekend*. It became impossible for us not to be together after she overwhelmed me with shit like that. I contemplated how it was possible for me to go from nothing but lovin' the dick to only being with her.

I'm not sure how she made her money but I knew it wasn't completely legit. She claimed to be a regular mutherfucker who had a couple of investments here and there, but wherever we went, people knew her and not just everyday people. Well-known performers and record label owners would stop her to make small talk and even ask her if they could do shit for her.

I was lovin' her image so it didn't bother me when she introduced me as her girl. She kept my pockets phat and I was there with open hands. After the third month, things started getting serious—on her part that is. We would go to the same fuckin' parties with all the same mutherfuckers and suddenly she was getting mad and pulling me to the side about dumb shit.

"Vita," she said one night we were at a party in the Hamptons, "who the fuck is that nigga I saw you huggin' on?"

I looked at her like *what the fuck*. "Who are you talkin' about?" I asked. *And I really didn't* know since I had hugged a lot of niggas.

"Vita don't play stupid wit' me okay?"

"Yeah whateva," I said, ready to leave after she brought that dumb shit to my attention.

Later when she dropped me off in front of my building and walked me to the door, she was still trippin'. I wondered why she was quiet the whole ride home and waited to get out front of my residence to start some shit.

"Vita don't do that shit again," she said like she was my mother.

"Fuck you," I said, trying to go inside and close the door in her face.

"Oh *fuck me*?" she said and grabbed my arm. "Vita don't fuckin' turn ya back on me when I'm talkin' to you. I saw that nigga Suave in your face and I don't want to see that shit again."

I looked around to make sure none of my neighbors were around before I got loud. "I can't control who the fuck knows me," I said, yanking my arm out of her hand.

"Okay then," she said and got in her car and sped off.

I don't know why, but she had made me feeling guilty about some shit that I knew I hadn't done. True, Suave was rollin' like that but I had never fucked him before. Once he had asked if we could hook up, but I knew that word would only get back to her. When I say she knew everybody, that's what the fuck I meant. I couldn't even count on tryna go and eat somewhere secluded. The owner would probably know her there too.

Like I thought, she called me the next day and told me to wait for a package. It was a platinum choker with *Vita* spelled out in diamonds. She did shit like that every time we got into it. When she found out that I was going back to Baltimore for any reason, she always accused me of seeing Quentin. In the beginning I respected her by going home just to do whatever it was that I had to. But after hearing the bullshit accusations so many times, I slowly let him back into my life.

He was cool after I told him about KC but I could still see that he was hurt. "Vita, like I told you before I'm here and it's gon' always be that way. When you ready I know it'll be me and you again," he said.

And just like Jewel told me when I was in the chair getting my hair done, I was right at Quentin's house that night sleeping with him like I had never left.

Nikola

Chelsea was worrying for nothing. But I could tell that her seeing Marco tripped her up, though. I saw his sneaky ass leaving the church and made a note to self to have him stopped before he could get on the boat. Of course, that was unrealistic since there were way more people at the reception than at the church. I was so busy making sure that everything was going in the right direction that at first I didn't see Omar.

He was finer than a mutherfucker! And fine was putting it lightly. I had met him the year before at a Jazz concert downtown at the Pier Six. I wasn't really into the old stuff but my mother had put me down with Frankie Beverly and Maze at an early age and I had always wanted to experience them live. Their one song, 'Happy Feelings' always reminded me of her cleaning the house on Saturday mornings.

Coming to the concert was one of the first times I was without Chanel or Chelsea trying to "make shit liquid." It was August and the heat was ridiculous. Although the concert was held under a large pavilion to block the sun I opted for a white linen dress and these sexy white Gucci sandals that said three things: I'm a lady, but I like to fuck, and it's gon' cost you. My hair had grown out a little longer but I had it covered with a floppy straw hat. I was there to enjoy the music, but at the same time scope the crowd for dollars. Some comedienne was on stage and I got up to get me a cup of Zinfandel.

Walking back to my seat, I saw him standing by the dock drinking from his bottle of Evian. From where I was standing he was a marvelous being and instantly made me forget about everything I was there for. His hair was plaited into single braids and then braided again into two. The man's appearance was immaculate. I could see that he had the sideburns trimmed around his face as well as the hair around his neck. His eyebrows even looked defined. He had on a black sleeveless shirt that looked like it cost a fortune, beige, linen cargo pants and matching sandals. I pretended to be moving with the crowd and slowed down when I got closer to him.

Everything about him was clean and as I got a look at him from the side, all I could think about was how gorgeous he was. I looked down at his feet and couldn't believe that his toes were pedicured. His feet and nails seemed to have a thin coat of natural polish. If I didn't have all of my shit together I would've felt like he could give me major competition. He had to be gay, I thought, because there was no way a real nigga could be that pretty and that *fine*. I passed him off as gay and started walking away. Before I could pass him he touched the small of my back.

"Excuse me," he said in this gentle voice, " but I have to tell you. You are absolutely beautiful."

I looked at him like he didn't know what the fuck he was talking about. I knew that I was pretty, but if me and him were standing together in front of a mirror, I would just have to leave him there by himself.

"Thank you," was all I said. But what I really wanted to say was, *Yes and you and me can make the prettiest babies the world has ever seen.*

"I'm Omar," he said, extending his hand.

I looked at his wrist and noticed the silver charm bracelet. "Nikola," I said.

"Your name is almost pretty as you." Instead of thanking him I smiled. "How old are you?" he asked.

"Nineteen," I said.

"Nineteen? Stop lying."

"I'm not lying," I said, enjoying the way he took his time to gaze over every part of my body.

"You look so much older," he said, shaking his head. "Help us all when you get older. You'll be dangerous. What a nineteen-year old know about Frankie Beverly?"

"I know about him. My mother put me down wit' his stuff when I was thirteen."

"Oh, okay. So Nikola, where are you sitting?"

"Row C," I said, hoping to get another peek at the perfect row of teeth in his mouth.

"I'm not tryna show you out, but I have a extra seat in row A if you want to join me."

Omar didn't have to ask me twice. Walking to the front, there was no doubt that every pair of eyes was on us. I think we both knew we were the prettiest couple in there. Omar told me he was supposed to be there with his girlfriend, but they had broken up a month ago. *So he wasn't gay.* Still, I had to know why we both looked like we had gone to the same manicurist.

Mr. Wonderful said he was a model and underneath all of the pretty boy exterior was a true nigga. That was enough for me so the next morning I was eating breakfast in his bed and wearing one of his shirts. Omar stepped out of his bathroom and his baby fine hair was all over his head. He wore a white towel wrapped around his waist. *What was he doing to me?* Staring at him for too long made me feel lightheaded.

Omar came over to my side of the bed and started sucking on my toes while he played in my pussy. After I came for what seemed like the tenth time in eight hours, we laid in bed and watched talk shows all morning. I never told Chanel and Chelsea about my secret night with Omar. I was the backbone of our trio and I couldn't let them know I'd slipped.

That night, we'd left the concert and came back to his place where he cooked dinner and listened to his Marvin Gaye collection. He was twenty-eight and had been modeling since he was seventeen.

Hearing him talk about past relationships, it was obvious that he hadn't found happiness yet. I never heard someone say their looks were a curse. But I was one to talk, when I had prejudged him based on the same thing. We sat there and drank a bottle of Moët while he massaged my feet. I couldn't even fix my lips to ask him for some money. Shit, I felt like I owed him something.

After spending that magical night together, we went to other Jazz concerts and did things like book readings and clubs in DC and Philly where the spoken word held an open mic. I was enjoying the simple things, like sitting in Barnes & Noble drinking frappucino or playing cards in his living room.

Two months of me sneaking around and I felt myself falling way too hard for him. My nose was wide open. I had missed out on a lot of chances to make money and Chanel and Chelsea were starting to ask questions. As far as Omar knew, he thought I did hair and when we weren't together, assumed I was away at a hair show.

Slowly, I distanced myself from him and got back into the groove of things, but it was hard to let Omar's face escape from my mind that quickly. I had learned to see past his pretty face for the other things in him that made him the beautiful person he was. Whoever the girl was that would finally settle down with him, she was in for a lot of happiness, because every moment with him would be satisfying.

Omar had continued to call me after I cut him off, but I never picked up the phone. I didn't know how to tell him that he was everything I ever wanted in a man, but was lacking the financial stability I needed forever. I knew that modeling brought him good money from the things I saw in his condo, but he had told me that he sometimes went months before anything came his way. I needed something more concrete.

I was deep in thought as I drove the streets of Philadelphia the night before the wedding, contemplating my situation. Each of us seemed to be doing her own thing, and though I knew that no one would ever come between the bond we had formed, things were changing.

Chelsea had her Charles and Chanel *thought* she had her Quentin. Me and her needed to sit down and talk because I don't think she was aware that I knew about the hold Quentin had on her. She reminded me of my mother in that aspect. I believed that my mother knew my father was doing his dirt all along, but was willing to accept it on the basis that he was taking care of home.

After leaving the party I just needed some time to myself. I was always so worried about the things going on in their lives that I hadn't given *Nikola* any thought. I was so accustomed to having things when I wanted them but I needed another plan to ensure that I would always have. I could do hair in my sleep and had thought about a salon, but my money was funny. The only smart move I had made was paying off my mother's house. Sad to say, but all I had to show for my years in the life were clothes, cars and jewelry.

That night I had on a bracelet and necklace that cost $85,000 altogether. That was equipment for a salon right there. Well, actually, Antonio had given me the set. He was an Italian jeweler in New York who had enjoyed my company many nights. I met him when I was in Manhattan shopping for a floor-length chinchilla.

Antonio happened to be getting fitted for his custom made matching male version. I caught his eye in the mirror. "You see something you like?" I mouthed.

He scrunched up his face and I immediately knew his language and ability to comprehend were horrible. I placed the house payment back on its hanger, walking towards him with that confidence I had acquired after my dealings with men of his status. He was dressed in a charcoal cashmere turtleneck with dark gray wool pants and his shoes cost nothing less than a G. *I was baggin' him fasho!*

When I was close enough to smell the D&G cologne, I whispered to him again, "You see somethin' you like?"

His familiar Italian accent further confirmed what I already knew. He was Carlito's long-lost brother. And later that night when I pissed on him to satisfy his sexual fetish, I walked out of his expensive penthouse with my new coat. A few more piss sessions and I had a jewelry collection that would've made the Big Tymers proud. I called him again to collect other expensive gifts but he said I cost too much. Ha! *Didn't he know he had to pay up to lay up,* or in his case, *pay up to get pissed on?*

A year later I was on Philadelphia's Broad St. the night before Chelsea's wedding. The infamous street was divided into north and south and I had entered the clean part where everything was lit up. It was about 2:30, so just as our affair was ending, the clubs were just getting started. I pulled up to the corner, across the street from a club called *Libations.* It was on the second floor of the structure and from what I could see the place was jumpin'. Outside there were convertible Benzes, Escalades with expensive rims, and sports cars. That was enough for me to pull into the adjacent parking lot and get ready to do da' damn thing.

Before I got out I checked my orange Coach bag for my fake ID, applied another coating of clear MAC Lipglass and ran my hands through my hair. When I opened the door to the club I heard the DJ mixing hip-hop with R & B, and the guy at the door was rocking his big ass to the beat. I almost thought he would topple off the stool, he was shaking his ass so hard.

"Ten dollars, and I need to see ya ID," he said in a dramatic drag queen voice.

I gave him a fifty and pulled the card from the zippered pocket of my bag. He looked at the picture and back at me, dramatically swinging the blonde wig.

"The birth date on here says January 1977. How old are you?" he asked.

"Twenty-four," I said, never stuttering.

I wasn't stupid. I had been embarrassed before when we all went to *Vegas Nights* in Atlanta when another doorman had asked me the same question. I had to slip the mutherfucker there at the door another hundred besides the fifty dollars we were already paying for VIP admission because he had caught me off guard.

"Here's ya change and have a good time," he said, giving me back the ID.

I walked up the stairs and had to adjust my eyes to the blue and purple lighting. I wondered why all of the girls were standing together near the front and figured they were just playing hard to get. I guessed they were too scared to approach the big ballers that I knew were in there holdin' it down. That was fine with me. It would just give me the chance to pick and choose as I pleased. I glided into the crowd and watched as they cleared the way for me. Like always, I didn't have to shove my way through or use any *excuse me's*. The crowds of females were happy to move out of my way for a chance to get a look at me in my orange halter and brown leather pants.

As I got closer to the back of the club where people were on the dance floor, it became apparent that I was in the wrong place. There was no sign of niggas anywhere. The phat rides I had seen outside belonged to a bunch of bitches. I couldn't believe that I had stepped into a lesbo club.

"Shit," I said to myself and turned back around to get the fuck out of there.

"Leavin' so soon?" a pretty, chubby-faced girl asked me.

"Umm, yeah, I'm in the wrong place," I said, taken aback by her features. I couldn't understand how somebody so pretty would want to look like a nigga.

"Didn't know this was dykes-r-us, huh?" she laughed.

"Sure didn't," I said still trying to get away from the crowd and out the door.

"So you leavin' based on that?" she asked.

"Well, yeah. I'm not gay," I said.

"So? Who said you had to be gay to have a good time? Come on and stick around. Nobody will do anything you don't want them to. Plus, you wit' me and nobody will even say more than hi."

I looked at all of the different things going on around me and saw that a lot of girls were dancing alone, and there were those that looked like they were ready to fuck right against the walls. Everybody seemed pretty harmless though. I had started moving my body to the music anyway.

"See, I told you it don't matter. Look at you doing your thing," she said.

I decided that I would stay for a while and walked to the bar to get me a Purple Rain. "Can you use Chambord?" I asked the bartender.

"I'll have the same thing," she said. We sat at the bar and she turned and faced me. "So you have a name, club wanderer?"

"Nikola," I said, quickly feeling warm inside after tasting the five liquors used to make my drink.

"That's real pretty," she said, sliding a twenty onto the counter. "So what part of Philly you from?"

"No part. I'm from Baltimore."

"So what you doin' here in Philly?"

"Hosting my best friend's bachelorette party," I said, taking another long sip of my drink.

"It's already over or you escaped?"

"Both," I laughed.

"Damn, your teeth are pretty," she said.

She was about to ask me something when a petite Spanish girl tapped her on the shoulder. "Hey, w'sup," KC said to her and turned back around to face me.

I could see that the girl was disappointed by the way she had been dismissed. I didn't want to be the cause of any lover's quarrel so I stood up to leave. "Listen, it was nice talkin' to you, but I got a wedding later on today."

She grabbed my hand gently. "No, don't go yet, she's just a friend. I wanted to ask you something... Oh yeah, is the wedding here in Philly?"

"No, back home," I said, faking a yawn.

"Don't get sleepy on me yet. Where at in Baltimore?"

"A Catholic church on Edmondson Ave. You know where that is?" I asked.

"Yeah, I know. Look, I know I wasn't invited, but you think I could see you again at the reception maybe?"

*Didn't I tell her I wasn't gay?* I was sure that she had the women falling at her feet, but she just wasn't my cup of tea.

"What did you say your name was?" I asked.

"Katrina."

"Well, Katrina, like I said before I'm not knockin' this whole scene, but it's just not me."

"I can feel that, but I'm comin' at you as a friend. You seem like the type of person I am. Takin' chances, wanderin' around cities and clubs you aren't familiar with. I like that kind of shit too. Look, if you won't let me see you at the reception, how 'bout I send you a roundtrip to NY next weekend and we hang out? Strictly friends tip."

"I don't know," I said.

"Well you got a number I can reach you at?" she asked.

"You got a two-way?"

"No doubt," she said and pulled the chrome device off her hip. "Let me beam you so I can make sure we won't lose touch."

I saw her screen name, *K Caramel* appear on my two-way screen. I sent it to my contact list, beamed her my info, waved bye and headed to my car. I was sitting at the corner near the club waiting for the light to change when a periwinkle Acura RSX cut me off. I didn't even know they were on the road yet. I'd seen them at an auto show a few weeks earlier.

Katrina jumped out, and for some reason had me looking twice at her in her Dolce & Gabbana T-shirt and tailored pants. I knew it wasn't the liquor 'cause I hadn't even finished my drink at the bar.

"Oh, it's like that?" she asked, looking at my car.

"Can you move your car so I can get outta here?" I asked surprised at my own flirtatious tone.

"Yeah, I can do that," she said, returning the smile. "But I forgot to ask where the reception was. I been havin' a taste for crabs and who knows, maybe we can hook up after ya thing is over."

"It's on the Bay Lady, but the boat leaves at exactly 5:30."

"I can do that, or will I be in the way of you and ya man?"

"I don't have one," I said, wishing she would move so the cars behind us would stop honking.

"That's w'sup," she said, using a phrase I had heard a lot of people from Philly say rather than a complete sentence to convey their true feelings.

"So Nikola, if I don't see you later on the Bay Lady, I'll be hearin' from you sometime this week to send that ticket, right?"

"Yeah, okay," I said and watched her go to her car.

Driving back to Chelsea's, I was actually giving it some thought. Katrina was obviously paid and as far as I was concerned, money had no face or gender.

I was in the middle of introducing the newly married couple on the Bay Lady when my eyes met Omar's. I couldn't believe the effect he still had over me after four months of not seeing him. I was glad that I didn't see him sitting with a female. However, his section *was* the pretty boy pack. Some of the guys sitting with him were just as attractive, but I don't think they had anything on him and his charisma. I gave him his own personal smile and looked to the other side of the deck where I saw the Western clique. All eyes were on me like I suspected. I could tell they hadn't stopped hatin' since the party in Philly.

Everything about me said that I was doing big things. While they were working their customer service and bank jobs trying to pay off the note on their little Hondas, I was shittin' on them in my brand new midnight blue Lexus convertible. Most of them didn't know what a true friendship was, and I bet were surprised to see that me, Chanel and Chelsea were all still hangin' tough. Chelsea's party had definitely been a blast, but there were some things in the air that had felt out of place.

Chanel wasn't herself. Her mood was distant, the same way she had acted in the car when we were going to the church. And suddenly I was regretting the pact we had made about marrying a nigga that could set us for life. I was sure that it would happen over time, but we had said we would give it a year, and within the time we had been living the life, there was nobody that I even considered husband material.

The niggas I had fucked that were businessmen who had stock and mutual funds that would set them for life were just too damn boring. Their life revolved around the next business move, and while I wouldn't have a problem spending their money forever, I knew that something would always be missing.

While everyone on the boat was eating, I chose the time to mingle and see just who had come out besides Omar. Mr. Marco had found himself a corner table where he wouldn't be in Chelsea's field of vision. I headed straight to his table and leaned over his shoulder. "Hey, you bastard, you don't know me, but I know your sick ass, and if you *even* try to spoil my girl's day, I'll have somebody throw ya ass off this boat so fast, you won't be able to say foot fetish." I straightened out my dress and felt his eyes burning into my back. *That's right nigga, get a good look 'cause ya ass will wish you never stepped foot on this mutherfucker.*

Walking over to the Western table to make sure they were still sick and jealous of me, I felt a hand on the small of my back. It was Omar and he was touching me the same way he had done when I met him.

"Looking good," he said and kissed my cheek lightly.

I knew I was. Chelsea was the hottest thing in there, of course, but Chanel and me were next in line. Our dresses were replicas of hers, only the front was a mini skirt with a small train in the back. Our sandals were four inches and the same baby pink as the beaded flowers in her dress.

"You do too. And you smell nice," I said, inhaling his fragrance as he pulled away.

"I know you're busy, but Nikola why haven't I heard from you in let me see… two months?" he asked, pretending to count on his fingers.

"Omar, I can't really talk right now, but if I told you, you wouldn't understand."

"Nikola, you think I don't know what you and your girlfriends do?"

I didn't expect that to come from his mouth. We were only on the boat for forty-five minutes and mutherfuckers were talking already.

"I told you. See, that's what I'm talkin' 'bout. Already you judgin' me."

"You know that's not even me. I understand you do what you do for a reason, and I want to know why. Nikola, call me. We can work it out. You don't have to do that."

I didn't have a chance to think about what he said because I had spotted Katrina. She saw me walking away from Omar and waved for me to come over.

"Hey," I said. "I didn't think you would make it."

"Oh, come on now. You know I was serious any time I came looking for you outside the club."

I was about to ask her what part of New York she lived in, and why she was in Philly when I saw Chanel with her hands in Quentin's face. I didn't even know he had been invited, but then again, Omar hadn't had an invite from any of us either. DJ Lil' Mic was still spinning tracks, but I could hear her voice over the speakers. That could only mean one thing. *We had a problem.*

Vita

Before I left Jewel's salon that night I got a call from Quentin. He said he saw my car parked in front of her place and I had better show my face at his front door. I got us some Chinese and was waiting for him to let me in at 9:30.

"Hey baby," he said, reaching out for a hug.

"W'sup Q," I said, letting my hands run through his thick, curly hair. He had taken out his cornrows and his hair was flowing freely.

Quentin wore a HOBO T-shirt and shorts and smelled like a fresh bath and baby oil. Outside it had just finished raining and my arms and face were both sticky. The AC felt heavenly as I stepped inside his hallway.

"Turn around," he said.

"Why, I got somethin' on my ass?"

"Nah, checkin' out ya'do. That's real nice," he said, fluffing my hair. "You got it colored or somethin'?"

"It's called highlights," I said.

"I likes, I likes. Damn, you look good. You a lil' thick ain't you?" he commented.

"I got us some Chinese food," I said, ignoring his question.

"I hope you got some chicken and broccoli and some shrimp-fried rice," he said, taking the bags of food out my hand. "'Cause you the only one I know who eats that chicken chow shit and what's that other mess? Shrimp egg foo yong."

"It's called chicken low mein nigga," I said, rolling my eyes.

"Whateva it is, you better watch out before you fuck around and start growing cat whiskers."

I laughed and watched him empty our food into the blue and white Mikasa bowls. He put our food on a large tray and we sat down on the navy rug in the living room. This was my favorite room in his house. The walls were all brick and he had three steps that led up to his fireplace.

"So, w'sup?" I asked.

"Vita, I haven't seen or talked to you in two fuckin' months, so don't ask me that shit. I need to be askin' you the same thing."

"You already know w'sup wit' me," I said, trying to avoid any conversation about KC.

"No, I don't. I know what you tell me, but is it the truth?"

"Is what the truth?" I asked, pouring soy sauce over my noodles.

He lifted my face and held my chin. "Are you happy Vita? I mean when I *do* talk to you everything sounds cool, but when I see you it's somethin' different."

"Nigga, yeah I'm happy," I said, brushing off the seriousness of our conversation. "True, we get into it like everybody else I know, but…."

I didn't know what the *but* was, so I ate my food and pretended to look at the taped episode of *Oz*. Although I would never admit it, Quentin was the one person who knew me better than I knew myself sometimes. Things were off the hook with me and KC, and I didn't know that it showed on my face.

She had started that shit again about me fuckin' around. I was so tired of her bullshit that I told her ass off the way I should've done in the beginning. I felt like she thought her money entitled her to treat me any way she wanted and granted her control over my life.

I told her I didn't want to be bothered with her anymore. In response she had pushed me against the wall and threatened me with the same shit I heard her say before. "Vita, don't fuck wit'me. You don't know what I'm capable of."

She left and I knew that was the end 'cause I had never let nobody put their fuckin' hands on me. I was almost in Baltimore when she called me on the cell and said she was sorry and had a gift delivered to my place. That quickly I had forgotten about her possessiveness and couldn't wait to see what she had for me.

Me and Quentin had just finished eating when I heard my phone ringing. I reached into my bag and saw her name on the screen. Quentin was sitting there waiting for me to answer it, but I turned off the ringer and closed my bag. He looked at me like he wanted me to say something.

"I'm gettin' in the shower," I said.

"While you in there, tell her I said hi!" he hollered after me.

I got a towel and washcloth from the hallway closet and closed the bathroom door. Turning on the water for a shower, I hit the memory button to call her back.

"Why the fuck you ain't answer ya phone," she said before anything else.

"'Cause I couldn't get to it. My purse was in the backseat."

"Where you at?" she asked.

"At Jewel's," I said, thinking quickly.

"Oh, you stayin' at another bitch's house now?"

I couldn't believe the dumb shit coming from her mouth. She acted like I was fuckin' my hair stylist or something. "*Please*," I said.

"So, why you not home yet?" she asked.

"'Cause I'm going out. I'll be home tomorrow."

"Vita you need to be comin' home tonight like you told me. I told you I had somethin' delivered to ya crib."

"And I can get the shit tomorrow," I said and hung up.

KC had me so heated that I didn't even care if she called Jewel looking for me. I forgot that I had just gotten my hair done and instead ran water for a bath. I threw my clothes into a pile beside the toilet and was about to test the water with my foot when Quentin opened the door.

"Vita what the fuck is that on your back?"

"What are you talkin' about?" I asked, straining to see what it was.

He touched a spot above my ass and I flinched.

"Ouch, don't press my skin like that," I said.

"What is it?" he asked me again.

"I don't know. It must've happened when we was fussin'. I didn't even know it was there."

Quentin got a hand mirror from the toilet basin and held it so I could see. There was an ugly purple and black bruise the size of a baseball covering the majority of my lower back. "That bitch," I said.

"And ya ass is tellin' me that everything is cool. I knew you was lyin'."

"Q, I don't need you talkin' to me like you my goddamn father."

"I'm not. This shit is just upsettin' me," he said and stared at me for a long time. "Vita, stay here wit' me, 'cause if you go back and some other shit, some worst shit goes down, that bitch is catchin' somethin'." I eased down into the tub and the hot water against the bruise made me frown my face. "Hurt?" he asked.

I nodded and rested my head against the sponge cushion, wondering why I hadn't felt any pain all day. I closed my eyes so I wouldn't have to explain myself any further, and heard him reach for a magazine from the iron rack beside the sink.

The bathroom was so quiet that all I heard was our breathing and the echo of water dripping from the faucet. Even with my eyes closed I knew he was staring at the gun wound in my thigh. Months later, even after we weren't together, he had apologized repeatedly for putting my life in danger.

I had made the run with him to Philly when the drug deal went bad. He had changed connects for the third time that year and even I knew something wasn't right. The Jamaican didn't hesitate to pull out and I was caught in the crossfire.

Quentin shuffled the magazine pages. Like me, he probably wanted to push the memory in the back of his mind as far as it would go. I figured he was going to sit there and read while I bathed. It was something he used to do when we lived together. He would go over the different articles in *ESPN* and *Maxim* and I would pretend to listen, although the stories in *Maxim* did sometimes get my attention.

After thirty minutes had gone by, I dozed off and awoke to him washing me up. He was finished with the front of my body and told me to stand up. Patting the bruise softly and soaping up my ass cheeks, Quentin rinsed off the soap and held out a towel for me.

Later, when I was lotioned down and sprawled across his bed in my black lace bikini shorts and bra, I asked him about the wedding. "Who's gettin' married tomorrow?"

"My boy from Philly," he said, pulling a black Armani suit from his closet.

"I know 'em?"

"Yeah, you dropped off some shit to him a couple of times," he said.

"Who? Charles?"

"Yeah. He asked me if I was bringin' you, but I didn't know if you was comin' through this weekend. So what we wearin' tomorrow?" he asked and looked at me like he was ready to fuck.

"Ain't that what you pickin' out now?"

"Nah, I need somethin' to wear tonight to his bachelor's party."

"Where is it?"

"Miami," he said nonchalantly while putting on his pants.

"Quentin, it's 10:30 now. What time you supposed to be there?"

"I was supposed to leave at eight, but I saw that you was here, so I'm catchin' the next flight at 11:20. You takin' me?"

"Where, to BWI?"

"No, the moon," he said, laughing.

"You a real funny nigga."

I threw on some jeans and a T-shirt and we were out the door in fifteen minutes. Even though we weren't going anywhere, I got excited driving Quentin to BWI. The old rush of adrenaline returned to the pit of my stomach as I remembered our many trips through Delta airlines.

"Vita," he said before he got out the car, "when you lay out our clothes, they need to be coordinated. You know 'bout that right?" he joked me.

I knew he was being sarcastic because when I finally moved in with him he couldn't believe that my collection of clothes and shoes outdid his own. And his already took up three closets. He had to have the walk-ins extended to make room for my shoes alone. My obsession with having more clothes than I would ever wear only came from having gone without for most of my childhood. It got so ridiculous, that the only things I repeated were coats and the hottest shoes.

"Yeah, nigga whateva. Did you forget who you talking to? Be safe aight."

"I will. See you at gate C at 2:35 tomorrow, right?"

"No, on the moon," I said and pulled off.

Before I went back to Quentin's I stopped at Walgreen's for a pregnancy test. We hadn't been together since December, but I had missed my period in February, which was a giveaway 'cause that shit never skipped me. It was the second week of March and still nothing.

I peed on the stick in his bathroom and went back to my car to retrieve two of the outfits I might wear to the wedding. Before stretching them out on the bed I brought them to my nose and inhaled the new smell. The feeling was almost as intoxicating as the look of the designer fabrics. One was a chocolate linen Versus dress and the other, a black Carolina Herrera black silk top with slit shoulders and exaggerated sleeves, and a black leather skirt. I thought about the brown Louis bag I couldn't wait to carry and chose the dress.

Looking in Quentin's closet the ringing of the phone startled me. I walked to his side of the bed and picked up the cordless, but still heard the ringing coming from his dresser. After I opened his top drawer I saw that I had missed the call and was about to call back when the name *Chanel* popped up.

"Hello," I said.

"Who is this?" she asked.

"Who the fuck did you call?"

"Not you. Is Quentin there?"

"No bitch, I am," I said ready to cuss her ass out.

"And who are you?" she asked.

"You got a pen and paper?" I didn't give her a chance to answer. "Well, remember that my name is Vita, the only bitch you'll ever hear him talk about."

I let her cuss, get loud and hung up on her. Looking at the names and numbers in his phone I saw hers more than twenty times in the last two days. *What the fuck did she want that was so important?* I cut the phone off, threw it back in the drawer and took off my clothes. Sliding under the fluffy goosed down comforter I turned on *Sex and the City* and fell asleep with the thought that those white bitches and their drama had nothing on me.

The bitch that had called made me forget all about the test, so when I got up at eleven the next morning to use the bathroom, I missed the toilet and peed on myself when I saw the plus sign. Instantly so many thoughts ran through my mind, the first being KC's reaction.

So many times I had tried to separate from her, but she was always back in the picture the next day or the next week. She had told me once that she hoped she never caught me in the actual act of fuckin' around 'cause she wasn't sure of what she would do. I laughed it off but in my heart I knew she wasn't lying.

Quentin's reaction was predictable, but I wasn't ready to deal with the same shit I had before. So, in the car after I had picked him up from the airport, and later when we went back to his house to get dressed, I kept quiet. I needed time to think about what I wanted to do.

By the time we were dressed we had missed the wedding and barely made it to the boat before it pulled away from the Harbor. It was obvious that Charles knew how to spend his money, or at least his new wife did from all the expensive shit I was seeing.

I forgot how much I missed home when I saw this nigga Mohammed. Him and his sister Marisa were the only mutherfuckers that I fucked with enough to call friends. A few weeks after I met Quentin in '97 I had hooked up with Mo.

It was about 2:30 in the A.M. and *Valentino's* was the only place open to get a bite. And after a long night of clapping my ass and giving lap dances, I didn't care how the food tasted. As soon as I walked in, I heard his loud laugh over everybody else's sitting at his table.

I asked for a booth and sat there and watched him and the other niggas sitting with him. It was about eight of them and they seemed like they were having the best time. I could tell that they had just left a club 'cause they were all dressed in mostly black and had on their Rolexes, iced out bracelets and necklaces.

What attracted me to Mo was that he was cute in a brotherly kind of way. He had a bald head, fat cheeks and sleepy eyes that made him look like his feelings could easily be hurt. But if somebody saw his big muscles they would think twice about even speaking to him. The other niggas looked like regular hustlers, and after I peeped them, I knew the detailed trucks in the parking lot belonged to them.

I was sitting there waiting for the waitress to come and take my order when he got up from his seat. I thought he was going to the bathroom, but he came over to my table.

"How you doin' this fine mornin'?" he asked.

"I'm straight," I said, already hearing in his voice how funny he could be.

"Why you here by yourself?"

"'Cause I just am."

"Ain't nothin' wrong wit' that. Me and my boys still waitin' for our food. You tryna chill wit' us?"

I thought about it for a second. I really missed being around people, but shit, what really was there to miss. I had never had anybody but me. "Nah, that's okay," I said.

"Come on Miss Enyce," he said, referring to the baby blue and gray Enyce sweatsuit with the matching Air Max I was wearing. "Don't make me tell everybody to pull up a seat near ya booth. It's about ten of us. Picture that."

I laughed and watched the waitress come around him with her pad. "Hi, I'm Patricia and I'll be your waitress. Are you ready to order?"

"Patty you can take her order at my table," he said and grabbed my hand to pull me from my seat. I laughed quietly at the quick name change.

I gave in and followed him to the table where all eyes were on me. I quickly wondered how many of them *knew* me.

"Listen up y'all," he said loud enough for anybody at the other tables in our area to hear. "This pretty lady... What's your name?" he whispered in my ear.

"Vita."

"Yeah, this pretty lady Vita is joining us so make room."

All I heard was chairs scooting across the floor and *w'sup's* as I sat at a corner of the table near Mo.

"Well Vita, I'm Mo, that's Chucky, Frank, Eric, Mickey, Kalif, Rich, Bums and Rock," he said, going around the table.

I felt like I had interrupted something 'cause as soon as I sat down everybody got tightlipped like they had to watch what they said around me. I was glad when the new waitress came to take my order.

"Anything to drink?" she asked.

"Southern Comfort and Grey Goose on the rocks."

Chucky was the first to speak. "Yo Vita, don't tell me you drink that shit too!"

"Yeah," I said like who the fuck was he to question what I liked.

"That nigga next to you drinks the same shit," he said, referring to Mo. "Let me ask you this. What the fuck does it taste like?"

Not a minute later, the waitress set my drink in front of me. "Taste it," I said and slid it to him and watched him take a sip. He let it roll over his tongue and tasted it again.

"This shit is aight. I always thought that Southern Comfort shit was for the oldie fogies."

I think all of them niggas was surprised when I drank after Chucky, but it wasn't a big thing to me. I felt like we all would die from something one day. After that, the regular conversation picked up again. Me sharing my drink must've been my initiation into their crew.

"Now, like I was sayin' before y'all little taste test," Frank said, "how the fuck was she a virgin before I got wit' her, and her pussy is wide as a mutherfuckin' manhole?"

Everybody was laughing at his joke and went around the table with similar stories about bitches and their lies. Mo leaned toward me and started a private conversation. "Vita, I don't know anybody who drinks this shit but me. I'm tellin' you, it's fate I saw you here tonight."

Just as I was about to respond, a girl walked in with the same eyes and fat cheeks as Mo, and a spiked haircut that framed her round face nicely. It was obvious that they were brother and sister although she was lighter. She had on *black* like the rest of them and I wondered what the deal was and *why all black*.

I felt a little out of place since I had changed into my comfortable clothes, but after dancing all night in nearly nothing it felt good to have something covering my body. She had on the same Gianfranco leather hookup I had in my own closet. I guessed then that I was sitting around big money.

"Vita, this is my twin sister Marisa," Mo said.

She looked at me and gave me a phony smile, but I didn't say anything or bother to return the gesture. The bitch wasn't doing me any favors. I pretended like she wasn't there and started talking to Rock since Mo was asking her something about a safe. I strained to hear their conversation and Rock's question at the same time.

"Vita, you a female right? So let me ask you a question. I met this girl the other week named Shannon. Yo, she's everything I want in a girl—a little shorter than me, thick as a mutherfucker, hazel eyes and a nice little haircut, and she real intelligent. But yo, every time I wanna hook up wit' her it's a problem. She invited me to her house a couple of times but it was in the day so I don't know what to think. W'sup wit' her Vita? She gay, gotta man, what?"

Instantly I knew the Shannon he was talking about. And he was right. She was smart, went to college and all of the other things he'd said, but it wasn't what he thought. She did a few parties with me and never stuck around long enough to get involved in the shit we did after the real party had ended. I was surprised he hadn't seen her face or mine before. They sounded like they were from B-more, but they couldn't be, 'cause the city was too small for them not to know.

Before I could answer him, Marisa interrupted me. "Rock, I told ya ass before that she was a fuckin' stripper so leave it alone."

If I knew them better I would've spoken up and defended Shannon *and* myself, but I knew it might start a bunch of shit between me and Marisa. Bitches like her were quick to judge shit they knew nothing about.

"Like I was sayin' *Vita*," Rock said, facing me again, "you think she is what I said or a stripper like Marissa keeps tellin' me?"

"So what if she is?" I asked loud enough for Marisa to hear me. "Does that change ya opinion of her?"

He thought about it for a while. "Yeah."

"Why?"

"'Cause I'm jealous and I wouldn't want to think about her doin' all that shit wit' a bunch of other niggas."

"Rock, where y'all from?"

"Here, but we live close to DC, why?"

"Well if I tell you somethin', it's between you and me."

"No doubt," he said.

"I know Shannon," I said, lowering my voice. "And, yeah, she dances, but it's not what you think. A lot of the girls I know do certain shit that goes beyond shakin' ass *but all of it* is for a reason. That's how we make our money. You got your hustle to survive, right?"

"Yeah," he said.

"Well that's what we do, and none of it is personal. How would you feel if she treated you a certain way based strictly on what you do?"

"Aight, I see what you sayin'."

Mo wrapped up his conversation with his sister and turned to me when the food arrived. "Vita, I heard what you said. Ignore my sister. Sometimes she don't think about the shit she sayin', you know?"

I didn't answer him 'cause I didn't give a fuck if that was his sister or not. She was like any other mutherfucker who needed to do their research before saying some dumb shit.

My corned beef hash and Marisa's steak and eggs was the last thing to come out, but they waited for us to eat and ordered more drinks. It was almost 4:00 when we left Valentino's. Mo pulled me to the side and asked if he could get my number since he wanted to invite me on a trip they were taking to the Aspens in December. I didn't mind going as long as his nasty sister wasn't tagging along.

I was almost seated in my car when he came running behind me. "Vita, can you do me a favor real quick?"

"What?" I asked, wondering where the urgency in his voice came from so suddenly.

"Somethin' just came up and we all need to split up. Can my sister ride wit' you and show you where to go?"

"To do what? I don't even know her."

"It's not what you think. Look I got you. I'm gon' take care of you."

"If it's not what I think, why do you need to take care of me?"

"'Cause this is somethin' I been waitin' on and it would mean a lot to me." I knew this mutherfucker wasn't trying to use me by inviting me to his table and talking all that shit about the Aspens. "Don't look like that Vita. I just found out when I got the page a few seconds ago."

"Well, tell me first or I'm bouncin'."

He reached inside of a black shoulder bag I hadn't noticed before and felt around. "Hold out ya wrist," he said.

I looked down at the diamonds and knew it was platinum. The first time I saw and felt the metal was on Violet. She had owned a pair of platinum hoop earrings and matching necklace and was rockin' it way before I had heard it on any of the rap songs or saw it in the videos.

"*Oh*, so you just give me your girlfriend's shit?"

"Nah, that never belonged to nobody. It's yours. *Now*, will you do it?"

"Mo, I need to know what I'm gettin' into."

"Bet. Marisa will tell you on the way there."

I sat in my car and waited impatiently for her to tell me what I thought I already knew. I needed to hear something to ease my fidgety nerves so I skipped to Biggie's *Life After Death*. Hip-Hop was the only music I listened to and old school R&B when the mood hit me. 'I Love The Dough' was ending and the 'What's Beef' intro was playing when Marisa tapped on the window. I was going to show her real beef if she got in the car with the same dumb shit she had pulled in *Valentino's*. When she got in, I knew she was trying to figure out how I could afford the Jag.

"Let them pull off first," she said.

Mo and his friends were in two black trucks, a Suburban and a Cherokee. I cut the heat down and listened to her directions. We were headed to DC before she spoke up. "This will only take a minute."

"What?" I asked still disgusted with her know-it-all attitude.

"I don't know what Mo told you, but all we do is rob mutherfuckers."

I quickly reached for my gun that I kept in my door. I was about to point it at her when she grabbed my wrist.

"Chill Vita, we don't rob people. Well, actually we do, but not everyday niggas like you. Big shit like jewelry stores, banks…"

"So where the fuck are we goin'?" I asked, wiping the sweat off my top lip.

"To this jewelry store outside of Laurel," she said, stretching out her legs. "Vita, I didn't mean that shit I said at the table. I didn't know. And Mo's my brother but so are all them other niggas. I just be lookin' out for 'em, you know?"

"I can understand that, but until you really speak about some shit you need to think twice 'cause it ain't no different from what you 'bout to do. And why the fuck ya brother need me to drive you?"

"'Cause the pigs won't hesitate to pull them over. With us they see two pretty bitches and look the other way, and I always hold the jewelry and shit. We never got caught with the money but jewelry is a dead giveaway. They find that shit on them and they straight goin' to jail."

Marisa told me they had just come from robbing a check-cashing place, which explained the black. The way things worked was that Mo or one of the other niggas would get with the assistant managers or head associates of the different places and learn the procedures, codes to alarms and safes, whatever they needed to get into the building and get 'em for everything.

Nine times out of ten, they were working with females who figured they had nothing to lose, plus I knew most bitches' panties dropped without hesitation when they saw niggas who looked like they had some kind of money. And, they would be stupid to turn down the quick five thousand they were getting that usually took them six or seven months to make on their barely above minimum wage jobs.

Marisa had gone to school for alarm systems and learned the different wiring, enough to disarm most alarms. She said the systems for the bigger banks were more complicated, but she was working on it. The kicker was this—she owned the alarm company linked to a lot of the places they hit up.

We were coming to the exit and she was slipping on some black Isotoners and black bug-eyed glasses. Pulling up to the back of a big jewelry store, I hadn't quite stopped before she jumped out the car. The preppy-looking black guy, who I assumed worked there had left the back door open for her and was pulling away in his broke down Camry.

Marisa said they had exactly nine minutes and thirty-six seconds before the police would circle the parking lot and the building. Not even two minutes after she was in, she was back in the car. "The mutherfucker that owns this ain't no joke wit' the surveillance. I almost missed the second box that controlled the cameras around the building," she said out of breath. She was pulling the tape out of the three videocassettes and breaking them in half. "Pull out and go to the side of that Amoco at the light."

Mo finally flashed us from the Suburban. My Jag followed them to a secluded park, and Marisa went over to his window. He passed her a bag larger than the one I had seen earlier. The three cars split up. Thirty minutes later me and Marisa were sitting outside of this gated community. Mo and the rest of them pulled up to the circular driveway at the same time.

I knew then how they could afford to live the way they did. Outside was a fountain and two big black doors that led to a spiral staircase. Before Marisa got out she told me Mo would call me the next day. That meant I wasn't invited into their house yet.

Me and Mo finally hooked up on a one on one and he took care of me. We went to Vegas and after spending $10,000 I stopped counting. Later in the hotel room this mutherfucker ate pussy like it was his daytime job. I couldn't let him get my mind, so I had to show him my skills. I started to go down on him but he stopped me.

"Vita, I need to be honest wit' you," he said.

"About what?"

"Why, you know... You lookin' for me to try to fuck but I won't."

"Why not?" I asked scared to hear some crazy shit.

"'Cause my dick ain't right. It ain't been right since I got shot."

"So what, it can't get up?" I asked, curious to see what a non-working dick looked like.

"Nah, I don't have no feelin' around my waist area."

My feelings don't get soft easily, but I felt for him that moment and even tried to work with him. We went out three other times and tried to get it up but had no luck. He never called me again. I figured he was embarrassed and left it alone. Me and Marisa hung out for a minute and over time I found myself trusting her, but she fell off too.

Standing there with Quentin at the wedding reception, I watched Mo come towards me and wondered if he had taken care of his problem. I waited for him to speak first.

"W'sup my nigga," he said. I thought he was talking to me but he reached out and hugged Quentin. "Hey Vita," he said and gave me a small hug.

I caught a glimpse at Quentin's face and if he was questioning me and Mo, I didn't see it. "Yo, where you at?" Mo asked him.

"I think Charles told me table twelve."

"Yeah, we up in that piece too," Mo said.

I saw Marisa, Bums and Rock already there at the table. I sat next to Marisa but I didn't have too much to say. She was on some ol' bitch shit when she stood me up the weekend we were supposed to go to Cancun for this huge party.

"W'sup Vita," she said. "Long time, huh?"

"*Please*. Don't even front like I'm the one to blame for that shit. Ya ass is the one who forgot how to meet a bitch at her house like we talked about. If you didn't wanna go, you should've used ya phone. You still got two of 'em right?"

"Vita, obviously some shit happened that was outta my control. How 'bout we do South Beach Memorial weekend, my treat?"

"Whateva, it's been like four years and you wanna hang out. Yeah, okay."

"Look, that Wednesday we hit up the big bank down on Paca St. We only had time to hit up one safe and be out. But we walked with nine hundred G's. Just think about what we could've got with more time."

"So, why you ain't call me or drop by?" I asked.

"'Cause we had to leave this mafaucka. I took care of the main alarm and some of the cameras, but the shit was difficult. We used masks for the first time and it was a good thing 'cause they had part of their surveillance hooked up to one of the breakers in the backroom."

"So could they see y'all was black?"

"Nah, everything was covered up. Our hands, necks, the only way they might've known is if they saw Chucky's ass walkin' like he was a pimp. How the fuck we gon' rob somethin' and his ass is boppin' and shit."

I laughed 'cause there was no way he could've been mistaken for a white boy. I was also relieved that Mo hadn't stopped calling me because I had done something wrong. My ego was like a nigga's when it came to my sexual performance. Marisa told me they had all left and drove to Mexico. I thought back to that time and remembered catching the story on the news.

The investigators said they were reviewing the tapes but had no leads at the time. They showed parts of the tape but it didn't click for me that it might've been them. The reporter never said anything about a female involved and there were only five of them on the tape. I guessed the rest of the clique was waiting in the car or taking care of other shit around the building. I was about to ask her if she was finished with the robbing business when I heard the voice come through the loud speakers.

"Good evening, and thank you for joining us as we celebrate the union of the new couple, Mr. and Mrs. Somerset," the voice said, leading everyone into a clapping frenzy.

I figured she was the planner and the bride's best friend 'cause she was just too much into it to be a casual acquaintance. Her and another girl two seats away from the bride had on the same dress. They were all a bunch of pretty, prissy bitches in my eyes, but the one on the mic was definitely model material.

Her high yellow ass couldn't fuck wit' me, but she came close. The bride reminded me of one of those goody-two shoe bitches who said shit like, "we can't fuck, but I'll suck ya dick." I could see her green eyes and fake-ass titties from where I was sitting and she looked like she had never had to want for anything a day in her life.

Bitches like that killed me because they were usually the ones that snagged big hustler-type of niggas like Charles. They didn't know shit about being down for a nigga when worst came to worst, and as long as the money was right, they were right.

The other girl had this chocolate complexion and reminded me of Foxy Brown only she was a little taller, real thick and her eyes were more slanted. I figured her to be one of those dark-skinned bitches who had to hear dumb shit like, "You real pretty to be a dark girl," all her life. Like pretty bitches don't come in all shades, but anyway, I could spot undercover dick-suckers a mile away. They weren't foolin' anybody but themselves.

I remembered why I liked Marisa when she said the shit I was thinking. "Look at those bitches frontin' like they owners of Fortune 500 companies and shit," she said, imitating the way they sat at the head table.

"What, you thinkin' like me now?" I asked.

"Nah girl, I know them. I went to Western wit' 'em until the tenth grade when they put me out."

"For what?" I asked.

"Sellin' weed."

I knew all about Western and their reputation for having some of the snobbiest bitches in the world and so her comment made me laugh real loud. "Marisa how the fuck you gon' be sellin' weed up that bitch? You knew they wasn't goin' for that."

"True, they weren't goin' for it, but those white girls were buyin' the shit more than the black ones, and I know I was gettin' like five hundred a week from them mutherfuckers."

"They used to buy it from you too?" I asked, pointing to the three musketeers.

"No, girl. They was in the books a lil' something but they all hung together back then too. Now it look like they done a whole three sixty 'cause back then they didn't look like that. Well the girl Chanel did, but the other two was plain Janes."

I knew I didn't hear her say Chanel. The shit would just be too much of a fuckin' coincidence if that was the one I had to cuss out the night before. I wanted to ask Quentin if he knew her straight out, but I knew niggas too well to try that approach, so I just put it out there without even tryna be slick.

"Q," I said.

"Yeah, w'sup," he said, facing me.

"I know you didn't bring me here on some ol' big dick shit."

"Girl, what you talkin'?"

"You knew she was gon' be here?"

"Who?" he asked, and that quick I saw in his eyes that he knew just who the fuck I was talking about.

"*Chanel nigga*, don't play stupid."

"Vita, get off that shit. I wouldn't do no dirty shit like that. I ain't think she was gon' be here. I mean I knew she was cool wit' Charles' girl but I ain't on no sneaky shit. A nigga got a million more things to worry about than some freak-ass bitch sittin' up at my man's wedding."

In a nutshell that meant he was fuckin' her, but it bothered me that he had called her a freak-ass when clearly her name was programmed in his phone. He must've seen the question mark on my face 'cause he felt the need to keep talking. "Don't look like that. You was away. A nigga got needs. *You know that*, but none of that shit is serious. When you on the scene everything stops."

That was enough for me, I thought, as I felt him rub my thighs under the table. I was glad I had worn the dress, 'cause seconds later I saw him suck on his finger and then he started playing in my pussy. If this Chanel bitch thought he was serious about her, I hoped she got a look under the table 'cause as long as I was in the picture she was looking at some serious competition.

Our table was joking the older people on the floor who had the nerve to be doing the Electric Slide when I saw her coming towards us. "Quentin I need to talk to you," she said.

I couldn't believe the bitch was bold enough to come over to our table. "Don't you see me fuckin' sittin' here," I said, standing to my feet.

"Vita," Quentin said, "I got this."

"Oh, *you* got this?" she said loud enough for the two tables near us to turn around.

Marisa pulled me by my arm to sit me down, but I wanted to know what the fuckin' urgency was. She could've left the shit on his voicemail.

"Nah, Marisa, get off me," I said. "This bitch sees me sittin' here and *still* came over. What the fuck is it that's so important?"

"None of ya fuckin' business!" she screamed.

"Oh, it's not?" I said, swinging at her face. I had put so much energy into hitting her that I got angry when I felt Mo holding me.

"Chanel, this is not even the time for this shit," Quentin said.

"Then you need to make some fuckin' time. 'Cause I ain't goin' no fuckin' where," she said, folding her arms.

Mo had left me enough reach to lean over the table. I grabbed Marisa's glass of red wine and splashed the shit on *Chanel* and her pretty little dress.

"You bitch!" she screamed before she got a slight hold around my neck.

By then Rock and Bums were standing in between us and so was her girlfriend, the wedding planner. "Chanel, don't mess up Chelsea's day. You'll see her again. Fuck this trash and Quentin," she said.

"Fuck me? Bitch you can wear that red shit too," I said.

After they pulled that bitch away I sat down and ate my lobster tails like nothing had gone down. Quentin thought he was slick. He told me he went to talk to his boy Scooby, but I knew he wanted to talk shit over with her. *And to think that I was actually considering coming back to Baltimore.* I washed down my food with the Perrier and decided that I needed something stronger.

On my way to the bar on the bottom deck, I took a detour to the bathroom to check my face and hair. Instead of using the mirrors near the stalls I stood in the waiting area where I could use the floor-length mirrors and make sure my whole outfit was still intact. Everything was quiet except the flushing of a toilet and two familiar voices. "Chanel, why you lose ya cool like that? Couldn't it wait until you saw him?"

I knew that was the wedding planner talking from having to listen to her annoying voice for the last two hours.

"No, I been tryna talk to him for two weeks. It's always some excuse. You know how he is. *I'm here, I'm there, I'm hemmed up.* Well fuck, I'm hemmed up too. For about three months now."

"What? Don't tell me you're pregnant." She must've shook her head 'cause homegirls's voice got real loud. "Chanel, what the fuck! You fuckin' that nigga raw?"

"Yeah, a few times, but he was the only one, and Kola don't give me that shit 'cause I know you slipped a couple of times yourself."

"True, but didn't you know you were pregnant after the first month of missin' your period?"

"No 'cause I still get it. It's not that heavy but I still spot for two days instead of five."

"Well, are you keepin' it?"

I waited impatiently for her to answer, but all I heard was the sink running. She must've been trying to clean the wine from her dress.

I left the bathroom, looking down at my own stomach and realized I wasn't far behind her. At that moment I was actually considering keeping it and walked past the bar. I had everything that I always wanted, but a baby would make me complete.

My memories of my mother Sandy were fading. From age six to ten, I spent a lot of time by myself since she was always running the streets or giving cocaine parties. My mother was beautiful and had the same defined lips as me, but I was too young to understand why her skin was getting darker and her arms and legs thinner.

For awhile she kept her habit in check, but by the time I was eight she didn't even get up to iron my clothes or fix me the routine breakfast of toast and orange juice. She had to snort a few lines just to get charged up and be able to walk me to school, but soon that wasn't enough.

I was basically living in our apartment on my own. I didn't have money to wash clothes or buy food, but our neighbor Ms. Sylvia, a short petite woman with hair that grew in white instead of gray, always set a plate for me in the evening. She didn't watch a lot of TV, but she had two large bookshelves filled with fiction, non-fiction and dozens of finished crossword puzzles. She introduced me to Donald Goines and after I read *Black Girl Lost* I was hooked.

Teachers in school wanted us to read shit by Mark Twain. Fuck that, Donald Goines was more real to me then any of that bubblegum shit. It was my escape. I had stopped going to school since I got into fights almost everyday behind the condition of my clothes since there was no escaping Toya and Leatrice, the middle school bullies who were bigger than the average ten-year olds. They would see me in the halls and push me against the lockers or sit behind me in class and pull my hair.

One day I couldn't take it and slapped Toya in the face with my notebook. The teacher moved us, but her and Leatrice were waiting for me after school and they continued to tease me on the strength that I stank and needed to wash my clothes.

I couldn't explain to them that I had no way of getting new clothes or completely removing the smell from my old ones with plain water and no detergent. So I dealt with it, and sat in the Enoch Pratt Free Library with my head buried in a book on the days I didn't feel like taking their shit.

About three years ago when I was doing my thing with Quentin and the dough was rollin' in, I ran into Toya downtown. She was going inside of one of those knockoff stores and I was going into a boutique that required appointments only. I told the owner Toni I would be back in five minutes. That's all the time it took me to punch the shit out of her.

It was obvious she didn't know who I was. I pretended to look at the weak shit they had on the wall while she held up a pair of raggedy jeans and asked me if they could go with a tacky-ass T-shirt with rhinestones spelling out the word *sexy*. I couldn't believe she had the nerve to ask me that shit. Didn't she see that I was rockin' nothing but Versace?

"Bitch please," I replied and laughed.

"Bitch?" she said, moving her neck.

"You don't know who I am, do you?" I asked her, removing my shades.

"Nah, and I really don't give a fuck."

"You don't have to," I said and handled my business.

The Korean owner threatened to call the police after she saw how I knocked Toya into a stack of unopened boxes. I gave her the same nonchalant laugh, put on my shades and went down to the boutique and waited for Toni to buzz me in.

At the reception, a glance at a familiar face jarred me from my daydream. I looked twice and knew I hadn't seen KC. It would just be too crazy if her ass had found out about the wedding and wanted to check on me. My mind was moving way too fast as I thought about the shit that had went down earlier with Chanel. *Had she seen me with Quentin?* I didn't mind drama, but I wasn't ready to go through a bunch of bullshit with her, so I left without telling Quentin. He would probably think I was still trippin', but I was fine.

In the cab to his house my thoughts went back to my childhood and the day I found my mother in the back of our apartment building by a dumpster. She was half-naked and I thought she was sleeping. I shook her shoulder and called out to her. A long time had gone by before one of her dopefiend friends came over and told me what I didn't want to hear. I screamed until I felt Ms. Sylvia's arms holding me tight.

I clutched my own stomach and knew there was no way I was letting my child go through that. He or she would always have anything it wanted. I decided then that I was keeping it. I knew Quentin would be there regardless, but even if he wasn't completely, it didn't matter. I had never depended on a nigga to do shit for me. This baby was my only family and the one thing that would make me whole.

Chelsea

Charles and I spent our honeymoon in Europe, the first week in Paris and the second in Venice. Paris was a surprise, of course since I didn't think he remembered me telling him that I spoke French fluently throughout high school. I spoke Spanish the same, but favored the French culture for their legends of love and sensuality.

We stayed at the *Costes*, located near the headquarters of the most upscale shops. The suite we stayed in ran $5,500 a night and was decorated with jewel-toned colors, heavy swag curtains, and lavish accessories dating as far back as the late nineteenth century. Downstairs was four dining rooms with different decorative themes, and every morning before we headed out we received massages.

There was always something to do in Paris. However, the only major highlights in Venice were the bridges over the street waterways, and a wine factory where we crushed grapes into our own personal bottle not to be opened until our tenth anniversary. There was also a plethora of shops and boutiques with more leather bags and shoes than I would ever be able to wear in a year.

The first day in Paris we ate at one of the outside cafés I had dreamed of visiting in high school while a violinist serenaded us. I could tell it was bothering Charles after the second song because he started clinching his right jaw. When the young Frenchman shifted the violin on his shoulder for another selection, he grabbed the stick and said, "Aight, that's enough of that shit. Tell the waiter we ready."

The poor guy seemed to only know French and stood there like he was unsure of what to do next. I tipped him and politely told him in French that we were ready to order.

"His ass was gettin' carried away, huh?" Charles asked.

"Yeah, I guess," I said, feeling a little embarrassed. I surmised that the saying was true. *You could take 'em out the hood, but you couldn't take the hood out of them.*

"You look sad," he said, touching my hand. "What, you want me to call him back over here?"

"No, that's okay, I'm hungry anyway."

"So, tonight is the night. You nervous?"

"Nervous about what?" I asked.

"Your first time making love."

152

"A little," I said, pulling the straw floppy hat over my eyes to disguise any signs of dishonesty.

"Don't be scared. I'll be real gentle, but only if you talk that French shit I heard you saying to ol' boy. That better not have been some dirty shit you told him either."

"No, I save that for you," I said and leaned over to whisper some French gibberish in his ear until we were finished with the meal.

After we ate, we went to the Flower Market where I bought gems from the French Riviera and later went next door to look at rare birds from around the world. I was just enjoying his company and being able to walk down the street holding his hand. I couldn't imagine having such a good time with anyone else.

On the way to the hotel I kept replaying the night ahead and how I would act with him. I had come too far to suddenly become honest. At the reception I kept seeing Marco's eyes scan my face like I owed him something. And I'm still not sure what Nikola told him, but as soon as the boat pulled up to the deck, he was gone. I guessed that my secret was still safe.

In the room with Charles later that night I slipped into the bathroom, showered and put on a white bustier with matching lace panties and a missing crotch. I had told him I was a virgin but that didn't mean I had to look like one. I checked the mirror before I walked out, applied a little gloss to my lips and took a deep breath.

He was lighting candles around the room and closing the curtains when I opened the door. I stood there until he turned around and realized I was watching him.

"Damn, you look good," he said as I watched the erection grow in his boxers.

"Thank you," I said, actually beginning to feel nervous.

"Come over here. You act like we're strangers or something," he said, holding out his hand.

I walked over like I was in a trance and sat on the bed while he kneeled in front of me. He lifted my leg and ran his tongue over my foot and then the next. I threw my head back and felt him running his tongue up my legs and finally between my legs. The wetness ran down my thighs and I laid back and got ready for the highlight of the night—or the biggest hoax of my life.

Charles' face was close to mine and I got excited as I smelled my scent on his lips. "I been waitin' for this forever," he said before he entered me.

I clenched the walls of my vagina real tight like I had read in a magazine to bring him extra pleasure, and watched his face tense up like he was experiencing the best feeling in the world. I pretended like he was hurting me, and with every pump, dug my nails into his back. Not to mention the vinegar and water douche I had concocted.

"Too much for you?" he asked, never stopping.

"No," I whispered.

We did it every way possible. The sun was coming up and I was more than exhausted. It didn't help that my legs were all Jell-O and my back was aching. If

Charles was trying to mark what was his, he had done it, and if somebody tried to tell me I wasn't a virgin before, all they needed was my account of our endless lovemaking. We decided to stay in and sleep the day away.

There was an amusement park on the lawns of the Pelouse de Reuilly with high-flying Ferris wheels, carousels, jugglers and fire-eaters. At the top of one of the tallest Ferris wheels I almost choked on my strawberry daiquiri when he said, "Girl, you took the dick like a pro."

"Oh, yeah," I said and laughed nervously. I didn't know if that was a compliment or an accusation.

Leaving Europe I had enough clothes to carry me into the winter and it was only spring. Although I too was a little surprised at the way Charles was throwing around money like it was nothing more than recycled paper, it amazed me that some of the European storeowners over there expected us to be strictly browsing when we entered the different shops.

Two months after our trip and I was still unpacking the boxes of clothes, shoes, furniture and dishware we had to have shipped from stores like Valentino, Yves Saint Laurent and Bernhardt. I felt like a real life Martha Stewart as I redecorated the house with new furniture and freshly painted walls.

I'm home by myself most of the time, and a week ago I told Charles that I felt so lonely without him at home some nights. He came through the door the next day with a Yorkshire Terrier named Freeway and a Brussels griffon I called Chi Chi. They're so small and at eight weeks, run around like two small kids getting into everything.

The other night we had plans to go to a Luau that was a surprise birthday party for his friend in New York. I would be meeting Smalls' girlfriend Randi for the first time. Charles knew I missed Nikola and Chanel since I didn't see them like I used to. He thought that it would be better anyway if I got to know Randi because he spent most of his time with Smalls. I didn't care who he wanted me to meet, I was just happy to be going out with him.

I loved to watch him pick out my clothes and he had laid out a silk banana-colored dress and matching leather sandals with wooden cha cha heels. "Leave the panties in the drawer," he said when I reached into the pile of Victoria's Secret.

I stopped and stared at him in the mirror. He was giving me that sexual look that always let me know he wanted a public favor later. My hair had grown out a little from the last cut Nikola gave me and my alternate hairdresser in Philly had a reputation for being one of the best, but when I got out of the chair, I always felt like something was missing. Charles didn't care what it looked like since his hands were in it all the time. And I was sure that before the end of the night he'd be grabbing it while I hit him off in the driver's seat.

I watched him in the mirror as he got dressed in linen pants and a matching shirt when I grabbed a daffodil from the liliqué vase on our dresser. I pulled the hair behind my ear and stuck in the flower with a bobby pin.

Liquid Dreams

"Umm you look good buttercup," Charles said as he came behind me and grabbed my breasts.

That was his nickname for me after we left Paris. A vendor had spoken to me in French and got fresh by saying I was the buttercup lover in his dream. Charles had asked me what he said and I lied and told him he said he was lucky to have a wife as pretty as the buttercups growing in his mother's garden.

"You do too. We look good together," I said and smiled at my secret.

When we went out we always made sure we complemented each other with his and her perfume. That night we had on 360.° I sniffed and smiled at the thought of us fitting together the way we did.

The party was at a spot called *Lulu's*, and instead of the two-hour drive I thought it would take to get there, we arrived in half the time. He was doing between ninety and a buck twenty the whole way in the shiny, red Range Rover we had driven off the lot a week ago.

I enjoyed the city for the bright lights and the activity that carried into dawn but I hated everything else about it. Exiting the Lincoln Tunnel, I instantly felt like the rat race was on. New Yorkers disgusted me the way they rushed and almost crashed bumpers, only to get to the next red light. No one, not even the pedestrians seemed to be relaxed. We had almost reached 38th Street when a silver Continental screeched next to us, trying to block us from moving into the far left lane to make a turn.

"I know this mutherfucker sees me," Charles said loudly.

"Calm down baby, you know how crazy these people drive."

"Nah, they haven't seen crazy," he said and rolled down his window. "Man watch where the fuck you goin'."

"Fuck off you asshole," the foreigner said as he quickly gave him the finger.

Not only was he nasty, but he continued to try and block us, and was so close that I thought his mirror would scrape the side of the truck. "What the fuck," Charles said and reached into the backseat while he pushed on the horn. Now that we're married I see a different side to him—his street side.

He couldn't find what he was searching for and grabbed an empty Corona bottle from one of the cup holders. Before I could stop him he had the car in park and had thrown it inside of the other vehicle's window.

I was glad it hadn't broken, but the driver still had a huge knot near the side of his forehead and his head wrap had fallen off. "You fucking crazy nigger!" he screamed while holding his head.

"Nigga?" Charles said and opened his door. "I got ya nigga."

It scared me as he pulled the black gun from a case under his seat. I quickly said a prayer and watched the driver turn the corner. "Charles!" I yelled. *"Let's go."*

I couldn't believe how fast he had changed into another person. His jawbone had tightened and I could see that he was gritting his teeth. He got in the truck and I eased back into the seat. "What were you thinking?" I asked.

155

"What you mean what was I thinking? I was *thinking* I was gon' bust his ass, that's what."

I could still see him twitching his jaw out the corner of my eye, so I kept quiet and looked out the window for the rest of the ride. Waiting for valet at the restaurant he leaned over and said, "I'm sorry if I scared you buttercup, but this city is ruthless. You know how it is. Shit like that can't get you all scared. You Mrs. Somerset, remember?"

I gave him a weak smile and looked at all of the couples going inside. I knew most of the guys were probably in the same line of work as Charles, but I wondered how many of their girlfriends and wives saw their significant others casually pull out guns, ready to shoot at anyone who rubbed them the wrong way. After my hands stopped shaking I realized how much I was actually turned on. I grabbed Charles by the neck and gave him a kiss that told him I was okay.

Inside, *Lulu's* looked like an island I had visited when the girls and I all took a trip to Hawaii. There were real palm trees and birds of paradise lined against the walls. Someone was at the door placing the multi-colored flowers around our necks, but I insisted on a bracelet instead. I was so impressed by the created atmosphere that I broke off one of the pink hibiscus flowers dangling from the ceiling and replaced the daffodil in my hair.

"Oh yeah, that's real nice," Charles said, pulling me closer to him. "You would really look nice if you got some streaks that color."

*Streaks?* "You think?" I asked him, wondering where he'd gotten that idea.

Inside of the reserved ballroom, there were four large floats and a grass-covered platform I assumed was the dance floor, along with waterfalls and fountains to give it a realistic feel of being on water. Simulated rain fell from two huge humidifiers in the ceiling and I hoped it wouldn't frizz my hair.

"Who paid for all this?" I whispered to Charles.

"Me, Smalls and a couple of these other cats."

Although I was aware of Charles' *money is no object* theme to life I was becoming concerned with the amounts he was throwing around. Even if they had split the cost, I knew he had put up most of it. And the things I saw weren't cheap. I had counted at least twelve exotic parrots perched all over the place. Each float sat at least twenty-five people and there looked to be a bottle of Cristal between every two seats.

Charles introduced me to Pudgy and Eddie, two guys I remembered from the reception. We spotted Smalls and his girlfriend. As usual he gave me a hug, only it didn't feel like the brotherly kind I was used to. "Chelz, this is my girl Randi."

I looked at her and recognized her face as well. Her resemblance to Chanel was uncanny. Her eyes were slightly slanted, her cheekbones high, and her most salient feature was the mole above her top lip.

"Hello," I said to her.

"W'sup," she said.

"Hey Chelz, me and Smalls 'bout to holler at these other niggas. You and Ran can sit and chill, talk and shit. You know," Charles said.

"Yeah," I said and took a seat next to her.

I shifted in my seat a little since I wasn't used to being in another female's company besides Nikola and Chanel. Randi, I could tell, was used to it since she was carrying on three different conversations with girls who sat there waiting for their men to return to them. Not having someone to talk to was fine with me since I could care less about trying to find the right shoes to match a Fendi dress.

"So," Randi said, breaking me away from my thoughts about a website I had started on my computer, "how does it feel to be with Charles?"

"What do you mean?" I asked, shrugging my shoulders.

"You know what I mean," she said in her baby voice. "Being wit' a nigga that runs shit, got it like that."

"For real!" the one girl said, sitting across from us with the crown and diamonds in the center of her side tooth.

"I guess it's cool," I said, not wanting to sound like a square.

"*Cool*? That shit has got to be lovely! I mean Smalls got it like that a lil' somethin', but... Huh, he still got a lotta work to do wit' these lil' niggas comin' up. They be tryin' 'em, you know?"

I hoped she wasn't waiting for an answer because I knew nothing about that. "Yeah," I said anyway.

"I told him he need to be makin' examples when they do that shit, but *nah*."

I didn't know who Charles thought I was to be hanging out with Randi or her set of friends who were sitting there openly passing weed. She offered me a puff, but I declined. It wasn't like I had never done it, I just thought it was something to be done in one's home or on a street corner.

"So, Charles is just cool, huh?" the gold-toothed bandit asked me. "Well, what about in the bedroom? Is it true that he can lay it down and make you feel like you need crutches?"

She turned and looked at the third girl who seemed to have a little more class than they did and laughed. I sat there feeling awkward and thought about what I should say next. *Where was Chanel when I needed her?* At the thought of her I looked towards the entrance of the room and saw Quentin. But what surprised me more than anything else was a pregnant Vita following close behind him.

She was prettier than I had remembered at the reception and Quentin was introducing her and holding her stomach like he was the proudest father in the world. There was no way Chanel could know about this since I had just talked to her a week ago and listened to her tell me how Quentin had helped her paint the other bedroom at her house and pick out a crib for *her* baby. I gave those ghetto mamas at the table the nastiest stare I could and got up to make a call.

I was in such a hurry that I almost walked past Charles. He moved his drink to the other hand so he could grab me by the waist. "You leavin' me buttercup?" he asked playfully.

"Umm, no. Just going to the bathroom," I said anxious to use the phone.

"So how you like Randi? A little too street for you, huh?"

I tried to find the right words since Smalls wasn't too far behind him. "No not really," I lied.

"Come on, I know you, girl. She's not that bad. Just a little different from what you used to. You know?"

"Yeah. Baby listen, I gotta use the bathroom real bad," I said, breaking away from him.

"Can I come?" he asked seductively.

"Maybe later," I said and kissed him.

I found a spot near the kitchen where nobody from the party was visible and pulled my phone from the tan Bottega Veneta leather bag. I didn't get an answer at her house so I called Chanel's cell.

"Chanel," I said, glad that I had finally gotten through.

"Yeah, w'sup?" she said out of breath.

"Nothing. Where are you?"

"Just comin' from Gymboree wit' Kola why?"

I suddenly felt so left out and wished I were back in Baltimore with them going to a surprise party or sitting with them in Chanel's living room looking at the baby clothes.

"Oh, you know what you're having already?" I asked with unintentional disinterest in my voice. I was slightly homesick.

"Yeah, a girl. I sent you the sonogram yesterday."

"Yes!" I said, excited that I would have a girl to dress up in pink.

"What you mean *yes*? We don't need another grown-ass girl to give us hell."

"Whatever," I said, hearing in her voice that she was actually disappointed with the gender. "How are things with Quentin?" I asked, suddenly not wanting to tell her what I had seen.

"As cool as things could be when dealing wit' him. So when you comin' through Mrs. Somerset?" she asked, quickly changing the subject.

"Next month. You think I forgot about your twentieth?"

"Nah, I know you didn't. So w'sup, you sounded like somethin' was wrong. Shit cool wit' you and ya shot caller?"

I laughed. "Yeah, things are cool, but I was thinking about you a few minutes ago when these two ghetto mamas started asking questions about my man. One of 'em even had the nerve to bring up his performance in the bedroom."

"No she didn't Chelz. Please tell me you told that bitch about herself."

"Well… Not really," I started to say.

"Chelsea, you really need to run yo shit. Bitches know you together and will try shit like that to see how far they can get wit' a nigga. Where are you?" she asked, as I heard her bite down on a pickle.

"New York," I said, still trying to beat around the bush.

"Oh yeah? Q told me he was goin' up there this weekend too."

"He *is* here." I regretted it as soon as the words slipped.

"Where is here?" she asked like she was scared to hear my answer.

"At this surprise party... With Vita."

I waited to hear her cut up, but all I got was a dial tone.

"Damn."

I stood there a moment and wondered how it must feel to love and give your all to someone only to have them step on your heart repeatedly. I had never experienced that with a man, but I had known the feeling when dealing with my father. Sometimes at night when I was alone, I would call my parents' house and listen to him say hello over and over again. Besides my marriage to Charles I didn't know where all of Daddy's ill feelings came from. I would be lying if I said it wouldn't mean the world for me to have him in my life again. He didn't have to like Charles but I at least wanted him to respect my relationship.

"Whoa!" Smalls said, jarring me from my thoughts.

I looked at his face and his build, and although he and Charles weren't related, they looked like brothers. Maybe it was true that two people began to look alike if they spent enough time together—third grade in their case.

"Hey Smalls," I said, returning the wide smile. "The party start yet?"

"Yeah, a few minutes ago. That nigga Malik ain't have a clue what was up. You remember him don't you?"

Charles knew so many people that I had a hard time keeping up with them, but I did remember names, and *Malik* didn't ring any bells.

"No, I don't think I do. He grew up with you two?" I asked.

"Yeah, you could say that. He did a bid wit' Charles and when these niggas had a hit on 'em at the Pen, he took care of it."

"Really," I said, wanting to know more of the story.

I was fixing my mouth to ask him another question when a tall girl, who's complexion was close to mine, came behind him and wrapped her arms around his chest. She was slender like a model, with curves on every part of her body and hair that was as bright as a crimson sunset. Her hot pants showed off her tattoos of snakes, Chinese markings and other detailed illustrations. A lavender, floor-length jacket barely covered her breasts that sat out and were adorned with the same claw prints as the ones on her thighs.

"W'sup big bro?" she said to Smalls.

"Nothin' much. Just chattin' wit' Charles' wife. I don't think you met her before, did you?"

"Nah," she said and let her eyes fall over every inch of my body. "You seen 'em?" she asked and focused her attention back to Smalls.

"Yeah, I think he went outside for a sec."

"Aight, bet. I'll catch you later," she said and walked away, never giving me a second glance.

*Didn't she know who I was? I was Charles' wife, not his girlfriend or a quick fling.* I hadn't thought like that all night because it wasn't necessary when I had been receiving the envious stares since we had arrived. I was enjoying the looks from the other females and here was somebody who had treated me like I was beneath her.

"Who was that?" I asked him.

"Dana," he said like I should've known without further explanation.

"From…"

"Oh, you know, somebody that's always been cool like fam."

"She a model or something?"

"Nah," he smiled. "Back to what I was saying. Oh yeah," he said snapping his fingers. "So you sure you don't know him?"

"Who?" I asked, becoming irritated and bothered by the smirk on his face.

"Malik," he said, giving me a chance to respond. "Come on, think back to a time when you were in DC at the *Marriott.*"

My heart stopped. Me and the girls had all went to DC plenty of times and had always stayed at the Marriott, but he had said it with so much more meaning that I knew exactly what he was getting at.

Malik was a memory that I had long forgotten, or at least tried to. We had met one night in Georgetown when I had to stop at a computer store and pick up some software that was only available there. The store was known to be the computer central for some of the biggest hackers in the world.

Walking out of there with my six-hundred dollar program, I was about to go in a store and try on some shoes I had seen in *Vogue* when I noticed him setting the alarm on his Lexus truck and walking into *Brooks Brothers.* I crossed the street, forgetting about the Manola Blahniks and followed him inside.

It was the dead of winter and I wore a long, gray suede coat with mink sleeves and collar. The matching hat fell over my eyes and I was able to watch him without seeming suspicious. I walked over to the suits and ties, grabbed a black suit tailored to perfection and inched closer to him. He wasn't paying me any mind as I watched him meticulously match one shade of blue with another.

I looked at his face from the side and liked the way his sideburns connected to his beard and how his thick, textured hair stood on his head. It was wild, but nicely groomed and his nails were clean and manicured as I watched them reach for a pair of seventy-five dollar dress socks.

"Excuse me," I said. "I'm getting this for my brother and I was wondering if you could help me find the right shirt and tie to match this suit."

"Umm, yeah I could do that," he said, staring into my eyes. "Your brother is a big dude, huh?"

"Yeah, two hundred forty pounds big."

Malik found a shirt and tie and talked me into buying shoes for my *brother* as well. I could have easily given the stuff to Reggie or Mikey but I didn't know their exact measurements.

At the register I realized that I hadn't looked at the tags. The cashier told me the total and I would only be left with a twenty for gas money. I couldn't believe I was spending $3,000 on some clothes nobody would ever see just so I could find out who the stranger was. I never liked to return stuff, but I was bringing everything back as soon as I got away from him. Besides, he didn't act like he was interested anyway.

"Thanks again," I said to him after I took the two shopping bags off the counter.

I was pushing the heavy glass doors open as he called out to me. "Wait up, you never told me your name."

"Why do you want to know?" I asked, still upset that I had wasted my money.

"'Cause I wanna see you after this, that's why."

I closed the door and shivered from the gusty winds cutting at my face. He had paid for his things and I followed him in his car to the hotel. I had done enough of that to know where his mind was, but it didn't bother me.

Sometimes I had a habit of letting my emotions get involved. Nikola had always teased me about *catching feelings*, but at that time I was low on money, and after seeing Malik dole out $12,000 like it grew on trees, I knew I had made the right choice. I was going to "make shit liquid" anyway I could.

We went to the hotel's restaurant and ordered two pitchers of blue margaritas, an entrée of quesadillas, potato skins and chicken fajitas. "So, what's your name?" I asked him as I dipped a quesadilla in sour cream.

"Malik," he said, touching my knee.

"So, what do you want to happen tonight Malik?" I asked feeling bolder as the tequila began to settle, already knowing what he wanted from me.

"Whatever you'll let me do."

We finished the food and every drop of the liquor. All that was left were blue Curacao-coated ice cubes. That entire time our conversation had only consisted of tiny bits of dialogue that in no way stimulated me.

"So, what's next?" I asked after washing down the last quesadilla.

"Me and you," he said, slurring his words.

"How much you got?"

He looked at me like I had confused him with someone else and raised his eyebrow. "You want me to pay you for sex?"

"Well, what did you think? That I would sleep with someone I know nothing about for the fun of it? Ha!" I said and laughed real loud.

"Well you *are* fine," he said and dug in his pockets. "Is this enough?" he asked and placed a row of bills on the bar.

I picked them up and counted $1,200. He must've thought I was crazy or just plain drunk. "Not hardly," I said and shook my head.

"Well here, but this is it," he said and laid another thousand on the bar.

If he thought I was stupid he had found the right one. But what he gave me would have to do until I could get what I really wanted. I didn't want to mess up my plan by asking him for more money and have him leave me there empty-handed altogether. I *couldn't* mess it up. At the time I was eighteen and still lived at home. I needed my own space and wanted to upgrade the '95 Millennia I was driving.

Before we could get off the elevator his hands were all over me. He thought his money meant open shop. "Slow down. We have all night," I said, removing his hands from my breasts.

In the room, he wasted no time getting naked. I looked at his muscular body and wanted to shake my head at something so sculptured gone down the drain. He could really have the whole package if he wasn't so shallow and could actually hold an intelligible conversation.

"Come on, let me see what you got. For 2 G's I shouldn't have to tell you anything," he said.

Just then there was a knock at the door. The drinks had been sent up. I wanted him to get as drunk as possible.

"Won't you get settled while I go in the bathroom and fix myself up," I barely whispered.

While he went to the door with nothing on, I laid my coat across the chair where he had thrown his clothes and quickly grabbed his pants. He was so drunk that I knew he wouldn't miss them. In the bathroom I locked the door and sat on the toilet seat while I dug around in his pockets. I knew he wasn't fooling me with that dumb expression, like he had never had to pay for sex or like he wasn't used to it. It was written all over his face. I dug deeper into the right pocket and felt his car keys and a money clip. Instead of money there were about thirty different credit cards, apparently all with different owners.

My eyes got wide as I saw the Diner's Club and American Express accounts. I shuffled through and took three of them with female names for myself. *What did he need with them?* I figured he had given me all the cash he had on him but decided that I would check his truck after he was drunk and dead to the world.

I took off my clothes and looked at myself in the mirror. If I didn't know myself I would say I was somebody else. I quickly turned away since my own eyes were scaring me. "Okay Chelz, you can do this," I whispered like I had done numerous times before, and pulled out one of the ultra sensitive condoms from my bag. Nikola wasn't there for "the talk" but it was time to "make shit liquid."

Wearing the matching lilac camisole and panties, Malik looked at me like his eyes were adjusting to sudden brightness. "Oh yeah, that's what I'm talking about," he said.

From where I stood I knew he had been drinking again. His eyes were glassy and I didn't have to look him over to see his erection. After I was on my back and he had poked me for what seemed like the hundredth time, I heard him grunt loudly like whatever he was trying to do wouldn't happen.

"Turn over," he said. I hoped he didn't want anal sex since I had never done it, and sometimes had problems with bowel movements. "Oh yeah it's coming!" he screamed.

I thought that what I felt on my back was semen, but after sniffing the air, I realized it was piss. I wanted to throw up, but I lay on my stomach and hoped he was done. I heard him panting like he was out of breath, so I went to get up, but he pushed me back down. "No, I'm not finish girl," he said and continued to piss on my stomach and breasts. What did it for me was seeing him point his dick towards my face.

"Oh, no you won't," I said and moved out the way.

I wasn't quick enough. Before I could move, he had saturated my hair and I felt sprinkles on my face. "Oh *my God*," I said and looked at him in disgust.

He was obviously turned on by his primal act because he climbed over me, pulled back the sheets and was out like a breastfed baby. I sat on the bed for a minute until I smelled the stench from my hair, and rushed into the bathroom to shower.

"The nasty bastard," I said as I touched my wet hair.

Once I was dried off and had on my clothes again I got the credit cards from his pocket, not caring about the names on them. I thought about taking his clothes and throwing them in a trashcan, but instead grabbed his keys. I had almost made it to the door when he turned over. *Please don't get up.* I waited until I saw his eyes close again and gently pulled the door behind me.

In the parking lot I turned off his alarm and lifted the back door of the truck. All I saw was a toolbox and a box of CDs. I checked under the seats and was ready to call it a night when I looked at the backseat and spotted what looked like an opening in the cushion. I felt near the seatbelt and pulled on the chair. Underneath were shoeboxes and two black Jansport backpacks. I unzipped one and saw hundreds of packs of marijuana. Two guns were in the other. I was scared that my fingerprints were on the zippers and quickly closed them, but not before I had wiped them with a tissue I got from my coat pocket.

I hoped the shoeboxes had what I was searching for and opened one of the four. Jackpot! There were bundles of tens and twenties.

"I knew his nasty ass was lying," I said aloud.

I grabbed one of each and put it back the way I had found it. I thought about Nikola and knew she probably wouldn't have taken any prisoners and took a whole shoebox or two. I didn't know how drunk he was and didn't want to take any chances on him coming to look for me, so I locked up everything, put on his alarm and dropped the keys outside of the room before I headed home.

I don't know how I could've forgotten about Malik since we had all shopped for months after that with the credit cards. I was still staring straight ahead when Smalls tapped me on my shoulder. "You remember now, don't you?" he asked, still giving me that stupid grin.

"Yeah, and your point is *what*?"

"My point *is*, that I know about you. I knew that shit was too good to be true when Charles told me he found his perfect wife. Who you think you foolin'?"

Everything he was saying was too much for me. I thought I would never have to worry about my past catching up to me and Smalls was standing there telling me otherwise.

"*What*, you told him?" I asked, scared to hear what he might say next.

"Nah, it don't matter. Y'all married now. But I know one thing. You need to be makin' plans to be doin' the same ol' freaky shit for me if you want this to stay between us three."

"Oh, really?" I asked, not believing he was blackmailing me. "And if I don't?"

He didn't hesitate to give me some more bad news. "You gon' be right out on ya ass that's what. You think everything is all sweet now, huh? You got ya fancy house, ya eighty thousand dollar car in the garage, money to blow everyday. Ya ass'll be right on a Greyhound back to Baltimore wit' those two other hoes, scrappin' up dollars to make yourself *wish* you had it like this again."

He knew he was controlling the situation and that scared me. I thought I knew him as Charles' best friend who would never cross him, but he was standing there holding the deck and ready to decide my fate.

"So what do you want?" I asked on the verge of tears.

"I already told you. I'll be in touch with you and when I do, you better be ready to give me what I want," he said and walked back to the party.

I suddenly felt so cheap in my three thousand-dollar dress and five hundred-dollar shoes as I listened to the thunder rumble outside. I walked to the entrance of Lulu's ready to leave and go back to the room at my parents' house with the pink wallpaper when I saw Dana with her hands wrapped around my husband's waist leaned up against the truck. *Just family my ass.*

No wonder he had made the comment about me getting streaks. He was hugged up with Charli Baltimore's long lost sister. I couldn't stop the tears from falling as I watched him look at her the way he had done the first time we'd met. I gazed into the sky for comfort but all I got were some gray clouds whose raindrops, I was glad, were falling harder than my own.

# The Chase/ 12

## Chanel

About two hours have passed since I came from Quentin's house. Chelsea called me at 10:30 from a restaurant in New York and told me he was there with Vita. Even if they had flown there, I assumed it would take them a minute to get back home if the party wasn't ending until two or three in the morning. It angered me that my suspicions of them being together again was on point, but I put it aside and made plans to do what I had been wanting to do for days.

A week before, I was on my way home from the twenty-four hour *Giant's* after picking up some Edy's Caramel Crunch ice cream and two jars of Claussen pickles. I had stopped at the gas station on North Ave. Closing the cap on my gas tank, I looked up and saw Quentin's metallic Tahoe speeding past. It was almost two and I knew he was finishing his runs for the night and was probably going home. If I knew him, he had just drove down my street to see if I was home.

Nikola asked me why I was keeping the baby after the way he had treated me at Chelsea's wedding, but I couldn't explain to her that he had become my addiction. I craved him and the excitement that came along with his company.

Besides the spontaneous sex that had gone down at the pool table that first time, we had done wild shit in a lot of other public places. The most vivid was an alley in the back of a club in VA. He had thrown me on the hood of his car and gave it to me, oblivious to the people watching us behind their curtains. There was never a boring moment, and besides, he had made it up to me shortly following the incident with Vita.

That bitch was so lucky it was my girl's big day. I couldn't get the wine off my dress, and Dara, one of Chelsea's cousins got off the boat and walked over to the gallery to get me a nice pantsuit from *Ann Taylor*.

I changed and ran right into Mr. Marcial. I tried to walk past him but he grabbed my wrist. "Chanel, why you always gotta act so crazy?"

"*Me* act crazy? You the crazy mafucka. How the fuck you gon' bring ya girlfriend around and not expect me to go off?"

"First off, I didn't go to the wedding so I wasn't even thinkin' you would be here. A nigga got a lot of shit on his mind. Why you always addin' to the extra bullshit?"

"Addin' to it? You know what Q, fuck you. After today forget you even knew me. I don't give a fuck if I ever see ya ass again. You or ya girl."

I quickly turned around to hide the tears in my eyes and started walking away from him.

"C, wait."

I don't know why I slowed down. Maybe it was the way he talked to me. I always liked to hear him call me that way. He sounded so gentle and I saw this other side to him that he tried to shield from the world.

"Quentin, wait for what? I'm tired of these mind games and shit. I understand she was in the picture before me, but I can't have you stringin' me along anymore."

"So, that's what you had to tell me earlier?"

"Not hardly," I said, trying not to look at his sexy-ass lips and dark eyes.

"Well, what was it?" he asked with that impatient tone I was used to.

"This ain't even the place now," I said, hoping he would ask me again.

"What time can I see you then? You gon' straight home after this?"

"Forget it. You not comin' through tonight just to fuck and bounce. That shit is gettin' old."

"Girl, what time?" he asked like I didn't have to worry about him leaving.

"Like 11:30," I said and turned away so he couldn't see the smile on my face.

I went to the top deck and saw Vita leaving the boat upset, and that made me feel even better. I hoped she had seen me and Quentin together and got angry enough to forget about him completely.

Later, while I was naked to take a bath, I looked at myself in the floor-length mirror. My stomach had definitely lost its flatness and my nipples were harder than ever. I moved my face closer to the mirror, but I didn't notice any drastic changes except fatter cheeks. If I had calculated things correctly on my calendar, I was three months pregnant.

I was sitting in the tub and flipping through *W* magazine when I heard Quentin ring the bell. I did a quick dry, slapped some powder between my legs and slipped on the white, cotton lounge outfit I had laid out on my bed.

"Damn, how long did it take that nigga to jump from the window," he said as I opened the door.

"Hey to you too," I said, kissing his cheek.

He had changed clothes and had on a Shooters T-shirt with gray sweats. He always wore something simple when he knew he was spending the night with me. "You look nice," he said, squeezing my ass though the pants.

Quentin liked when I wore white. He said the contrast with my skin tone always made him want to tear me up. "Thanks. You hungry?"

"Yeah," he said, gazing at my pussy through the drawstring pants. "What you got?"

"What you want?" I asked, untying the string.

"You know what I want," he said and wrapped my arms around his neck.

Quentin lifted me off the ground and had me against the wall for at least twenty minutes. Satisfied, we laid in my queen-sized canopy bed and I let him eat my pussy until the sheets were wet.

"So, what's so important? What, you need somethin'?"

"No. Q, do I look different to you?"

"Different like what?"

"My body, me?"

"You felt a little heavy when I picked you up, why you think you need to go on a diet or something?"

"Oh, that's what you think?" I said, hitting him in the chest.

"Ow! No, you know I like you the way you are. Thick in all the right places."

"I'm pregnant," I blurted out.

"You pregnant? By me?"

"Who else, nigga?"

"Chanel don't play innocent. I know 'bout dem niggas."

"You've been the *only* one for the last four months," I said, not believing he had the nerve to question me.

"How long?" he asked.

"Three months."

"What you wanna do?" he asked, moving the sheet so he could look at my stomach.

"That's why I need to talk to you. We need to think about it before it's too late."

"Too late for what?" he asked, lifting his head from the pillow. "Fuck that Chanel, I know you ain't gettin' rid of it. You act like I'm not gon' take care of it."

I turned over and faced the window. I was glad he had said the things I wanted to hear, but Vita was still an issue and I wasn't bringing a child into a baby mama drama situation.

"What's wrong?" he asked.

"Quentin, everything you said is fine, but…"

"What, you still trippin' off that girlfriend shit? Look, she's gone. I guess back to NY to be with that girl. I'm not chasin' that anymore. You carryin' my seed. If you tryna make this work, then leave it alone."

I turned back towards him, laid my head on his chest, and went to sleep with thoughts of us as a family. In my dream he was in our backyard teaching Lil' Quentin how to shoot a basketball while I sat on the steps and taped them on our camcorder. My dream came to an end when I woke up in the middle of the night and he was gone. I grabbed the pillow and inhaled his scent, wishing that he had only gone to use the bathroom, but even that was only a dream.

After he found out about the baby he was at my house for two weeks straight and then shit changed. I noticed a shift in his visits and he was only there on Sunday evenings and Tuesday and Thursday afternoons.

Things were good after that, but only for a minute. I was still concerned about the living situation and asked him again about his place. *If we were making things work, why couldn't I at least see where he laid his head?* He told me for the hundredth time that it wasn't safe. Especially since I was pregnant he needed to be on point like never before. His excuse was that he had to get shit on lock since summer was around the corner. He claimed he had to get on his grind so could take care of home when the baby came in the fall.

Quentin had over a hundred corners in Maryland and Virginia and needed to make sure they had enough product to cut down on the competition. I knew business was first and that's what turned me on, but my hormones were up and down and that meant I was extra needy.

During that time I never had a problem getting through to his cell or his house. But suddenly I was getting his voicemail again like I was when all we had was sex. And that wasn't even the problem. I had tried to call his house and his shit had been changed to an unlisted number. Again I was left in the dark so when I saw him passing me at the Amoco I had jumped in my car and decided that I would follow him until I got some answers.

The lights on a Benz were already obvious so I cut off the fog lights and stayed two cars behind the Tahoe, glad the extra height on his truck would make the chase easier. I saw that he was getting on I-83 and I knew the light didn't take long before it would change back to red. The brown van was taking its time making the left turn. Quentin was almost exiting the ramp so I pressed down hard on the horn.

"Drive your fuckin' car!" I screamed to the gray-haired man, hoping he could read my lips when he looked into his mirror. He was still taking his time to move his raggedy piece of shit so I went around him almost hitting the side of another car.

"Asshole!" the redneck screamed out his window.

I was too focused on catching up to Quentin to respond. I saw his taillights and sped up, exceeding the fifty-mile per hour speed limit. At one point I thought I had lost him when a Cloverdale truck cut me off. I understood then where road rage came from.

We finally got off at one of the Towson exits and I waited to see where he was going next. We made a right turn at the first light and I followed him down four back streets. I had to stop three times to let a car get in front of me. I finally saw his brake lights and turned mine off, parking at the corner behind a huge tree.

I looked around at the neighborhood and would have never suspected that he lived in such a rural area. He got out his truck and I bit my lip as I looked at his fresh Iverson braids and tried to figure out when he had them done. He looked around and walked two doors away from his truck towards one of the biggest brick houses on the block. I watched him walk between two large bushes located on the pathway. *Why was he entering his house through the back door?*

To make sure it was his house I sat there a while longer. I looked on the floor and remembered my ice cream. Reaching over, I was glad I had a plastic spoon in the glove compartment I hadn't used from my trip to Wendy's earlier. By the time I had put a dent in the box, he was leaving out again and had on sweats. *Yeah, it was his house.* I saw his cell phone in his hand and flipped mine open to tell him how sexy he looked.

"Chanel, what are you doin'?" I asked myself out loud. "You sittin' right in front of this nigga's house 'bout to call him."

He walked over to a red Jag that I didn't know he owned. I couldn't believe how little I knew about my baby's father. Quentin pulled out a Disney Store bag from the trunk with what looked like a huge Winnie the Pooh sticking out. I smiled and thought about the theme we were doing for the baby's room. So I *was* on his mind when we weren't together. He must've been making a space for the baby at his house and was getting it ready for us.

Thinking he was in for the night, I pulled off and drove home, still vowing to check out me and Lil' Quentin's new place. Knowing he was making plans for us at his house suddenly made everything okay, like the one-nighters and having to wait on him to ring my phone.

Two days after I followed him, I found out the sex of the baby. Dr. Desai told me she saw no signs of a penis and I was disappointed. Gladly Quentin couldn't make it to the appointment. He had pumped me up the whole five months hoping for a boy and I was scared to tell him that Lil' Quentin was going to be called Quenette or some shit. Later on that night the bell scared me since I wasn't expecting company.

"Where's the picture of my lil' man?" he asked before I could open the door for him.

"I didn't even know you were stoppin' through tonight," I said, mad that I hadn't had a chance to make up a story.

"Yeah, since I couldn't make it to the hospital earlier. So, where is it?"

"What?" I asked, knowing exactly what he was talking about.

"The picture."

"Oh, let me get yours off my dresser."

I went into my room and looked at the sonogram, still not believing the tiny being was growing inside of me. I had gone to Monroe St. earlier for a half-bushel of crabs. I felt her kicking more than she had ever done. I guessed the Old Bay was too much for her, but finished off every one anyway.

The phone rang in the living room and I heard Quentin press the talk button. "No nigga, I'm here," he said and hung up.

I quickly came back into the room to find out who had called. "Who was that?"

"One of ya lil' niggas."

"Q, don't answer my shit if you can't take a fuckin' message or bring me the phone."

"Whateva. Where's the flic?"

"Here," I said, handing him the one with her back to the camera.

"Where's his dick?"

"The doctor said he wouldn't turn over so she couldn't be sure. I laid on the table for forty-five minutes while she pushed down on my stomach to get his ass to turn over," I lied.

"He probably just wanted some quiet time like his daddy," he said and laughed. "Aight C, I'ma catch you later. I still got some shit to take care of tonight."

"Oh, so that's it? You just came here to see the sonogram and not me?"

"Don't start. You know I'll be over here tomorrow."

"Yeah, sure you will. Oh, and another thing. Why can't I get through at ya house?"

"'Cause I'm never there. Plus, these bitches keep callin' and hangin' up. Shit, my cell still works."

"When you choose to answer that shit," I said, becoming turned on by our little beef.

"I swear," he said, shaking his head, "you always know how to bring the drama."

"So get the fuck out then," I said, hoping he would go off on me and fuck me real wild like he did whenever I provoked him.

"Yo, you need to grow up," he said and closed the door behind him.

I let my back slide down the door surprised at the tears in my eyes. I didn't understand why I was crying, but shit, that was becoming normal. I had cried the other day after seeing a homeless man dig through a trashcan. While I wiped my face I started thinking that he was still with Vita.

So Chelsea calling me the next day only confirmed what I already knew. I was glad Nikola had just left. We had gone baby shopping earlier. She would try and talk me out of whatever I was going to do. She had already told me how stupid I was to be having the baby. I wasn't for another speech.

I got in my car and drove back to the house I had followed him to. I looked around to make sure no one was home and called a locksmith to come out to the address I was peering up at. He said he couldn't be there for another hour. When I promised him double the fee he would charge me, the van was there in twenty minutes.

"This *is* your house?" the dark man with the potbelly and gray beard asked as he pulled out his tools.

"Why wouldn't it be," I said, holding my own large belly. "I left my keys beside my bed."

"I guess so," he said and looked at me like he still had doubts. "A pregnant woman as pretty as you wouldn't lie."

"Exactly."

"So, when's the big day?" he asked while staring at my stomach.

"The middle of September," I said, covering my nose. He smelled like he had been smoking a Black & Mild and the sweet smell was making me nauseous.

"When my wife was carrying our twins she had cravings for all kinds of crazy mess. Shoot, one time she told me she wanted some chalk. Ain't that somethin'?"

It was pitch black outside and I was not feelin' this man's conversation about chalk. All I wanted him to do was open the door, take his $500 and forget that he'd seen me.

"There, it's open. Goodness, you got enough bolts on this door. You live alone or something?"

"Yeah," I said, glad I didn't hear any alarm going off. "My husband is in the Navy."

"A lot of time at sea, huh?"

"Yup."

"Okay, it's gonna be $760," he said and handed me a receipt.

"Why not five?"

"Because there were two extra locks to jimmy."

I reached into my bag and handed him the eight notes I had tucked at the bottom. "Keep the change," I said, anxious to get in the house.

"Thanks, and good luck with your bundle of joy."

"Yeah, okay," I mumbled and pushed open the black door.

I felt against the walls for a light and the first thing I saw was a black and white picture of a woman who had the same eyes as Quentin did. She looked like she was from the Philippines and had dark hair that was pulled back into one long French braid. I never saw Quentin smile, but I figured that he might've looked just like her when he did. I had asked him about his family and he mentioned his mother only once, like she had been the only one he was close to.

Instead of going into his living room first, I went into the sandstone kitchen and opened his refrigerator. It was filled with fruit and water and I knew that's how he kept his smooth complexion. I expected there to be cases of Corona but the only signs of liquor was a bottle of Grey Goose and Southern Comfort on his counter. His freezer was stocked with enough meat to feed ten African villages, and I wondered if he cooked for himself most of the time. The granite-topped island in the center of the kitchen near the wrought iron table was full of cookies, pickles and peanut butter. It looked like he was having the same cravings as me. I grabbed three cookies from the bag and walked into the living room.

I smiled at the signed Michael Jordan picture. I had bought it at an auction with Chelsea when she went looking for a Tiffany lamp. It set me back about three G's, but I knew Mike was his favorite and seeing him happy made me happy. Sitting on the deep-cushioned couch, I imagined him in front of the TV during basketball and football season.

I got up and felt along the walls in the hallway, looking for his room. I came to the bathroom first. It was almost the size of my kitchen. There was a Jacuzzi Whirlpool bath and walk-in shower with a glass door. I didn't go all the way in. A bunch of female products lined the sink. Quentin had enough hair to use some of the shampoos, but I knew he wasn't into Aveda's facial shit. I was suddenly tired of my tour and ready to find out the real deal.

His master bedroom was around the corner and I expected to smell his cologne as I entered, but the familiar fragrance of Chanel No° 5 greeted me. I searched the room for a light like my life depended on it and found a lamp beside the bed. Before I went snooping I picked up the phone off the night table and called my house. Just like I thought, the shit was on and working.

He had two large closets and I opened the one closest to the door first. There were all of the different shades I had seen on him, mostly dark colors and it was organized and separated into everything from stacks of Azzuré jeans to Armani suits. I pulled some of his shirts to my nose and inhaled them like I was testing a new scent. I didn't see any shoes so I assumed the second closet was filled to the ceiling with Timbs and Nikes.

I opened it and had to take a step back. The rows and rows of Donna Karan, D&G and Prada were making me sick to my stomach. It was more ridiculous than my own collection, with tags hanging off of every visible sleeve or skirt.

"That mafucka," I said scared of what I would do next.

Remembering what I had seen on Vita before, I knew the shit could only belong to her. I sat on the edge of the bed and looked around the room. So, that's why we couldn't make shit work. 'Cause she was back. I stared at the expensive-ass comforters and sheets on the bed and let the tears fall as I imagined him doing everything for her that he could only do for me on that one night he spent with me during the week.

I became angry as I watched my tears stain the army green linen dress. My eyes were burning. But I finally got myself together. The thing that I feared most had been realized. I held my stomach as I contemplated a baby with his face and his tendencies. I knew then that I couldn't keep it. I didn't want it anymore and the same thing went for him. *How could I have let myself become so stupid?* I got up and almost ran into the kitchen. There was a huge butcher knife that would do the job lovely.

I started with the living room and slit every cushion on his expensive chairs. I looked at the stuffing and got some satisfaction but it wasn't enough so I went straight to the bedroom and slashed every suit and shirt that was in his closet. I thought about Vita for a second and was going to say fuck her and leave it alone. But I remembered the wine on my dress and pulled every piece of clothing, purse and hat out and threw them on the bed. I had been experiencing shortness of breath a lot lately and I was feeling so exhausted, yet my anger wouldn't allow me to sit down.

I went back to the kitchen and got the bottles of liquor off the counter. It was too bad the Southern Comfort was the only thing that would stain something. I got all of her light-colored clothes and went to work. Everything else I drenched with the Vodka. *Try getting that smell out, Vita.*

I looked up from what I was doing and noticed a familiar picture on his mirror from across the room. It was the sonogram I had given him the night before and I wondered what Vita said when he told her I was pregnant. I felt a little better knowing she had probably been upset about the baby, but he was crazy if he thought he was bringing our baby around another bitch.

I went across the hall in search of the baby shit I had seen him get from the car and walked into a room filled with nothing but blue. He had four oak shelves against the wall stacked with clothes and I counted at least twenty pairs of Nikes. *Oh, no he didn't think my baby was staying there with them.* It was time for me to leave before I tore up all of that baby shit too.

Before I left, I looked back at the wall in the living room. "And give me my fuckin' poster," I said as I snatched it down.

Back in my living room I didn't even bother to change my clothes. I laid in the middle of the living room in the fetal position and called out to somebody, anybody who was listening, but my cries went unheard.

It's been two months since the *break-in* and I don't regret a thing. Especially after Quentin called me the next day with some bullshit story about having to go out of town. That translated to me that his ass was making a move. I was pleased at the thought of me shaking him up. He probably thought somebody was tryna rob him or some shit, stupid-ass nigga.

After I talked to him that one time, I got my home number changed and bought a new cell phone. I had cut him off along with everybody else. And I was miserable. My twentieth came and went and I got fucked up! As wrong as I knew a quarter bag of weed and a fifth of Hennessy and Coke were at six months, I downed it all, secretly wanting to miscarriage or die, whichever came first.

I only leave the house to go to McDonald's or look for my mother. I had gone past her house and there was an eviction notice on the door. When it rains, it mutherfuckin' pours was all I could think. Things were bleak for me. I missed Nikola and Chelsea, but didn't want my problems to become apart of their shit.

I was sitting on my bed trying to comb out my tangled mess when I heard my bell ringing. I put down the comb and contemplated answering it. I stared in the mirror on the wall and was disgusted with myself. I felt like a fat, bloated-ass pig as I looked at my cheeks and hands. And I was so wide that I hadn't seen my feet in weeks.

Whoever was at the door was being an asshole by holding down on the bell for so long. I got up and wrapped a rubber band around the mop on my head, and turned off the *Who Wants to Be a Millionaire* show. I had worn the same red and black Western T-shirt for the last two days, but I wasn't changing. The uninvited guest should've called if they wanted a prima donna bitch.

"Who is it!" I yelled.

"It's me."

I already knew who the *me* was. The voice was embedded in my head like a song on repeat. "Me who?"

"Come on, stop playin' and open the door."

"What the fuck do you want?" I asked.

"I need to talk to you, that's what I want." I unlocked the door and walked over to the couch. "Do I have to stand here and bang like I'm crazy?"

"It's open!" I yelled again as I sat back in my spot at the center of the couch.

Outside it was almost 100° and Quentin had a tan that made his skin look nice and toasty. *Cut it out. His ass did you so wrong.*

"So, where you been? I been comin' past here like every other day. And ya car is here, so w'sup?"

"Shit," I said, keeping our conversation as simple as possible.

"Shit? That's it?" he asked like he hadn't used the phrase before.

"That's what I said."

He came over and sat beside me, lifting my shirt so he could touch my stomach. "How's my lil' man?"

"You mean your little *girl*," I said, tired of the bullshit.

"Oh, for real? Well, hey, daddy's girl."

I could tell he wanted to question me about the sudden change in the sex, but was scared I would tell him to get the fuck out.

"So what you want? Ya *girlfriend* leave you again?" I asked.

He sighed real heavy, flipping channels and pretending to look at *Real World*. "C, I came through 'cause one, I was worried, two, your numbers aren't the same, and three, 'cause I'm not gon' say fuck you. You 'bout to have my baby."

"You think?" I said and looked at him like I could spit in his face at any moment. "You been sayin' that *fuck you* shit for awhile now, and it don't have to come from ya mouth. Everything you do is enough to tell me just that."

"Like what?"

"I'm so glad you asked," I said, going into the kitchen to make myself busy. I also knew that if I moved around it would give me a chance to get my thoughts together. I could feel myself getting a little appetite so I put the perfectly fried fish I hadn't touched from *Lake Trout* into the microwave.

"Where you goin'?" he asked from one of the stools at the counter.

"To take a shower," I said and dared him to ask if he could come.

"How long you gon' be?"

"You on my time right now so it don't matter."

I looked back at him and it was the first time I saw him smile. I remembered the picture on his wall, the woman's pretty teeth and small dent in her cheek and had to stop my own smile from showing.

As I let the water hit my stomach and worked the detangling conditioner into my hair, my mind started going. I felt like it was time for me to lay my shit down right when dealing with Quentin. Maybe we weren't together because I had been too cutesy with him and played that dumb *fuck me* role.

I didn't have to go back into the kitchen for my food once I was done showering. Quentin had my food sitting on the pale-green maple table. I sat in the lime chenille armchair and questioned his new attitude. For the first time he seemed to be more into me than he had ever been. He was telling me how pretty I looked and how he missed me. I was ready to cut the bullshit and tell him that I knew why I couldn't call his house and why I had never seen it. I wasn't quite sure what his reaction would be when he found out I had cut up his things, though.

"Why are you acting like this?" I asked.

He stopped kissing my stomach and looked at me. "Like what?"

"Like we have this happy family and we're so into each other when the truth is you're a fuckin' liar."

"Whoa! Where is that shit comin' from?"

"Quentin, don't look at me like you aren't. How long did you think I would be a fool for you?"

"A fool for me? I never asked you to. And what are you talkin' 'bout?"

"Stop playin' dumb! I know the real reason you couldn't stay here. Not because you tryna get shit together on the streets or because bitches are playin' on ya phone. It's because you got somebody. And don't you sit there and fuckin' lie to me. If you can't tell the truth then don't say shit. Just get up and get the fuck out."

The look he gave me said he knew I had been to his house. He got up from his spot on the floor and walked to the door. I didn't want to turn around and look at him because I feared that his back would be the last thing I ever saw. And because I didn't want to hear the door close, I stood up and went into my bedroom. I was ready to cry but I had done enough of that, so I turned on a CD that had pulled me through harder times and sang until my chest was hurting.

*My Life* was coming to an end and it I felt like somebody was watching me. I looked at my doorway and it was Quentin. I screamed and threw a pillow at him.

"Damn, I didn't know you sounded like that," he said.

"It's a lot of shit you don't know," I said, turning down the volume. "So, why didn't you leave? You wanna try and tell me another lie, is that it?"

"No," he said and walked over to my huge picture window.

"Well, what do you want. Why do you stick around, knowing I'm not who you want?"

"Chanel," he said, still looking out the window, "if I lied to you it's 'cause I didn't want to hurt you. I know that shit might sound fake, but I care about you. I mean it's more than that... Love, if that's what you want to call it. And yeah, there have been mutherfuckers before you, but... Man fuck it, I can't do this."

I couldn't let him stop. He was actually showing emotion and I needed to know how he felt about me. I needed to know if I was something more to him than a baby's mother or just another female who offered him good sex. "No go 'head. I'm listening," I said.

"Look I'ma leave this joint here and you tell me what you want to do," he said and left the room.

I looked where he had been standing and noticed the signature blue box. My heart was doing the familiar cartwheels it was used to whenever he was around, only they were multiplied with anticipation.

I opened it and didn't hesitate to slide the diamond-encircled band onto my swollen finger. "Q!" I yelled. I went into the living room and kitchen but he was gone. "Shit," I said, still smiling at the new addition.

I picked up the cordless to call Chelsea. I heard footsteps coming from the bathroom and dropped the phone. "So, I guess you like it," he said.

"I wish you stop scarin' me like that," I said, holding my chest.

"Does it fit?"

"Yeah," I said, holding out my hand. "How did you know my size?"

"The lady asked me how you looked. You know, you, your body. I said you were thick like I like and had a six-month belly."

"You mean seven," I corrected him.

"It was six back then."

"You hungry?" I asked.

"*Oh*, now a nigga can get some friendly treatment, huh?"

"Whateva," I said, feeling like blushing.

"Come on let's go out and get somethin' to eat," he said.

"Where?"

"It don't matter. A nigga's just hungry."

I got dressed in some real clothes, a white Richard Tyler pantsuit with black leather trimming and a white head wrap for my damp hair.

We had never been on a real outing where I felt like we could celebrate something or just be able to sit down and talk. I learned that his favorite food was anything Asian and he learned that I ironed my underwear and sheets. I hadn't felt so sexy in months and when we went back to my place, I remembered how good it felt to have his hands and lips explore my body like it pleased him to please me.

The pregnancy had definitely turned me into a freak because I finally gave in and let him fuck me in the ass. He came on my back and we laid there for an hour in silence. Then he asked me the question that changed my life forever.

"Chanel, I need to ask you somethin'."

"Yeah, w'sup?"

"In two weeks I need you to do me a favor."

"And what's that?"

He cut on the TV and I listened to him tell me about his plans to push weight in Philly. Everything he said would've been fine if only it wasn't Charles' turf he was about to fuck with.

I had just passed the Delaware Memorial Bridge exit when I started second-guessing my role in Quentin's plan to be the nigga at the top. Now, he never said outright that he was stepping on Charles' toes purposely, but I saw the fire that burned in his eyes when he told me how shit was supposed to go down.

I was driving a green Blazer with proper tags and registration, and if the police stopped me, the car belonged to my brother. That was the thing I was scared of since I was carrying a half a million dollars of China White.

Because of China White's resemblance to heroin but with a higher potency, users almost always ended up hooked. Not only was Quentin a knowledgeable seller but a researcher. He had followed its effects in Philadelphia from '92 when it was the hot thing on the streets. Quentin had started his hustling career selling weed. It was safer than other drugs, he said, but the profits were too slow for him. So at seventeen, he turned to cocaine. And while other niggas were using their hustle money to buy tennis, clothes and jewelry, he was saving. $75,000 later and he started supplying shit. The rest was simple.

There were so many overdoses with China and other ill side effects in such a short period of time that its popularity died quickly. His solution was a college roommate named Jason. Quentin had gone to College Park for two years on a basketball scholarship and lost it after he was caught selling a gram to another student. His coach helped have the charges dropped, but he couldn't do anything about the scholarship. He was out of there since basketball was the only thing keeping him in school. He was still tight with Jason who happened to be a biochemistry major.

Jason was already making money with all the research he'd done for all the major hospitals in MD, but he owed Quentin from their days in college when Jason was almost put out. He couldn't afford school after the first semester because his parents divorced and refused to pay his tuition. Quentin gave him the $8,000 he needed.

The other name for China White was Fentanyl and Jason knew how to produce it. He also knew how to cut down on the high potency that resulted in minor effects like uncontrollable shaking and constipation. Quentin told me he had suggested the drug be cut with laxatives and Jason joked him and said that he was in the wrong profession.

Before I was supposed to meet with Rook, Quentin's connect in Philly, I had to stop in Laurel, MD to pick up the stuff. I figured Jason to be a preppy nigga with thin-framed glasses, khakis and a polo shirt. The glasses existed, but they were stylish Fendi frames, and he wore a black tailored suit with a plain T-shirt and expensive shoes. I was surprised.

"Hey you," he said when I met him in the driveway of a brick garage.

"W'sup," I replied, admiring his pretty teeth and fresh-smelling cologne. If I didn't like the thug type, his ass might've been the one I was crazy about.

"So, where is it?" I asked, looking around like he should've had the shit on a pulley.

"In here. You might want to back the truck up so I can load it in the trunk."

After everything was tucked away I asked if I could use his bathroom. The rest of the ride to Philly had to be nonstop and I didn't trust me stopping anywhere until I had gotten rid of the shit. I looked around and to anyone else driving by, I'm sure Jason's private lab looked like all of the other property.

There was a large house connecting to the space that was big enough to hold three or four cars. Inside was something completely different. It reminded me of one of the brand new labs they had built at Western during my senior year with bright fluorescent lights, freshly painted walls and shiny equipment. I was impressed by his obvious intelligence as I looked at all of the chemical equations he had worked out on his blackboard and charts.

He noticed my interest. "You know about chemistry?" he asked.

"A little. It was my favorite science in school."

"Where did you go? Don't tell me. You look like one of those intellectuals from Georgetown."

"No, not hardly," I said, suddenly wishing I had gone to somebody's school. Even Quentin had two years of college.

He didn't press the subject any further. Instead we talked about chemical combustion and the new chemicals being added to the periodic table. It felt good discussing something outside of my everyday life that had only consisted of shopping and watching soaps and music videos.

Jason hugged me before I drove off. "Be careful," he whispered in my ear.

I wondered then if what I was doing was okay. Things didn't feel right as I drove through Delaware. I soon was greeted by the *Welcome to Pennsylvania* sign, but I brushed off the strange feeling and tapped my left hand to the oldies playing on the radio at two in the morning. I looked at the ring on my finger and realized I hadn't told Chelsea or Nikola about the engagement. I planned on meeting with them ASAP so they could plan me an off da' hook engagement party.

Despite the nervousness I was feeling I noticed the excitement in the air so late in the evening. Traffic was light but everyone seemed to have an important destination. Maybe some hot new club or restaurant. It was nice being in a city that stayed awake past 1am.

I was too busy searching for another radio station that I didn't notice the state trooper in my mirror. I told myself to calm down, and put on my signal to move to the middle lane. I was going the designated sixty mph, but I slowed down to fifty-five. I looked up and he was behind me again. I prepared myself and watched the red and blue lights spin like Mickey Mouse ears I used to get from the circus. He motioned for me to pull over and I waited until a car had passed to get over in the right lane.

While I sat and waited for him to run the tags and all of that other bullshit I started biting away at the acrylic on my left thumb. I saw him sitting in the car and wondered what was taking him so long. Quentin had told me that everything would check out if I was pulled over, but I was still shook.

He finally approached the window and I already knew he was going to be a headache. He straightened his hat and tapped on the window. "Evening. Why are driving the interstate without a seatbelt?" he asked in a southern accent.

"Well, as you can see I'm eight months pregnant and sometimes it's really uncomfortable," I said in the best professional voice possible. "I'm wearing my lap belt, though. Does it matter?"

"I'm afraid it does. Ma'am I'm gonna have to see your license and registration."

I passed him the papers and the fake ID with the side view picture. He took them and walked back to his car. Ten minutes later he was back at the window and I could see in his face that there was a problem. "Ma'am I'm gonna need another picture ID."

"Why?" I asked, beginning to panic.

"I ask all of the questions. Now, if you won't cooperate, I can call for backup."

I started thinking quickly and remembered the 9MM I had under the backseat. It was only supposed to be for emergencies, but he was putting me in a tight spot. I quickly weighed my options. If I gave him the only other ID I had, he would confirm the other to be a phony. If I lied and said I didn't have any other one, he would ask for a social. Either way, I was fucked. No matter what I did it meant arrest or worst, a search.

"It's in the trunk in one of my bags."

"Well, pop the trunk lady."

I thought fast. "I have to open it with the key. It's jammed."

"Well, it's too much traffic for you to get out. Hand me the keys and I'll get it."

"I have like three identical bags. You won't know where to look first. How about you help me out the passenger side."

"Okay, I can do that. My mother always told me it was bad luck to search a woman's personals."

*Was he a rookie or what?* I figured him to be young, but not dumb. Even I knew he wasn't supposed to let me out unless I had been drinking or something. The windows were tinted and on the other side of the truck I saw him making his way around to help me out. I reached for the gun and released the safety like Quentin had showed me.

I watched him struggle to open the door. "Come on, lady. I don't have all night," he said and started banging on the door.

That quickly the hesitation was gone. He didn't care about me and if I had to go to trial for all the shit I had on me, his cracker ass would be the top witness testifying against me and sending me away for ten to twenty.

"Fuck that," I said and hid the gun under my leather duffel purse. I let him help me down and handed him the keys. "Here you go. Sometimes it's too hard for me to open."

"I'll take care of that," he said and made his way to the trunk.

My world stopped. Before he could reach the back tire, I took a deep breath, aimed the gun at his neck and pulled the trigger.

# No Pain, No Gain/ 13

Vita

After I left the reception my gut told me to go back to New York. Not because I was mad at Quentin, but because I needed to know if my eyes were really fooling me. I had called KC's phone the whole way up I-95. I got her voicemail each time. It was the same thing at her house. I knew something was wrong because she never cut her cell off. She wasn't even replying to my two-way messages.

I drove up Park Ave. to my building and almost jumped out without putting the car in park. Violet's car was missing.

"Calm down, Vita."

Maybe it had been towed. New York had so many unclear signs as to where a person could park. But no, it couldn't be at the pound because I had parked the car in the same spot for the longest time.

I left my car double-parked and went straight to the front desk. "Mr. Humphrey," I said to the concierge.

"How are you, Ms. Horace?" he asked.

"Not good. Listen, was my other car towed or something?"

"I thought you moved it to the garage. There was a message on your door that a parking spot was finally available for you. About two hours ago I helped someone with the door and noticed it was gone."

"Well, did you see who got in?"

"No, I didn't see anyone."

"Fuck! Call the police for me," I said and angrily pushed the door open.

While I sat in my car and waited, I tapped the steering wheel and hoped that KC wasn't behind the shit. If she had found out about me and Quentin, I would've rather fought her than have her hurt me like she was doing.

"Please let my car be okay," I said over and over again.

I gave the officer a description and filled out the papers. Everything seemed to be okay in my apartment. That is, until I went up the spiral staircase to my bedroom and saw my jewelry thrown across my dresser. Every piece looked like it was there except the platinum pieces she had given me.

"Oh my goodness," I said as I sat on my bed. "That bitch was in my damn house."

I got up and walked through again to see if anything else was missing, but nothing else was out of place. I fell back into the center of my bed and stared at the ceiling for an hour until I heard my phone ringing. I didn't have to look at the caller ID to know it was her. "Where the fuck is my car?"

"Damn, hi to you too," a familiar female voice said.

"Who is this?"

"Marisa, nigga."

"Oh, hey," I said, remembering I had given her the number earlier. "I'm in this bitch 'bout to go crazy."

"What happened? And why you leave the boat without sayin' peace?"

I told her the story and got even angrier than I was before. "I'm tellin' you, she got my shit."

"Well, how long before you find out?" she asked.

"It won't take me long to know she did the shit, but finding it in this city, who the fuck knows."

"Well, call me tomorrow, even if you don't hear anything."

I felt so drained and just wanted to sit in the tub. I looked over at my windowsill and decided to start Mario Puzo's *Omerta* while I bathed. Instead I chose to write in my journal. I hadn't done that in awhile and it was my way of keeping in touch with Violet. All of my entries began with *Dear Violet*. There were two that I addressed to my mother, but that was only on her birthday and the first time I lost a baby.

I reached for the leather-bound book and noticed that it was out of place. I always set it between my Donald Goines collection and *The Coldest Winter Ever*. Now it was behind Freud's *Interpretation of Dreams*. If she had read my shit, that would be too much of a violation. I held it and it felt different. All of the pages were intact but I knew shit wasn't right. It felt so weird sitting there, knowing she had probably sat where I was, reading and rereading some shit. I had said stuff that I would never say out loud, things that I had tried to block out, and now she knew all of it.

I picked up the phone and used my star 69 feature to call Marisa back. I got her voicemail. "Call me before tomorrow. More like tonight. I need to take care of something."

I got a call from the police two days later. What I heard made all of my plans with Marisa justifiable. There was no denying that KC had clout to get away with this kind of shit. And it was crazy, 'cause despite the hurt, I could respect her for holding to her promise. I had no problem with that. However, pain and revenge were the issues and if I didn't show her what *I* was capable of, she might not ever know the kind of bitch she was really dealing with.

Nikola

The engine from a motorcycle made me want to jump out of my skin as I walked up the steps to KC's house. She must've been as shocked as me because she stopped to turn around. "Who da fuck is ridin' at three in the morning?" she asked herself.

Before KC could reach the top step to open the door, two motorcycles, one white with a spider web pattern and the other, black, with the Grim Reaper's face, screeched around the corner. The two riders, who I couldn't tell if they were male or female, reached into their holsters, aimed guns and started shooting. The popping sound forced me to jump over the granite railing, landing on a huge rock.

I lay there and could still hear the vrooming from a distance. When the air was quiet I slowly got up, afraid to go to the top of the porch. My left hand was throbbing and I had a headache that felt like I had been banging it against a brick wall. I called out her name but I didn't hear any sound. I went to walk up the steps and tripped over her leg, hitting my chin on the step. I was in so much pain, but seeing her with blood covering her chest and neck made me forget everything I was feeling.

"KC," I said, touching her face.

She didn't speak and I started slapping her cheek. Hearing the sirens approach us, she opened her eyes. Most of the neighbors were standing outside in their nightclothes, and I assumed they had all called for an ambulance.

At the hospital I got three stitches where my hand and wrist met and she had to have three bullets removed from her shoulder blade, arm and leg. While she slept under the inducing effects of morphine dosages, I answered to a police officer. She asked me to give her an account of the evening and I told her about everything that went down, from the time KC picked me up at La Guardia until we were almost gunned down in front of her house.

A week after Chelsea's wedding I had started receiving a different type of fresh, rare flower everyday along with a *How was your day* message in my two-way. I wanted to tell KC she needed to slow down, but I didn't talk to her until that Friday night. She called to make sure my first-class roundtrip for New York on Saturday morning was confirmed. Before we hung up I reminded her that it was on the *strictly friends* tip.

"No doubt," she said.

Besides a couple of white entrepreneurs I had fucked, no one ever flew *me* first class except *me*. Even so-called ballers who wanted me to come and visit them didn't have enough sense to upgrade from coach unless I bitched, which was often.

It was 11:30 when I walked up the ramp. KC was standing there talking on the phone. She saw me, closed her cell and embraced me like we had known each other forever. She had the same sporty look I had seen her in before: designer T-shirt, cargo pants and expensive shoes.

"That outfit is nice," she said, referring to my Calvin Klein pants and tee.

I didn't want to give off any unnecessary, sexy vibes so I chose to dress as casually as possible. "Thanks," I said, moving the hair from eyes.

"You hungry?" she asked.

"Starving."

"How many bags you got at baggage claim?" she asked, leading the way to the escalator.

"None, it's only for the weekend. All I have is this," I said, holding up my Louis Vuitton case. I never traveled with too much. If a nigga was flying me somewhere he could buy me clothes when I got there.

Now that we were away from the club scene and in her town, the first thing I noticed about her was this air of confidence I recognized in myself. She walked like she owned the world and wouldn't settle for less. We reached the front of the airport and she had a car waiting for us. KC immediately gave her driver, Montaco, directions to a restaurant in Manhattan.

"Even though it's almost twelve, you still have a taste for breakfast or you want somethin' else?" she asked.

"Breakfast food is fine since I'm still on A.M. time."

"I feel you."

For the rest of the ride we discussed the recent elections. She said she had mad respect for Bush even after he was able to bamboozle America with the Florida *miscounts*. I wasn't too sure about the respect part of it, but we both agreed that money had played a major part in it, and that the saying was true—*money talks and bullshit walks.*

At the restaurant I felt like royalty. There were so many important people having brunch in their seven hundred-dollar loafers and khakis who made it a point to come over to our table. She introduced me as an important friend from Baltimore and I was receiving the same respect. I had never had so much fun that early in the day. I wanted to ask her what she did for a living, but knew the tables would turn back to me. *Fuck it, we were both grown.* She made her money the way she knew how, and so did I.

"So," I said after we were able to enjoy our food, "you know a lot of people. You come here a lot, huh?"

"Just when I gotta taste for these buttermilk pancakes, crisp bacon and sausages that taste like they come straight from a pig farm."

"Oh yeah," I said laughing.

"There you go wit' that smile. So Nikola, what do you do with your time?"

*Shit, I was supposed to be asking that question first.* "You mean as far as hobbies, work, what?"

"All of that."

"Well I just like to enjoy life. I feel like sky's the limit."

"That sounds like one of my sayings. What else? You work?"

I thought for a second and listened to the clanking of the expensive glassware and Oneida silverware. "Everyday is a business move," I said, hoping she wouldn't delve any deeper.

"Then that makes us two of a kind, 'cause business is always on my mind too. That is, in between having fun."

"I feel you on that," I said and finished off my drink.

Another round of mimosas, an hour of traffic later and we were at a spa whose cheapest service ran $2,200. She requested two deluxe treatments, and after an Oxygen Facial and a Hot Stone Massage I was in heaven. KC really knew how to make a guest feel welcomed. She was also down with the hot shit.

Later as I enjoyed the two hundred-dollar paraffin pedicure that entailed tiny strips of Pucci print with Swarovski crystals being sealed on my toenails, she didn't question Pucci as a misspelling. Instead she asked if I had ever owned a dress with the expensive print.

"What you know 'bout that?" I asked, raising my eyebrow.

She laughed. "I gotta stay on top of the shit y'all wear. A lot of niggas don't do that. They pick up anything wit' a name brand and think they lacin' y'all. I like to see a woman with that exclusive shit. Feel me?"

KC sat in a chair across from me with her phone and didn't wait for a response. It was then that I was dying to know exactly what she did for a living. She talked to various people like they all owed her something. And she never asked them if they had performed some task for her. When her phone rang it was them reporting to her.

"That looks nice," she said, standing over the manicurist. "You like?"

"Yeah, I thought Baltimore was the originator of rhinestones, but this goes way beyond anything I've ever seen."

"Look, I need to run Uptown and take care of somethin', but it'll only be for a couple of hours. I'll leave you this," she said, handing me her American Express. "Montaco is still outside. He'll take you wherever you need to go."

For once, I was speechless. I didn't have to demand anything from her or initiate the events of the day. "You comin' back down here to meet me or what?"

"Nah, I'll see you at my house. Oh, and I'm not sure what clothes you brought with your *one* piece of luggage," she laughed, "but some friends of mine are throwin' a party."

"Is it formal?" I asked, anticipating whatever was about to go down.

"Hell nah, but whateva you get to wear has to make a statement. Shit, why am I even tellin' you this? Every time I see you it's on some ol' other shit."

She walked away and I couldn't help relishing in all the attention. Goodness, if she was a man she would be the catch of the fuckin' year. I watched her walk through the revolving doors and thought about what other surprises she had for the evening.

"Your girlfriend, she nice," the brown-haired Dominican said.

"She is, isn't she," I said, surprised at my own reply. "You have openings for hair?"

"Oh yes! I been wanting to do yours since I saw you. So nice and thick, you know. Nice texture and long."

I sat in her chair for two hours like I was a Barbie doll. I couldn't believe she had charged me $270 for some shit I had been doing forever. I couldn't deny how nice the layers and auburn highlights were, but $270? It was time for me to get my shit together. A hair salon was definitely the next thing on my agenda.

"Where to next?" Montaco asked when I got in the car. It was only 4:00.

"I need to shop."

"What do you like? Valentino, Prada, Gucci..."

*Ding! Ding! Ding!* I wanted to say. "Take me to all of the above."

We got to Fifth Ave. and I felt out of place riding from store to store with my Calvin Klein T-shirt. That was a first for me. My shit was usually tight but this atmosphere was different. The only thing that said I was fit to shop among the wealthy was my expensive hairdo. "You want anything while I'm out?" I asked him.

"No, I'm fine. Call my phone so I'll know when to circle the block for you."

He gave me the number and after I programmed it, I dialed my mother. "Ma," I said after hearing her voice.

"Hey baby, I was just thinking about you. Why haven't I seen you in two weeks? My hair is all over my head."

"Mommy, you know how busy I get. Like, now I'm in New York. I called to see if you wanted me to get you anything."

"Kola, you know I'm fine. What are you doing there?"

"Checking out some prices for the salon equipment."

Whenever I handed her some money or bought her anything expensive, I always told her it came from something hair-related. When I bought her first car, I lied and said the money came from hair services I had performed at a big fashion show in Chicago. She hugged me and told me how proud she was. I had even overheard her conversations with my aunts. "Kola is so creative with her hands. Next week she's doing a show in California."

I couldn't tell her the truth. She was the one person I knew who wasn't judgmental, but she was still my mother. "You sure you don't want anything?" I asked her again. "Women's Day is coming up at church and I saw a *bad* hat at one of these boutiques. All of the sisters will be checking you out."

The familiar laugh made my day. "Oh, okay, but Kola, don't get me anything too extravagant. You know how you can get."

"Okay, love you too ma," I said and hung up.

The first thing I did was go hat shopping. I couldn't decide between two pillboxes and three different straw brims with lavender, tan and yellow trimmings, so I got them all.

At the register, it was the first time I looked at the card. Katrina Chisham was the name at the bottom. After I went to Prada I didn't have to travel any further. It had everything I wanted down to the shoes and bag. I knew that American Express usually had a never-ending limit, but I decided to spare KC the damage of my unfeeling spending habit, and called it a day. After all, the dress alone was $7,300.

It was 6:30 when Montaco came for me and 8:00 when he pulled up to her house. KC's home was like some shit I had only seen in *Metropolitan Home* with Greco-Roman architectural structures, glass windows and large, loft-like space. She was standing in the doorway when I reached the top of the steps. I heard D'Angelo's *Voodoo* and was glad most of the songs had an upbeat tempo because I wasn't ready for seduction, something I knew she was probably good at.

"Have fun?" she asked.

"It was cool," I said, and looked at all of the detail she had incorporated into her home. It was so big that we had to take an elevator to the top floor. I followed her to one of the extra rooms, still awestruck by the layout.

"You like blue and orange, right?"

"Yeah, they're my favorite colors," I said.

"I figured that," she said and turned on the light to a room that was the size of the entire apartment my mother and me had lived in.

It was like she had designed the room with me in mind. The walls were a fusion of sky and royal blues, and the headboard of the bed was covered in orange, crushed velvet.

"Your place is really nice," I said, laying my bags on the bed.

"Thanks. So what did you get?"

"Did I ask to see what you were wearin' tonight?" I teased.

"My bad."

"Oh, here's your card," I said, digging into my bag.

"Nah, don't insult me. Hold on to it. You might need it when I call you to hang out the next time."

To mask my surprise and delight, I changed the subject. "So, how long do we have to get ready?"

"Shit, take all the time you need. The party don't start until *we* get there anyway."

She was right. After I watched her tackle New York's busy streets in her Lamborghini like she was in a demolition derby, we arrived at a restaurant in Upper Manhattan. It was early spring and the weather was unusually warm. It only added to the excitement of the restaurant's appearance. Inside there was indigo lighting, silver walls and a second floor that served as a dance floor and lounging area with couches and flat screens that flashed instant pictures of everyone's activities, whether they were eating dinner, holding a drink or smoking cigars as big as polish sausages.

I assumed that she and her friends had rented out the whole place. As I looked into the faces of the beautiful women, (some feminine and others who wouldn't know what femininity was if it slapped them) I realized that I was in the company of NY's finest—the lesbian connection.

Outside I had noticed the limos, the Benzes, the Beamers and one or two Bentleys that were almost identical to the one she had parked in the back of her estate. I hoped I wouldn't be bored out my mind with conversation about the Stock Market.

Most of the women were Black except a few Hispanics and Asians. She introduced me to everyone and I was glad that I had decided on the black halter dress with the low back. None of them could have worn it the way I did or been able to pull off the strappy six-inch heels either.

Stopping at each table, we sat at one of the booths with high leather backs and I took in the atmosphere again. There was just too much going on for me to remember the names of everyone she had introduced me to. But I figured that I should at least get to know who was at our immediate table.

There was Nina who sat to my right with an accent that reminded me of my grandmother who lived in Rhode Island. It had that New York edge to it, but was more sophisticated. She was friendly, but talkative and had the biggest eyes I had ever seen. Her girlfriend, who they called Meechi, was the same way only she was more serious. Then there was Michelle and Tekila who couldn't keep their hands off each other, and Kelly and Jasmine who both had bright red hair and matching tongue rings.

"So, let me tell you how I had to bust his balls today," Nina began. "This fucker tried to talk about the Japanese Market and how he was representing two of the biggest investors in Tokyo. Said I could learn a lot from him. '*Oh yeah*' I said. At the end of the day I had both of his fuckin' clients. Oh, he was definitely fuckin' wit' the right one."

They all broke out into loud laughter and I sat and listened to their other stories of *pussy power*.

"Order whatever you want," KC whispered to me. "The cook will make you anything, sushi, ribs, whatever. She was voted number one last year for the best cuisine in Manhattan."

"Where is the waiter?"

"He'll be over soon. One of them anyway. There's like 125 people here tonight and they all can eat."

I was having fun. They all seemed to have some kind of control and didn't care if they had to piss on a man to get what they wanted. It was intoxicating. I felt so empowered by their need to break the *glass ceiling*.

While KC gave the cocktail waitress my order for a Purple Rain, I turned to Nina who was trying to get my attention. "Your earrings are nice," she said.

I touched the platinum *falling rain* earrings with diamonds that KC had had sitting on the dresser when I got out the shower. "Thanks," I said.

"Nikola, right?"

"Yeah."

"Wouldn't you agree that a woman could run the country better than a man?" she asked.

"Only if we learned how to make decisions without letting our emotions get involved."

"That's a first. I haven't heard that from a woman besides her," she said, pointing to KC. "So how do you two know each other? You used to have something serious together?"

That's the emotional shit I was talking about. She asked me a question and then wanted to answer it for me.

"Nina, stop being so nosy," KC interrupted. "I already told you who she was."

"Oh, okay," she said and changed the subject. "So who does your hair? It's nice."

I answered the rest of her questions and was glad when the food came. She would finally have something to keep her mouth busy. KC ate from my plate of steamed shrimp and lobster bisque while I tried every sushi roll in front of her. When it looked like everyone was finishing their last bites, the music got louder and she said she wanted me to see the upstairs.

We sat on one of the deep orange and chocolate couches made for two people and one of the waitresses set two blunts in front of us like they were mints.

"You puff?" she asked.

"It depends on what's in it."

"Oh, I only get the best. That chronic! It's from a dude in Cali who grows the shit on the mountains. You should see it. The trees grow like fuckin' cactus in Arizona."

"How is it that you know so many people, and why is it that we can smoke this so freely?"

She laughed like I had told a joke. "Here, let me light that first," she said and held the silver lighter open. I puffed in and waited for her to begin talking. "Well, I own this place and I know so many people because things just work that way. You know how it is when you lead a certain lifestyle and certain mutherfuckers make their way into your life?"

"Yeah," I said, completely lost and left in the dark. "Is everybody in here gay?"

"Most of 'em. And the rest are a bunch of females who want to come to the other side, but enjoy the excitement of strikin' the match and blowin' it out before they give it a chance to burn their fingers. Does that bother you?"

"What?" I said, fully aware of what she was asking me.

"Being here and knowin' who you're around."

"No, I'm actually having a lot of fun. More fun than I've had in a minute."

"You know, ya hair is nice," she said, looking at me like she was seeing my face for the first time. "Every time I've seen you it's always perfect. Who does it?"

"I do."

"That's right. I forgot, you just told Nina that. You got your license?"

"I need to get it so I can open a salon," I said, suddenly wishing I were able to say I owned something to validate myself.

"I can get you a license, that's not hard. Did you have a location in mind?"

"Nah, not yet."

"You look like a stylist."

"Oh, you've dated that many, huh?"

"*What*, you callin' this a date? I thought this was a *strictly friends* type of thing."

"Don't joke me," I said, wondering why I had even let the comment slip.

"I'm just messin' around," she said and went to the bar for some more drinks.

While I watched her wait for the bartender to shake my drink, a girl I had seen looking over at our table all evening, came behind her and wrapped her arms around her chest. She was my complexion and wore her hair naturally curly and wild. KC turned around real quick like she was disgusted and pulled away. I strained to see what she was saying and wished I could read lips better. The girl asked her why she hadn't called and KC told her it was because she was busy and grabbed our drinks off the bar.

"A lot of admirers, huh?" I asked, still watching the girl who looked at me like she wanted to shoot darts from her eyes.

KC laughed and passed me the Collins glass. "That's how it seems, doesn't it? Every time, every time."

"So was that your ex?"

"Oh no. Just somebody who got too attached."

"Was that a problem?"

"What, the attachment part of it? Nah, I don't mind that, but it's a problem when feelings aren't mutual. I like to chase. I hate it when a woman is more into me. It turns me off."

"But wouldn't you take that as flattery?"

"I guess, just not the kind I want," she said and shrugged it off.

The alcohol and weed was allowing my conversation to flow more freely so I asked her the question I was dying to know. "How did you know you were gay?"

"How did you know you were straight?" she quickly shot back.

"I'm sorry," I said, feeling like I had hit a sensitive spot. "I didn't mean to offend you."

"I know you didn't, but I think both questions are the same."

"Well, I'm straight 'cause I just am."

"The same thing here. I just am. Now, how many times do you get that question?"

"Never," I said, regretting the can of worms I had opened.

"*Me*? I got that all my life. From family, people I didn't know. How do you explain that you like the smell of a woman, the feel of her breasts, her hands, her hair," she said and touched the edges of my hair.

"I'm sorry," I said, and felt like those other women she had been talking about earlier.

My question didn't affect our vibe for too long. Minutes later we were back into another conversation filled with jokes and more weed smoke. That's the thing I liked about her. She could've let my remark put a damper on the mood, but she quickly flipped the script and turned things back to normal.

So I shouldn't have been surprised when we were at the hospital and I watched her remain calm after she realized what had happened to her. "You have fun tonight?" she asked, as she tried to lift her head.

"For the most part," I said, rubbing my hand.

"Ooh, you hurt yourself?" she asked and reached over to touch my wrist.

"It's nothing."

"No, it is. I'm sorry if I put you in that situation. That was just the work of somebody tryna scare me. If they wanted to, they could've finished the job."

"But who would want to scare you like that?" I asked, concerned about my own life.

"Somebody who couldn't accept the truth or take heed to warnings."

*Who the fuck was I dealing with?* She talked like she was in the Mafia filled with nothing but organized crime.

The next day I had helped her get settled in her room and asked if somebody was coming to help her until she got back on her feet.

"Nikola, don't leave yet. If you're scared we can go to my house in Philly. I'm just used to you. I feel like I've known you for awhile."

"I know you mean well, but I've never had to duck bullets, and exciting as this whole experience has been, I have a life I need to get back to."

"What? You need money. I'm not tryna mess up ya paper. Whatever you need this week, I got you."

"But why don't you want your family to take care of you? Where are they? I mean, look at you. You can barely sit up. I'm no doctor."

"I didn't ask you to be, I just want you around."

I thought about Philly and figured it would give me the chance to see Chelsea and check out KC's *other* house. After all, it was only for a week.

Her X5 was gassed up and we were on our way to Philly. That house couldn't touch the one in Long Island, but came close. Soon, a week turned into a month, and a month into two. She hadn't crossed the friend line but even I had come close a few times. There were other things about her besides the money that made her attractive. Our conversations flowed with ease and even on bed rest she was a go-getter. That was the biggest attraction.

I had only gone home once to drop the hats off to Mommy and visit Chanel, but that was the last time. Chelsea, who was thirty minutes away, was out of sight, out of mind. It was like she had dropped off the planet. Nobody answered their phones and Chanel had even had hers changed. It wasn't my fault I couldn't reach her on her birthday. I had still sent her a bracelet with her birthstone and a singing bear, but she never called.

KC, on the other hand, was adding excitement to my life everyday. Since she couldn't get out and do the things she was used to, I was meeting with the people she dealt with from day to day. I learned that she had a lot of dealings with real estate, and the people I met with used the property to engage in gambling and other illegal activities. When they handed me the business envelopes, I passed them the deeds to their property. Once I looked inside and there was a cashier's check for $83,000. I wondered exactly what kind of property they were buying.

It was strange knowing that she trusted me enough to share so much with me. One day we were sitting in her room playing Monopoly when she decided to ask about my personal life. "Niko," she said, using the nickname she had started calling me after my second week of staying with her.

"Yeah, w'sup?"

"Why don't you ever talk about your relationships?"

"With who? I don't have one."

"I don't just mean the intimate ones. I mean with your mother, your father. You close to them?"

She was sounding like a therapist. "With my mother, yes. My father, that's something I don't want to get into."

"That's cool. And what about the intimate ones, what happened to the last one or does it still exist?"

"I've never been in one. Even in high school, I never let myself become, as you put it, *attached*."

"Why not?"

I hadn't thought about it. The only real relationships I had ever maintained were the ones with women. Even after my father, the guys I had known hurt me in some way and left. And my mother's side of the family only consisted of women who dogged men every chance they got.

Our Thanksgiving dinners and other holiday events never went without their stories about finding their husbands with this woman or getting their asses whooped. It was pitiful that I had never had any constant, positive male images in my life.

"Scared to get hurt I guess. Not wanting to feel those things that come with it."

"I feel that. So now do you feel safe? With me... Knowing where I'm coming from when it comes to women."

I laughed nervously. "I haven't given it any thought."

She must've known I was lying because she leaned over and kissed me on the cheek. I didn't know how to react so I sat there and pretended to look at the TV hanging from the wall. She leaned over again and turned my face to hers. "I know this might be hard for you to believe, but I would never want to hurt you."

And then she kissed me again, tracing her tongue around the outline of my top lip. I had tried to fight the things I had been feeling, but it was useless. Even if I never saw her again so many questions of *what if* might pass through my mind forever.

She was running her fingers over my neck when I heard the sound of my phone going off with the urgent ring, letting me know they had left a message. Whoever was trying to get through wasted no time calling back. I got scared and automatically thought about my mother. She had been complaining about a chest cold and I kept telling myself that I would go home, but I never did. *Was this my curse for letting time go by?* If she was in the hospital I hoped I would have at least one more chance to talk to her.

"Hello," I said when I answered it.

"I-I need you to come and get me," the frantic voice said.

"Hello," I said again. "Who is this?"

"It's me! Please hurry! I'm beggin' you. I don't know what to do."

"Calm down Chanel," I said when I realized it was her. "Where are you?"

"I need you right now. Please come," she pleaded.

"Listen. I can get there quicker if you tell me where you are."

I listened to her sob. "I'm at the Motel Six right at the exit before you get to the Delaware exit. Hurry up! I don't know what to do."

"What room?"

"Umm," I heard her say and fumble around like she was searching for the key to the room. "Room thirteen."

"Okay hold tight. I'm like forty-five minutes away, but I'll try to get there faster."

"Please just come on. And bring me some gasoline," she said before she hung up.

*Room thirteen and gasoline, what the fuck?* What had she gotten herself into? I just knew it was that fuckin' Quentin. I told her that he was a mutherfucker.

"Where are the fuckin' keys?" I said loudly. "They're never where I left 'em."

"Wait, wait what's wrong?" KC asked.

"Shit, I don't know. I gotta go and get Chanel. She's cryin' and shit like she 'bout to slit her wrists or somethin'."

"You need me to go?"

"Nah, I'll see you when I get back."

I couldn't contemplate a serious relationship even if I wanted to. As long as I was bailing one of them out of their shit my heart would remain unattached.

Forty-five minutes later I was pulling into the parking lot of the motel. I didn't see her car anywhere and wondered how she had gotten to Delaware. I banged and kicked on the door until I saw her move the curtains. She cracked the door and pulled me inside.

"Oh *my God*. What happened?" I asked as I looked at the blood splattered on her neck and clothes.

"Close the fuckin' door!" she screamed.

I locked it and looked at the room. The sheets were stripped off the bed and there were two suitcases like she was about to take a trip. Her eyes were red and her hands were shaking.

"Sit down and tell me what happened."

"No! We can't stay here. I need to get away as quick as possible."

"Okay, let's go. I'm parked right out front."

When I loaded up her suitcases and started to back out of the parking lot, she stopped me. "Wait, wait. Pull over there," she said, pointing to a hidden spot near a bunch of trees. "Where's the gasoline?"

"In the trunk."

"Well, pop the shit. I don't have all fuckin' night!"

I waited for her to get out and watched her wipe the doors of a Blazer with the pillowcase she took from the room. Then she covered it with the gasoline I had picked up at Rite Aid. I had so many questions for her when she calmed down. She lit the match and stood there in a trance. I looked around at the other rooms and all the lights were out. I hoped we were the only ones witnessing the shit and honked twice. "Come on!" I yelled.

On the highway, she rolled down the window and threw up until her shoulders were heaving. I reached over and rubbed her back. "Chanel tell me what's wrong. You're doing more than scaring me. I need to know somethin'."

"I killed a police officer," she blurted.

My hands started shaking after she told me that and I tried to piece things together. "Before you start tellin' me the story, did you wipe down the inside of that truck the same way you did the outside?"

She shook her head yes and started crying again. I wanted to stop at a roadside café but she had the blood on her shirt and we needed to get off the highway as soon as possible. I was sure the police were on the prowl like roaches.

I listened to her tell me the story and shook my head when I heard Quentin's name. "You should've let him transport his own fuckin' packages. Look at you. Your goddamn stomach is hanging over your pants. He wasn't thinkin' about you *at all*. Did you call him yet?"

"Yeah, I told him that shit went wrong and he went off. He said that I couldn't do shit right."

"Just like I thought. Chanel, I know it's too late to say this, but niggas like Quentin don't give a fuck about you when shit goes wrong with *their* money. As long as you benefit them, shit is sweet."

"But he proposed to me," she started to say.

I looked down at her finger and wondered if she knew he had played her. She was starting to sound as naïve as Chelsea.

"Where are we?" she asked when I pulled up to the front of the house.

"I'll be back in five minutes. I'm getting you a change of clothes and we're going to see Chelz."

I walked inside and called out to KC.

"I'm in the bathroom!" she yelled back.

"I'm not comin' near there. Ya ass stanks."

She laughed. "I'm just pissin'."

I was in my room packing a bag when she hopped in the room on her crutch. "What's wrong? Why you leavin'?"

I didn't know how much of the story I could trust her with, but remembered that she had shared a lot with me. So I replayed everything. It was obvious that she was used to coming up with solutions to crime, because the whole time I was telling her about Chanel I could see her mind going.

"Hold up," she interrupted me. "She was on I-95 right?"

"Yeah, why?"

"Because she had to go through a toll or two. You can believe that the fuckin' police are going to review the tapes as soon as they can."

"Shit! Shit! Shit!" I said, pulling on my hair.

"Wait, don't look like that," she said, touching my hand. "A friend of mine might be able to help. Where you goin' now?"

"To Chelsea's house."

"Well leave ya phone on. I'll call you in about forty minutes. Nikola," she said before I walked out the door, "I'll take care of it, aight?"

I gave her the smile she was used to and prepared myself to clean up Chanel's mess and some other shit that I couldn't smell yet.

Vita

Memorial Day Weekend had finally arrived and it was the last time I really would have a chance to party before I would be on bed rest. After that shit went down with KC I called Quentin and told him I was coming back to Baltimore—for good.

I hadn't visited a doctor yet, but Jewel told me about Mercy Hospital. They had a reputation for the most comfortable and successful deliveries, especially with women who couldn't carry their babies to term. I met with Dr. Desai the Monday after I moved back and she explained the procedure she would perform at the end of my fifth month. Even though there would only be minor stitching and a shift in my cervix, Quentin sat there and asked more questions than I did.

There really wasn't anything serious to it besides me having to lay around for three months bored out my mind. Quentin was trying harder since things were so fucked up with the last baby. I had finally told him I was pregnant and his face lit up. He started planning the room and a party with all his niggas and the few bitches I fucked with. It was like we had this silent understanding between us that said he knew I didn't have too many close friends, and a party would be better than a baby shower. But shit with Quentin wasn't sweet immediately.

I hadn't been there two nights before the calls started coming in at three and four in the morning. I realized that things were going to be a little different since I had been away for awhile, but it didn't take him long to adjust. I told him that he either had to get his number changed or I would move into my own place. The calls ended up being the least of my worries.

One night we went to New York for a surprise party and the shit was like that. I ran into so many people I hadn't seen in awhile, and they were all astonished to see a pregnant Vita. I took pleasure in Charles' wife's startled expression. She took one look at me and my stomach and rushed to use the phone. I knew how bitches were so I could hear the conversation in my mind. "Guess who's here and pregnant?"

So it was no coincidence that upon our return to Baltimore in the early morning hours that the house looked like a fuckin' tornado had blown through. Quentin swore that somebody had tried to rob him, but after seeing my shit, I knew what time it was.

"Q, which one of ya bitches did this?"

He looked at me all confused. "Vita, ain't no bitch do this. Some stupid nigga found out where I rest and probably came lookin' for some shit."

"Really now? Well explain this," I said, holding up a dress with an alcohol stain. "Ain't no nigga gon' do some bullshit like take the time to slash my shit. This is the work of a bitch. Now I'm not gon' ask you this question again, but is there somethin' you want to tell me?"

I knew his ass and I could tell if he was lying. He was so sure of himself most of the time that I never sensed hesitation, but I saw it all in his face. "Nah, it ain't shit you need to know except we movin'," he said and looked away.

"Guess again nigga. *Ya ass* is movin'. I'm goin' to South Beach and when I get back, I want all of this shit dealt with. Fuck the clothes and all that other mess. It can be replaced. You need to handle whateva mess you got yourself into, 'cause when I get back I can't deal wit' stress and plain ol' bullshit." I got closer to his face so he could understand how serious I was. "Fuck those days of you not givin' a fuck if the baby I'm carryin' is healthy. I could give a *fuck* about you runnin' the streets and whateva else it is you do wit' those whores. I want you to tell me now, do I have to find another place or what, 'cause you know I'll be aight either way."

This was the second time, besides when I saw him cry that he looked crushed. But everything I said was the truth. He was standing there telling me he had nothing to share. I knew about the other baby. And I couldn't be mad at her. I would've done the same thing, even some tire slashing, 'cause there was no telling what kind of garbage he was filling her head with.

"I hear you," was all he said before he ran my bath water.

I never played him and he knew I wasn't going to bullshit any issues I had with him, so like always, I put the shit on the glass before we went to bed that night.

"When she gettin' the abortion Q?"

"What?" he said, choking on the bottled water.

"You heard me. When?"

"She will," was all he said before he got up to roll a Dutchie.

I already had mad love for Quentin, but him lying to me challenged his credibility and changed the way I looked at him. True, I had been away for a minute, but he was the same nigga that said I would always be number one. *Number one* meant taking care of shit like unwanted pregnancies before I found out. But I had to come to terms with the fact that he was a nigga first, and just like he did what he wanted, I was gonna have to be the bitch I was and *do me*.

I was five months pregnant and I felt beautiful. My hair had grown out six inches already and my nails were growing without the acrylic. I had stopped using Aveda to get rid of my blackhead problem, and my skin was clear and glowing. I got more hollers than before, like the security at the airport. Quentin was dropping me off at BWI so I could head down to Miami and one of the airline agents tried to push up on me.

"Darling, you are finer than the best wine."

"Man, watch who the fuck you talkin' to," Quentin said, appearing from the side of the truck with my two bags. "That's my wife."

"Quentin, chill out. You know he's just tellin' the truth," I said, making him more jealous.

"Yeah, aight," he said. "So, when you come back the new house is gon' be tight. Did you want somethin' different besides that Pooh shit for his room?" he asked, pointing to my stomach.

He had a habit of doing that, like the baby was in a stroller already. He even got up every morning to talk to the picture on the mirror like it was a real snapshot. There was a visible dick, but no face.

"Quentin, what's wrong wit' Pooh?" I laughed, already knowing what he would say.

"You know what's wrong wit' his faggot ass. I can't tell if it's a boy or a girl. Now Tigger, that's a O.G."

"Really? Well, you can put *some* Tigger in there, but it's all about Pooh, okay?"

"Whateva," he said, and kissed my neck while he played in my hair. "Call me if I need to come and get you early."

"Doubt it," I said and dug in his pockets. "What you got for me?"

He reached inside of his jacket and with a quick move, pulled me close to him and slipped the bag of money that I was sure was filled with nothing but fifties and hundreds, into the pocket of my long jacket. "Vita, don't show ya pregnant ass while you down there either. I got niggas lookin' out in South Beach."

"I bet you do," I said, and grabbed his ass.

"Love you too," he said and waited until I was inside the airport before he pulled off. His history with customs kept him out of the airport if it wasn't necessary.

Marisa was already in Florida since she had to check into the hotel by 12pm. *The Marlin* was the place to stay during the Memorial holiday. It was more than chic, and celebs were everywhere. We had connecting suites on the same floor with some familiar TV faces. I had even spotted members of the Wu on our floor.

My suite was all that. I could see the beach from my window and the water races had already started. Marisa was in my bathroom checking to see how identical everything was compared to hers.

"Damn Marisa, why you ain't tell me shit started this early?" I yelled to her.

"I didn't know. I'm not the event planner down this bitch."

I turned back around and couldn't believe the sights on the beach. Bitches who looked like whales had strings in their asses. "See, I wasn't sure about my swimwear, but look at these chicks. She got enough stretchmarks to... Shit I don't know."

"V, look at you. Pregnant and everything you still got a model body, and ya stomach looks real cute, like a beach ball. Shit, you haven't heard?"

"What's that?" I asked, scared to hear what she would say next.

"Niggas fall over each other to get to pregnant pussy."

I laughed real loud at that one. "You crazy as hell!"

I knew she was telling the truth. A lot of pregnant women underestimated the sexual energy they gave off. I was ready to flaunt mine everywhere.

It was a blazing 95° outside so the first thing we did was hit the beach. The stares said one thing: people weren't used to seeing a pregnant woman in the open with so little clothes. I had on a red and white Chanel halter bikini with matching flip-flops, and a floppy candy cane hat. Although I had been taking my clothes off in front of strangers for years, I found myself becoming paranoid. However, my confidence quickly returned when I noticed the same whales I had seen from my window. They were parading up and down the sidewalks like they were on a catwalk in Milan.

At the dock we rented our jet skis and met up with Black and Bugsy whose tongues were hanging out their mouths when they saw me. They were from down South and owned the biggest car detailing business in Miami. They were also giving us the lowrider to show off at the car show the following night.

"Damn, who is this?" Black asked Marisa.

"Nigga, *ask me* if you wanna know," I said, putting him in his place.

"Oh, I like you already, Red. You nice and feisty."

*Red* was a name they gave to girls my complexion and *Black*, I guessed, is what they called darker girls. Personally, it was a turnoff, and there was no guessing how he got his nickname. He wasn't ugly but he wasn't the type of nigga I would usually have on my arm. Bugsy was just okay too. He was tall and built like Black with diamonds in both ears, only he was brown-skinned.

It was amazing to me how a little dough could make the *aight* niggas model material. The bitches were practically flashing them to get their attention, but a mouthful of golds and a southern drawl didn't excite me. I was more into having fun than anything else.

I could tell that Marisa and Bugsy had fucked with each other before from the way he touched the back of her hair. She had cut the spikes away and her hair was now its natural texture with tiny, but cute texturized curls that framed her round face.

"I see you liked them earrings I sent you, Red," Bugsy said to her in his accent.

"Yeah, thanks again," she said, touching the five-carat studs.

"So when you gon' be my gull?" he asked her.

"When you leave your wife," she shot back. "I heard about the phat-ass villa you got her in Palm Beach."

"Boa, I tell ya, y'all females can talk," he said, obviously caught off guard by her knowledge of the house.

"Yeah, you think a bitch told me, but ya ass forgot that I got eight brothers to put me down wit' bullshit niggas like you."

"Whateva, hop yo ass on that ski and let's race."

We had a blast on the water. I didn't say anything, but I had never taken a swimming lesson a day in my life. The only thing that saved me was the orange lifesaver and my hands gripping Black's waist, who did enough tricks to send me into early labor. We went up against nine other couples including Marisa and Bugsy, and won three of the five races.

By the time I got back to my room it was 7:00 and all I wanted was a nap. All Marisa wanted to do was hit up Bugsy's pockets. She had been talking about this platinum and diamond Harry Winston watch the entire day and swore that he was going to buy it. I wanted to ask her why she couldn't just steal it, but knew it was her way of getting him back for the bankroll he had dished out for his wife.

I woke up two hours later to the vibration of a drum and what sounded like a parade on the main street. I could tell that Marisa had been in my room to cover me up and was still out running her hustle, but I was ready for the next adventure. Plus, I had an appetite that couldn't be ignored any longer.

After a shower, a light application of MAC, and a bend with the flat irons, I made my way to the lobby. My lavender linen halter dress with matching Coach shoes and bag was just right for the live atmosphere. There was a reggae band from St. Lucia who was rockin' everything from Bob Marley to the go-go beats that originated in DC. I was trying to get a table when I heard my name.

"Vita, is that you?"

I turned around and tried to see through the crowds of faces. I heard her voice again and saw a woman with the same wispy hairstyle as mine. As she got closer I realized that I had never seen her before, and prepared myself to give a beat down.

"Vita?" she said again when I was close enough to smell the Big Red she was chewing.

"Yeah," I said, cradling my stomach.

"I'm Kristen.... Violet's best friend from California."

If it wasn't for the music, I think I would've passed out. I didn't think anybody else knew Violet besides Jewel and here was Kristen Rivera, a well-known porn star, telling me she was her best friend. There were the gray eyes and signature scarlet hair she had rocked most of her career. Even though Violet was a private person, we shared a lot. But I had no idea she was friends with Kristen Rivera.

"Umm, how do you know me?"

She pulled me by the arm and hugged me for a long time. When she let me go she was crying so hard. "I'm sorry. It's just that this is so unreal to me. Can we leave here and go to another spot?"

She didn't have to ask me twice. I was scared, but eager at the same time to hear what she had to tell me. For that moment I was believing in miracles and thinking that maybe Violet had survived. I started replaying the kind of bogus-ass stories and plots I had seen in movies and the soaps where the actor mysteriously survives everything short of being eaten alive by a bear or some shit.

We ended up at the *Lola Bar and Lounge* where much of the South Beach party crew came to chill with a mature crowd who sipped martinis and listened to the blues and funk. I sat across from her in one of the denim chairs while a waitress took her order. I waited impatiently like an anxious child who couldn't wait to hear a bedtime story. I had even forgotten how hungry I'd been.

"Vita, you sure you don't want anything?"

"No." I wanted to say *yes* but the wait was making me crazy. My insides were doing all kinds of crazy things.

"You look just like the pictures, only prettier. And older, of course."

"What pictures?" I asked, confused.

"I'm sorry," she said, wiping her eyes again, "but Violet was like my sister. We came from that same place of not knowing and not having shit. You know, makin' something out of nothing, and when she told me about you, it was like she had found something to finally bring her happiness, something to live for."

"I did all that?" I asked, feeling like a little girl again.

"*Yeah*. I guess you were staying with her for about three months when I found out how much you meant to her. I was in Cali and had gone to do the film thing and I called her to come out there with me. She said she had you to look after."

"So she put everything on hold for me?" I said, more to myself than to her.

"I wish I could've met you at the funeral, but I figured it was all too much for you. The last few years have been rough, huh?"

"You ain't lyin'," I said, suddenly feeling another presence besides us two. The warm breeze coming through the patio had the hairs on my arms standing up.

My meeting Kristen was for a reason. I started crying. I had never gotten used to that loneliness that I had felt all my life, and she was proof that a person's soul could live on and reveal itself, bringing the unexpected.

"This is too much for me," I said. "Two months ago the only memory I had left was burnt away too, and now you just come from nowhere."

"She loved that car," she said, already knowing what I was talking about. "One time we drove to New York thinking we would be the next big models, you know because we were taller than the average girls. And you could tell they wanted to laugh at our big titties and wide hips. Violet knew modeling was my dream. She just went along for support 'cause she was so beautiful that I think she could've got a fuckin' contract just by walkin' the streets and being her everyday self. So, instead of going back to Baltimore, we drove all the way to Canada in that car and she told me jokes to cheer me up. I was Thelma and she was Louise. My fuckin' backbone."

That was the real shit that I missed. We sat there another two hours, and I laughed and cried at things I never knew about the person who had been the closest to me. Kristen was leaving to go back to L.A. for another movie and gave me her number and address. She said she would send me the pictures Violet had mailed to her and I promised to stay in touch.

I walked back into the hotel, unaware of all the activities going on around me. Marisa hit me on my two-way, but I told her to chill with Bugsy and that I wasn't feeling too hot. I didn't want to be alone, but I wanted quiet. Since the reggae band had cleared out, I decided to take a seat at one of the stool tables in the corner.

Everything seemed to be so much bigger than me at that moment. Not in the literal sense, but as far as life and death. In four months I would be responsible for another life. Only being concerned with myself was coming to an end—the same way things had been for Violet when I showed up.

I looked out the window at the streets filled with people and wondered if they were living for the moment or if they had ever felt what I was feeling—that time was too short and life not promised. I had never been so deep in thought and the shit was giving me a headache. I was relieved when the waiter came to take my order. "Give me Southern Comfort and... I'm sorry, a virgin piña colada with extra ice."

I looked up from the menu and I saw them—Charles with Dana. They were holding hands and drinking from the same pineapple-shaped glass. It was no secret that she was his bitch in the utmost respectful way, but he was married. If he was going to flaunt her in public, he could've shown some respect for his new wife. I didn't know Chelsea, and even though I wasn't too fond of her friend, she didn't deserve that shit. I bet she didn't even know he was using her ass. Marriage to him was just an excuse to make himself seem legal.

I *wish* I would've seen Quentin anywhere in the United States with his bitch. I hoped he had enough sense to take them hoes out of the country or anywhere that wasn't in the plain view of so many people who rolled in the same circle. But, I had to remember who I was talking about. Charles didn't give a fuck if he was caught. And Dana wasn't his only one. Big Willie niggas like him could never have *one*. She just happened to be *that* bitch like me, who would always be number one for whatever reason.

In her case, she had helped him get to the top and was getting everything his wife should have had. She had the fuckin' mansion up in Connecticut, a new Benz whenever some new shit hit the dealership, and just ridiculous amounts of money to keep her happy for a long time.

Dana was from Jersey but she had gone to Jewel's once for hair coloring. She was in the chair telling her business like they all did, and she told her she would never marry Charles, and the woman who did was a fool. That was the one thing I remembered about her whenever I saw her. It was like placing a phrase with a face. Her words of wisdom, I knew, came from her own mother who ran with the Big Willies of the 80's when crack had hit the scene. She married Big Mike, Dana's father. They lost everything when the Feds came.

Seeing her made me think about Quentin. I had counted the change he slipped me at the airport and there was about $38,000. I figured that he had to be sitting on at least four mil. Not that I had ever seen him with that much money at one time, but even if the amount was close, it was time for him to pull out and become legal. He had so much potential that it fucked with me sometimes.

"Excuse me," a deep voice said, forcing me to draw my attention from the plate of baked chicken and rice covered in teriyaki sauce.

"Yes," I said, wondering what fragrance department the man attached to the voice had stepped out of.

"Even if it's for a moment, I want to talk to you."

The only people who were known to approach a person like that were the Feds, and I instantly thought they were coming for me to get to Q. I set my fork on my plate and tried to figure him out. He was dressed in a black T-shirt that hugged his muscles just enough, Diesel jeans, a black Kangol hat and he stood about 6'4."

"It depends…. If you're the police, keep on walkin' 'cause I don't know shit."

He laughed real deep and I saw the small bulge in his neck move. "If I had that authority, I would've locked you up a long time ago."

I realized that he was a lot older than most of the twenty-something's running around South Beach that weekend. He wore a neat-shaven beard and his eyes were full of experience. My pregnancy had me wanting sex more often, but for him, it was a different kind of attraction, one void of a need for a fleeing one-night stand.

"A long time ago? Do I know you?"

"I feel like I do. I saw you earlier in the lobby. The ah, lady that embraced you seemed so compelled to you. I felt the same way when I saw you get off the elevator earlier today and when I saw you again…"

"Oh, so you're a stalker too?"

"Nah, I was just sitting here deep in thought and you appeared again. I couldn't let you slip away. You do that to people all the time?"

"Do what?"

"Have that effect on them like you did with the young lady earlier."

"You don't even know the half. She just came from nowhere, so unexpected. Never mind, you wouldn't understand," I said, feeling uncomfortable because I was telling my business to a complete stranger.

"No, please continue," he said and touched my arm softly.

"Well, she was friends with the only person I called family and it was kind of overwhelming to meet somebody…"

"Who had ties to someone so dear to you," he said, finishing my thought. Damn, he was eloquent.

"Exactly."

"You mind?" he asked, pointing to the empty chair across from me.

"Go ahead," I said, noticing the strength in his arms and hands with every movement he made.

I don't know what it was about him that had me feeling open. He wasn't even my type of man, that thug, pants saggin' kind who used the word *nigga* like it was *supposed* to be in all his sentences.

"What's this all about?" he asked, holding my left wrist where a purple and pink tattoo that had to be colored every three months, connected into a bracelet.

"That's a part of my memory. You know, to the person I was telling you about."

"Really? So violets was their favorite flower?"

"No, her name."

He saw that I wanted to change the subject and looked out the window. "So many Black voices gone unheard," he said to himself more than to me.

"Excuse me," I said, looking to see what he was talking about.

"Oh, I apologize. I'm going into my own world of trying to save my brothers and sisters."

"What are you, a raise-ya-fist activist?"

"So I've been told," he said and studied the expression on my face. "I'm sorry. I'm not tryna mess up the whole excitement theme goin' on down here, but the sistas," he said, shaking his head, "lack so much respect for themselves. And the brothers don't help. They disrespect them and call it love."

He had definitely fucked up my mood. If I wanted to hear some empowerment shit I could make a visit to Lexington Market when I got back to Baltimore and listen to one of the Muslim brothers shout their messages over the loud speakers.

"If that bothers you so much why are you even here?" I asked.

"With you or here in South Beach?"

*So he was being cute.* "Both," I said, contemplating how he would react if I told him I had lived most of my earlier years doing a lot of the things he was so against.

"I'm here doing research on the Black male and female relationship."

"And you chose South Beach as your place to study?" I asked. "There are no real relationships here. Everybody is here to get sucked or fucked."

"My point exactly. I need to know why, and how is it that they can give so much of themselves to these brothers who are as lost as them."

"You don't need to do research to understand that. Everything is about dough here."

"So, it's a cash attraction before anything else?" he asked, making me forget what I was going to say next.

"Well, yeah. What did you think it was about, *love*?"

"Not initially, but isn't that supposed to come as the relationship progresses?"

I laughed again. "What time period are you from? It's 2001, and love is the last thing on a person's mind when gettin' paid is the issue at hand."

"And what about you, sis?" His voice had probably fucked up the minds of so many women.

"What about me? I'm here to have fun and you aren't helping."

"I didn't mean to get all serious on you. I just wanted to hear what was on your mind."

"What are you, a writer, teacher or somethin'?"

"Both."

"You never told me your name. I wouldn't mind reading this book."

"It's Kahlil."

"Oh, like Kahlil Gibran and *The Prophet*?"

"*You read that?*" he asked like I was one of the lost souls he had preached about earlier.

"Now I'm ready for you to get up." *Was he amazed that I knew how to read or some shit?*

"Why, did I offend you?"

"*Hell yeah!* You sound surprised that I'm able to pick anything up besides *Don Diva* magazine. And you're sittin' here probably assuming so many things about me. Shit, I'm probably part of ya little study."

"Before I tell you what's on my mind, what's your name?"

"Vita," I said, picking up my fork to finish the food that was barely warm. I was ready for this conversation to be over.

"Vita, I won't lie to you. The first time I saw you I wondered what would bring a young, pregnant woman down here to engage in the things that take place. But the longer I watched you, your mannerisms, your spirit, I really wanted to know you. I found you... breathtaking. And to answer your question, I never assume anything before I know what's up, the facts. Frankly, I find you to be very intelligent. I wanted to know your story, but not for a book. For me to be able to say I knew her, I knew a part of her. You don't ever feel that way about somebody you pass on the streets or see at a store?"

"No, I don't think I have," I said. He was intriguing and I felt more than flattered. In that moment I felt... sexy.

I would have never expected Kahlil to be a writer or professor of Sociology, but he did remind me of a young Malcolm X in the making. We sat there until the bar shut down and discussed books that I had never admitted to reading to anyone else and talked about the wild and romantic experiences he had had with women.

It was the first time that someone of his stature had approached me that way. I don't know if it was the linen dress and the fact that I had on clothes for a change, but he was on another level. I was feeling the mental masturbation, and pretended to be someone else. Taking my clothes off every night required me to be somewhat of an actress on stage but this was different. In pretending, I was actually revealing a part of myself I was forced to ignore if I were to survive in the world I lived in.

His thirty-three old mind was taking me to the places I had only read about when I was eight and trying to run from the world. He made me feel like there was more to me than a stripper with a pretty face. But deep down I always knew that.

I told him everything that I had kept bottled inside for so long. The emptiness I felt everyday when I thought about my life and never knowing a family besides the few friends I had met since Violet, the degrading things I had done while dancing that I had never even mentioned to Quentin. Kahlil was like this protective, trusting figure, and I knew I wouldn't see him again.

And as refreshing as our conversation had been, my mood saddened when I knew it was coming to an end. I had cried and laughed in the same breath. *What kind of conversations would I have with Quentin when I returned home?* I would just have to turn my hustler dick into new, intellectual dick.

"Vita, you stupid," I told myself.

My private joke made me feel a little better while I watched Kahlil leave to catch his flight. He said he was going back to Philly to start a new section in his book, and though he wouldn't admit it, I think my story was enough to leave him locked in a room for months.

I sat there another thirty minutes after he had left and reflected on the things we talked about. I had never allowed my mind to leave the confinements of gettin' money. *What else was there to life?* It was too late to become another person. My life had been mapped out for me.

"I told you I was gon' make his ass pay," Marisa said, breaking me out of the daze by waving her wrist in front of my face.

"Let me check it out." I now knew the meaning of *blinding ice*. "Yeah, this is definitely worth ninety-four G's," I said, walking towards the elevator.

"A hundred after taxes," she corrected me. "V, I *know* you aren't goin' to bed. Shit is just poppin' off. Plus, I wanted you to meet Syreeta and Shani. Everybody is partyin' at *Level* tonight."

"I don't know. I'm not really feelin' the club scene right now."

"Why, because you got dick on your mind?" she joked. She must've peeped me in the corner with Kahlil. "You look like you just lost ya best friend. And I'm here so that can't be it."

I laughed. "Nah, just tired."

"Aight, we won't stay long. Plus, Bugs don't know I know, but his wife s'posed to be up in there. You know a bitch always gotta check out the competition."

"Yeah, I know 'bout that. Security tight?" I asked, remembering that I had left my fake ID behind.

"Why? You got ya ID right?" she asked.

"Umm, yeah but not my fake one."

Marisa raised her eyebrow slightly and I realized that I had never mentioned my age to her. "V, how old are you?"

"Twenty," I said without blinking.

"Get da fuck outta here. So that means in '97 you were... Sixteen!" she said after she did the math. I still didn't respond. "You a grown-ass for real. Fuck it, we rollin' VIP anyway."

I laughed at Marisa's reaction to her new discovery. Walking out the hotel onto Ocean Drive to wait for our car service I could still feel her looking at me. "Chill girl, it's the titties that get everybody," I said.

We laughed again and followed the rest of the crowd who obviously had no intentions on clubbing anywhere else besides *Level*. Once in VIP Marisa introduced me to the twins. Syreeta and Shani were the two girls who had carried out the shit with KC. They were two motorcycle freaks whose only request from Marisa were two new BMW bikes that would make them the envy of other bike riders. The only thing that gave them a rush more than riding at 120 mph was toting and shooting guns.

The atmosphere in the club was live. The DJ was giving the crowd what they came for. Even the southern booty-bouncin' shit was off the hook. We sat in one of the VIP sections and I looked at the twins' faces that were the same diamond shape with widow's peaks. While everybody else was dressed in bikini tops and hot pants, they wore tight-fitting leather. I wanted to remind them that we were in hot-ass Florida.

"What's her face," Shani said, "was scared as hell when she realized we were coming for her."

"Who, KC?" I asked, anxious to know how things went down.

"Yeah, her and her girlfriend."

"Girlfriend?" I asked.

"Yeah, she leaped over the steps like she was used to it."

"And what about KC, what happened with her?"

"I think we got her in the arm."

"You *think*?"

"Yeah. We don't look at the results. Whateva happens afterward is *whateva*."

I looked around and wondered where Marisa had stepped off too. I wanted to use her phone to call KC just to make sure she was still alive. I didn't want to talk. I just needed to hear her voice.

Everybody was singing the hook to the Mary J. Blige and Jadakiss remake of the Soul II Soul classic when I caught up with Marisa. I had paged her with a, *Where are you* in her two-way and waited for mine to go off with a reply, but it never came. "Didn't you get my page?" I asked her.

"Nah, it's on silent," she said after checking her screen.

The bass from the speakers were making me queasy and there was something else going on that didn't feel right. "You ready?" I asked.

"V, we ain't been here a hour. Lil' Quentin bothering you?"

"Yeah, and shit feels a lil' off in here. You don't feel it?"

"Nah," she said, reaching out and squeezing some nigga's ass.

"Aight, well I'ma see you later. Knock when you get in," I said and started walking away.

"V," she said after she caught up with me, "if I didn't tell you, I'm glad ya ass is here. It wouldn't be the same without you."

"I know trick. See you at the room."

I hadn't reached the door when the pushing started. I heard the DJ over the speakers telling the crowd to stay calm, but it was too late. The music had stopped and the bullets were flying.

Chelsea

"No, let's get a hotel," I pleaded with him.

"Bitch, I ask *all* the questions and give *all* the orders and I say we do this shit here like we been doin'," he said, and grabbed me by the hair.

"Okay, but just not in my bedroom."

He laughed and shoved me inside of the room anyway.

It was a Tuesday night, and like clockwork for the last two months, Smalls had come by and raped me repeatedly until he got tired. He knew that Charles left every Monday for Connecticut and returned on Wednesday, but it was like he wanted him to catch us. A few times he had purposely stopped by on Wednesday, and when Charles came through the door, pretended like he was waiting for him to come home.

The very first time we were together he had called the house knowing I was there alone. "You by yourself?" he asked when I picked up the phone. I didn't say anything because I knew it was him, and wasn't looking forward to whatever he had planned. "Yeah, you there," he said before hanging up.

Minutes later he was knocking at the door. I tried to ignore it, but he started ringing the bell until I had no choice but answer it. "What the fuck took you so long?" he asked, pushing me aside and walking to the kitchen where he opened the fridge and helped himself to a sandwich.

I sat on the couch not knowing what to say. Before I came to the door I had tried to make myself as unattractive as possible. I tied a scarf around my flip style and threw on some sweat pants and footies. I didn't feel cute, but he thought otherwise.

"Oh yeah, you look real good."

"Can we get this over with?" I asked, ready for him to leave as quickly as he had come.

"*Oh*, don't rush me. You'll know when it's over," he said, plopping down next to me.

He turned on a sports channel and started watching basketball like I wasn't even there. Thirty minutes of listening to him yelling at the screen past and I was ready to get it over with. I got up, but he pulled me by the wrist back down to the couch. "Oh, I see, you ready for big daddy now, huh?"

The smile that I had always thought to be so warm had turned into one filled with deceit and nastiness. He cut the TV off and stood in front of me. He dropped his jeans and a black dick that looked like a big, burnt sausage was almost hitting me in the eye.

"Go ahead, I see your eyes. Taste it."

I had just learned how to give good head with Charles and Smalls was getting ready to force me to do something I had never enjoyed before my husband. I leaned into him and gagged as soon as I felt it hit the back of my throat.

"I can't, it's too much," I said, hoping he would change his mind.

"You a fuckin' lie. I know my man wouldn't spend all this time chasin' a bitch wit' trashy head. Do that shit before I show you the right way."

I hesitated again and after getting the same result, he grabbed the back of my neck and forced it inside until I didn't have a choice. And while he moaned with pleasure, the tears fell from the reoccurring need to throw up and the sensation of lips that had become dry and cracked.

After an eternity of gag reflex I felt his lower body jerk and tried to pull away. He took his hand that was supported by the arm of the couch and grabbed my head with both of his hands so that I wouldn't miss his ejaculation. I tasted him and threw up all over the floor.

"You think that throwing up shit is gon' get you out of gettin' fucked? I'm glad you think so," he said and lifted me from my knees onto the couch.

I closed my eyes and started counting. I thought he would enter me from behind, but he spread my butt cheeks and searched until he found my rectum. I screamed as I felt him tear away my skin and tried to muffle my cries into one of the pillows. When he was finished, I laid there, not wanting to see his face or the satisfaction he had gotten from bringing me so much pain.

"Same time next week," he said before leaving.

I only remember being too sore to get up, and if I did, it was the next day. My muscles hadn't ached that much since the days of me running ten miles at some track meet. And even then, it didn't hurt as much. The smell of my own vomit made me remember what had happened and I ran to the sink to continue throwing up.

I was finally able to sit on the toilet and it felt like I was removing splinters. Charles came home that evening and wanted sex. I couldn't tell him that every hole on my body was ripped, so I blamed it on my period.

Smalls would always leave his mark in the worst kind of way. Once, he covered most of my visible body parts with hickeys and I had to tell Charles that it was a breakout from some peaches I had eaten. I was tired of lying to him and lying on my back. If it wasn't for Smalls it was for Charles who I only got to see two days out the week if I was lucky.

I already knew about Dana, but I had learned about another girl a month after the party in New York. She lived right in Philly. Coming from the dentist in Center City, I took a back street to avoid all the traffic on City Line Ave. I saw his car first and as I turned the corner I almost missed him. I looked into my mirror and he was standing in the doorway kissing her neck and reaching into her robe.

# Tiffany A. Womble

I pulled into a gas station and cried until there were no more tears. I drove home slowly, feeling like *I* was the *other* woman. He had told me he was out of town, but he was really there in Philly, right under my nose. But him whoring around was minor compared to the things I learned two weeks later.

It was three in the morning and I was just getting to sleep when the door opened. I heard Smalls' voice first and then Charles', who sounded like he had been drinking. The other two guys, I assumed, were Bishop and Flipper. I had met those two on my trip with Charles to one of his barbershops.

They were in the backroom counting money. Charles tapped on the door. I could tell he didn't want me to know what was going on, because he let them finish up before I went in. But it was too late. I had seen the drugs and money machines and already knew what was up. He hadn't taken me to the shop since.

I heard the TV come on in the living room and figured that Charles thought I was in Baltimore. But I had changed my mind. My Porsche wasn't in the driveway because I had dropped it off at the detailer earlier so he could change the color to forest green. It was different, but pink was beginning to make me sick.

"Yo, you got the new Scarface DVD?" Smalls asked Charles.

He disgusted me. He was just at the house the other day looking through our collection like he had invested in it himself.

"That's Chelz's shit. She got it."

"Oh, word!" Bishop said. "Wifey fucks wit' da face?"

"It's like he's fam to her or some shit. Every time I come in she be watchin' the shit like she analyzin'," Charles said.

"You 'bout to put her down?" Flipper asked.

"Neva that," Charles said, like he thought the idea was ludicrous. "I got Dana for that."

I eased out the bed and tiptoed to the step to hear them better. I listened to the refrigerator door open and knew it was Smalls' chunky ass feeding his mouth.

"You know they say the quiet girls the ones who carry their shit better than the niggas in the game sometime," Flipper, said, taking up for me.

"Doubt it!" Charles and Smalls said in unison.

"She know 'bout her?" Bishop asked, referring to Dana.

"And if she do! A nigga gon' do what he been doin'."

"Playas forever!" Smalls chimed in.

I couldn't believe that he was outright disrespecting me in front of his closest friends and making me seem so gullible at the same time.

"So, you sayin' you would never put ya own wife down?" Bishop asked him.

"Hell nah! Chelz? Man she don't have the heart for this. Her favorite fuckin' color is pink. That ain't gangster. Now Dana.... You know she gon' be a ride or die bitch 'til the end. Chelz.... You get the picture."

"Where is she?" Smalls asked in that grimy voice of his.

"Went home to visit her girls."

210

"Those freak bitches," Smalls said, like he knew my friends personally.

"I know, right?" Charles said, agreeing with him.

Now I was curious to know what he thought about *me*. Was I just his home bitch, the one he knew would take care of his bills and keep the house tidy?

"So back to business," Bishop said. "What you gon' do about ol' boy Q?"

My ears perked up when I heard Quentin mentioned. I had found out that Charles put Quentin down with a few connects in Philly two years ago, but that was as far as he went concerning the connection. I bet Dana knew more about it than I did.

"I'ma handle mine. He been tryna step on toes for a minute. How fuckin' stupid to try and move China. That shit don't do what it's s'posed to on the streets no more," Charles said.

"And I heard that side bitch of his was helpin' him move that shit," Bishop said.

"Who Vita?" Charles asked.

"Nah, ya girl's friend. The one that sang at ya wedding wit' the big titties."

"Hell yeah they big," Smalls said. "I was tryna holla at baby, but she was trippin' and shit like her pussy was made out of gold."

"Chanel?" Charles said.

"Yeah!" Bishop said like they were playing a guessing game.

"She gon' get hers too. A bullet don't have no name," Charles said.

My heart started beating out of control, the way it did when someone confronted me about fighting after school. I wanted to run to the phone and warn her. I felt trapped. I didn't know *who* I was living with. He was a stranger. And I knew that I couldn't call what we had love. Any time he could tell his boys that he had no problem taking out my best friend. It was frightening.

"So who you gon' get to do the shit?" Smalls asked.

"Won't you do it nigga! You got all the mutherfuckin' questions," Charles said.

"Nigga, I handle mine. Just tell me when."

I was so tired of his bravado. All he did was run his mouth, and it was making me sick to my stomach.

"Aight, we gon' see. The last fuckin' time you used ya nine was, let's see…"

"Fuckin' never," Flipper said.

"Yeah, aight," Smalls said like his ego was bruised.

"What you 'bout to get into?" Bishop asked Charles.

"After I give you the shit, goin' to Morgan's house. Shit, Chelsea ain't here, and that's the newest pussy I got."

"I hear that," Bishop said.

"That's who you should've married," Smalls said. "She real wholesome."

Charles laughed real loud. "Yo, I know I'm drunk 'cause ya ass need to get smacked for that dumb shit."

"Nah, because you know I ain't lyin'."

"Shit, I asked Morgan, but she was tellin' me she couldn't marry me 'cause she had to finish school and shit. What the fuck! I told her I would buy her pretty ass a school."

I heard them all laughing and walking downstairs to get whatever he had to give them. I sat at the top of the stairs feeling like I was at my lowest. I knew then that I had to do something about my situation. My marriage was a joke after only four months, so there was no use in trying to hold onto it. But I *was* going to hold on to the title of wifey. It would be important for whatever I planned.

I had never gone snooping but there couldn't have been a better time to do it. I prayed that Charles wouldn't come back upstairs for anything, because I didn't want him to know that I was home or had heard anything. I heard the TV being turned off and listened for the front door to close. Minutes later I heard three cars start up and pull off. I slid to the side of the window and moved the blinds back to make sure his car was gone.

As long as I had been in the house I never went downstairs unless I was washing clothes. Once I thought I had heard him on the phone, but I didn't know where the sound was coming from. I figured that he was probably upstairs and I was hearing him through the vents. I was still tiptoeing through the basement like it wasn't my house when I saw the door that looked like it was a part of the wall. I wondered when Charles had had it done, but remembered that he had lived there before me. I pushed on the space but nothing happened. I laid my back against it and found I was in some secret room. It was like the antique revolving doors I had only seen in black and white horror movies. It was dark and I was afraid of what I would see when I found a light.

I felt both of the nearest walls, but they were blank. It was like a game of Blind Man Bluff as I slowly walked across the plush carpet. I hit my knee on what felt like a glass table and my hand touched the shade of a lamp. I pulled down on the switch, and like I suspected, I was in his hidden office. The glass I had felt was a huge desk with a phone and a large chair. There was a matching table in the middle of the floor that had six seats with glass legs, and that was it. I wondered what was so special about a room with no furniture.

There were file boxes to the right and I started from the top. I opened the first folder and there was journal tape with dates and large amounts totaling $600,000 and higher. The dates went back to 1995. I was only fourteen then. The second drawer had more folders with names on the front. My mouth hung open as I read the names— Dana, China, Mona, Talia, Morgan, and finally, Chelsea. My hands started shaking as I set the others on the desk and opened mine.

Inside were receipts but not the regular kind for miscellaneous items like clothes and shoes. He had papers for my two cars, my wedding dress and ring. I braced myself and opened the one with Dana's name. Hers was thicker and I was ready to knock the desk over when I saw a deed to an estate in Connecticut, numerous titles to expensive cars and jewelry. The deed to the house, excuse me, her estate, dated to 1998 and was worth 1.2 million fuckin' dollars.

The other folders all held deeds to houses in Jersey, New Rochelle, and Philly. I did some quick math and everything had to be worth two million, and who knew how much money he was giving them when he made his *trips*. I sat there and searched for some kind of answers. I didn't know what to do with the information I had found. It was just too much. Maybe things would be okay if I was the one coming out on top, but it wasn't that way, and I was his wife.

There was another drawer and I almost didn't want to see what was there. I took a deep breath and inside of the last couple of folders were court papers to trials where he had been tried for counts of attempted murder and conspiracy to distribute cocaine. I wasn't surprised at his criminal background, but I was curious about who had represented him in court. I was sure that he had given them tons of money for getting him off. As I was thinking that, a business card fell out with Attorney Bloomberg printed in gold lettering. I put all his papers away and slipped the card into the pocket of my robe.

Before I left, I saw another spot in the wall. But when I turned it around it stopped halfway so I had to reach in and feel what was there. I felt paper and knew it was money. Behind that were cold pieces of metal and I didn't have to feel for a handle to know they were guns.

Back upstairs, I cut on the DVD player and watched *Scarface* a second time that day. But my focus wasn't on the story like it usually was. It was like a second voice to remind me I wasn't alone. The one thing I did pay close attention to was Montana's ease with a gun. *Was I capable of taking a life?* Charles sure didn't think so. He didn't even think I could handle the everyday shit he did for a living.

I couldn't believe how stupid I was. I thought I would live the perfect life, but I was fooling myself. He didn't care about me. He was making plans to kill my friend. I looked at the clock on the wall and watched the long hand go around until the sun was coming through the windows. I got up from the couch to finally get some sleep, but it was impossible. I had become a new person and the new Chelsea was putting away the pink dress forever.

Smalls pushed me on the bed, but I didn't put up a fight like I had done the other times when he insisted on fucking me in my own bed. I took a good look at his face and smiled at the thought of him with a gun in his mouth.

"What you smilin' for?" he asked. "You finally ready to take the dick like a big girl?"

"Yeah, I am, but I want to give it to you in another way. You remember my friend Chanel?"

His eyes got wide and he started rubbing his dick. "Yeah. And?"

"Well I told her about us. She said she didn't know why I was complainin' since Charles wasn't packin' like you."

"True," he said, like I was telling him what he had been waiting to hear.

"And she tryna be wit' you too… Tonight."

"Tonight?'

"Yeah, tonight," I said seductively. "I mean I'm tryna fuck you now, but she wants to be wit' you too so if you want me to tell her ya hands are tied that's fine. We can all do it another time. I want to experience you now without all the fussin' and shit anyway."

"Damn girl, you off da hook tonight. All of us?" he asked, like he wasn't hearing me right.

"Yeah," I said, reaching for the phone and pretending to call her.

"Who you callin'?"

"I'm calling her to tell her we gotta do it another time."

"Nah, don't do that shit. Where she at?"

"The *Marriott*. You know about that right?"

He laughed. "Hell yeah."

"But I gotta tell you, even though she's into ménage, she don't fuck for free."

"None of y'all hoes do."

"So, you got somethin' for her?"

"Yeah, I got somethin' for her aight."

I could read his mind and I knew he had no intentions of giving up anything, money especially. He thought that any female should be proud to experience the shit between his legs.

I thought he would have a problem with me driving his brand new Q45, but he insisted. "All my hoes drive me around," was his response.

Before I got behind the wheel I checked my bag to make sure everything was there. "You like honey don't you?" I asked and held up the honey bear-shaped container.

"No doubt. What the fuck happened to you? You hit ya head or somethin'?"

"Why you say that?" I asked and started up the car.

"'Cause you on that shit that I like now. Showin' me the freak I knew you were."

I didn't say another word until we were halfway to the hotel. I pulled over and reached into my bag.

"Why we stop? We got another fifteen before we get there."

"I know, this is the part where I make shit exciting. Turn around so I can blindfold you."

"Fuck no! I need to be lookin' at my surroundings. A mutherfucker can never be too safe."

I expected him to protest, but I was ready for him. "Chill for once. This is all a part of the shit that's goin' down tonight. I call it the freak show. We've done it plenty of times before," I said and looked him directly in the eyes to show him I was serious.

"Damn, you look like a different person. I never paid attention to ya eyes, but damn, do you have to look at me like that? It's bad enough they look like cat's eyes and shit."

"Just turn around," I said and forced his head towards the window.

I waved my hand in front of his face to make sure he couldn't see and pulled off. I wasn't having second thoughts, but I wanted to know why he had treated me so badly. "Can I ask you somethin'?"

"Shoot," he said.

I laughed at his choice of words. "What would you have done if I refused to give in to you. You know, when you told me you knew about Malik."

"What, if you said I couldn't fuck you?"

I shook my head at his uncaring heart. "Yeah."

"I knew you was gon' do the shit. You didn't want to give up the lavish life. I figured ya ass out before I met you when Charles told me Marco's freak ass knew you. Any bitch that knows him got to be doin' some nasty shit for him. Charles figured that shit too, but still thought you might be a virgin, 'cause he know Marco ain't want sex. The only thing that gets that nigga off is pretty feet and enough coke to support that habit."

"So he bought a lot of drugs from y'all?"

"Shiit, that nigga was on a thousand-dollar a day habit."

Smalls was doing better than I thought he would. I didn't think he would offer that much information, but that was all I needed to hear. There were no more rules to life anymore—not his anyway. We were almost there and my nervousness was being outweighed by anxiety. I looked at the clock and it was 3:13. How lucky, I thought. I pulled into an abandoned lot that had been a warehouse at one time and drove until I saw the empty garage I had searched for all week.

"When I was in high school one of my favorite classes was anatomy," I said, and reached into my bag for the .38.

"Oh, I get it. This is a part of the freak show. That anatomy shit got a lot to do wit' my body and what y'all 'bout to do, right?"

"Right," I said and drove into one of the compartments that was used for storage before it became abandoned property. "Well, my favorite instrument was the scalpel."

"Never mind. I don't want to hear that shit. All I can see is my dick on the side of a road."

"You are so full of predictions tonight," I whispered and turned off the car with my left hand.

"We here?" he asked and felt the door for the handle. "Can I take this off or you guidin' me?"

"You can take it off," I said and held the gun near his cheek.

I wish I could've captured the expression on his face with a camera. It was a cross between constipation and fake toughness. "What the fuck, where are we?" he asked and looked at the brick wall in front of him.

"In hell. That's where you want to be right?"

"What are you talking about? This shit is a joke, right?"

"Oh yeah, I got the jokes Smalls," I said and gripped the gun in case he tried to knock it from my hand. "Shit was a joke when you tore my rectum or how 'bout when you bit on my clit. That shit was real funny." I waited for him to say something, but all I got was heavy breathing. "Oh, you a fuckin' asthmatic now? Now *that shit* is funny. Ya fat ass wasn't breathing heavy when you pinned me down and shoved ya nasty dick into my mouth, were you?"

He caught his breath long enough to talk. "You liked that shit. Ain't no nigga ever handled ya ass like that, and you loved it. Go 'head tell me. I wanna hear that shit before you do this. You probably can't even do the shit, can you? Scared to take this dick and scared to pull the trigger. Do it, what's stoppin' you," he kept repeating.

I wasn't slow. I knew he was using his words to buy him time, but he wasn't fast enough. While he reached under the seat, I looked him in the eyes and pulled the trigger. I watched the blood trickle down the window and looked at his mouth hanging open. It was the way I wanted it to be.

I reached into my bag and got my gloves and the scalpel. I avoided looking at his face and unzipped his pants. I couldn't believe it. The nigga was dead and still had a hard dick.

"This is what got you in trouble," I said and made one incision.

Blood gushed down the seat like water and I quickly stuffed his manhood into his mouth. I took the honey bottle off the seat and opened the tip. Inside was gasoline. I poured every drop into his mouth. After I wiped the steering wheel and door, I took the gloves off and grabbed my bag. I struck a match and threw it at his face. Him and his car would be nothing but burnt metal by the time the fire trucks came.

I ran towards my car that was parked behind a dilapidated dumpster. I had paid the detailer an extra $1,500 to bring it to the exact spot and told him he never saw me. I almost missed it since it was such a dark green. He had even cleaned the carpets and hung my favorite *Morning Fresh* Car-Freshener on the mirror. Now that was how service was supposed to be. Barely slamming the door, I put the car in third gear and tried to make it home before the sun came up.

Driving into my suburban neighborhood, I noticed the X5 and wondered who had stopped by so late. It was almost five and the birds were beginning their morning calls. Instead of pulling into the garage behind the truck, I parked in front of the house and waited to see if anyone was inside. Five minutes went by and the door opened.

I squinted to be sure it was Nikola and couldn't understand why she was in Philly. She motioned for me to get out and I turned off the car. I walked across the damp grass and stopped when I saw Chanel come behind her. She looked like hell. I thought about Quentin and hoped nothing had happened.

"It took you long enough," Nikola spoke first.

"I had to go to Kinko's," I said. "What's wrong with her?"

"Open the door first," Nikola said, reminding me of the same Kola who always had to be in control.

I opened the door and got a chance to look at my reflection in the mirror. I was glad they hadn't seen my face in the light. There were small drops of blood on my cheeks. I left the two of them in the foyer and ran upstairs to change.

In the bathroom I turned on the shower and got in without checking the temperature. "Shit!" I screamed when I felt the scalding water. Since my new transformation I had never cursed this much in my life. I'd always considered it *improper*. Ha!

After I adjusted the water, I looked at my hands and couldn't believe I had done it. I felt the skin on my face and remembered the look on Smalls' before I lit the match. The only thing separating life from death was a beating heart and I decided then that his would cease. He was better off dead.

Downstairs, Nikola was pacing the kitchen floor and Chanel was rocking back and forth in one of the armchairs.

"What happened?" I asked Nikola.

"Well, I'm glad you could join us. Kinko's my ass," she said.

"Look, I don't have time for that shit. That's where I said I was, and I'm not explainin' shit to you."

Chanel stopped moving and looked at me. "I killed him Chelz, I did it."

I walked over and sat in front of her on the floor. "Killed who, Quentin?"

"She just should have. He almost had *her* killed," Nikola said.

"Wait, back up. Who are you talking about?" I asked.

I jumped when I heard the phone ringing and watched Nikola race for her purse. While she answered it, Chanel told me what happened. I wondered why I wasn't feeling like her. She was really messed up. When I looked at her stomach, I realized I hadn't seen her since she was three months. Maybe her pregnancy made her more emotional.

"Chanel you gotta calm down and understand that I know how you feel right now."

"How you know Chelz? You probably ain't never even seen a gun."

"Don't assume shit!" I screamed. She looked like I had scared her so I changed my tone. "I'm sorry, but don't do that. We haven't really talked in two months so you don't know what I've seen. Things have changed, but I'm gon' tell you like I had to tell myself. Things are going to be okay. You didn't mean it did you?"

She shook her head no and started crying. "I had to or he was gon' take me away."

"Right. You didn't mean it, but you had to. Think about the outcome of things if you hadn't done it. He would've taken you away and what about your baby? Would you have wanted that?"

"No," she whispered.

"So chalk that shit up. It could've been worst. I know what I'm saying is probably sounding like nonsense, but you gotta know that *I know* what you're feeling, and it's going to work out. You believe me?"

She looked at me the same way Smalls had done in the car, like she was seeing me for the first time. "I believe you."

Nikola put her phone away and walked into the living room. "Everything is cool. Remember I told you about the person I know on the inside? Well, she took care of it. You want me to run your bath?"

"No, I'm cool," Chanel said, starting to sound like herself again.

I watched her get up from the chair and go upstairs. "You can get in my bed or sleep in one of the extra bedrooms," I told her.

She stopped at the top of the stairs and I watched her shoulders drop. "Thank you," she said and disappeared.

I turned on the radio to one of the jazz stations and propped my feet on the ottoman where the anniversary wine from Italy had been chilling since I left. It was Wednesday and I was glad Charles wouldn't be coming home. I probably wouldn't see him again until he felt like he needed to update his records or started wondering why he hadn't heard from Smalls—whichever came first.

"What's wrong wit' you?" Nikola asked.

"Why do you ask me that?" I asked, popping the cork off the bottle.

"You seem different. What, you tanning your skin now?"

"Sometimes. Have some wine," I offered.

"Nah, no thanks. And your hair, since when you start wearin' it like that?"

"Just started."

"Why the fuck you can't give me a real answer? *Sometimes, just started.* What's wrong wit' you?"

"I'm fine," I said, inhaling the sweet aroma leaving the goblet.

"No, ya ass has changed, that's what."

"Change is good, *very good.*"

218

Chanel

It seems like so much time has passed since that night when everything went wrong in my life. I got home and Quentin asked for the suitcases back without even glancing at me. I knew then that it was time to live for me. I was always told that therapy was for the mentally ill, but if I didn't fit that description, I don't know what I could've been classified as. My hair was falling out, and by my eighth month, I had lost fifteen pounds. The only thing that made me walk into the therapist's office was Dr. Desai's serious admonishment that I would lose my baby if I didn't get help.

Things were clearer after my fourth visit with Dr. Dixie. I found out that a lot of my unhappiness came from my refusal to open up. I had never talked to anyone about my issues with my mother, and a missing father certainly added to the feelings I had bottled up.

I never brought up the murder, though. I would call Chelsea at two and three in the morning when I had a nightmare or thoughts about what I had done. It was so crazy how she always knew what to say. Once, I had toyed with the thought of her experiencing the same thing, but erased it after remembering her fear of anything with more than two legs. Sure, marrying Charles had changed her, but not to the extent of having to kill someone.

We had all changed. Nikola had finally smartened up enough to save some of that money and open her first salon in the area where her mother and me lived. She said she would be opening a second one in Philly at the beginning of the New Year, but was too busy taking classes to brush up on her skills. I could tell that she felt responsible for a lot of the things that had gone wrong with our little pact, but therapy taught me to tell her that life leaves us no regrets, only lessons learned.

As for me, therapy isn't needed any longer, now that I have Minyah. I thought it fit her perfectly, and because I want her to have her own identity, she only has one name. She looks like a Black China doll. There's no denying her father's genes, but that's another story. Ironically, she arrived on his birthday. I hoped that him turning thirty would make him more of a man.

Her clear gray-green eyes were wide open when she entered the world at 11:30pm. They reminded me so much of Petey's that I got chills. I kissed her eyelashes and hoped she wouldn't want to run the streets like her mother. The day I was supposed to leave the hospital I had a few visits. Besides Nikola and Chelsea, who were lugging gifts through the door, my mother brought one of her own.

I forgot about the stitching and hollered when I saw Rico behind her. He was all buff from working out during his bid in the Pen and looked older than twenty-five. He sat on the edge of the bed and cradled Minyah like a delicate piece of art and kept telling me how beautiful she was. I was glad she would have him around since it didn't look like Quentin would be more than a piggy bank.

Aside from therapy, the most important lesson learned was the one I got from experience. I had taught myself to let go, and that's what I had to do with him. If I ever forgot about how wrong Quentin had done me, all I had to do was think about the day Minyah was born.

After waking up from my nap, the nurse told me I could see her in the nursery. I got to the room and there was someone else on duty. She asked me for a last name and I had to give her *Marcial*, Quentin's name. Her face got sad and she told me that I could come with her through the neonatal unit. I just knew I had seen Minyah, but I followed her anyway. She made me cover my face and wash my hands. When I saw the baby that she thought was mine, I stood there and cried.

Inside of the incubator was a little boy no bigger than my hand, with tubes prodding his mouth and nose. She told me that it was okay if I touched him since preemies needed more contact for better development. Opening the small door, his little body jumped and he flinched as I touched his leg.

I blew him a kiss and left the room in disbelief. I had read his bracelet and his mother's name was Elvita. How ironic. I asked the receptionist if all the new mothers were on the same floor and she nodded her head. I started walking in the opposite direction of the unit and stopped at one of the rooms when I saw Quentin. He was leaned over Vita, who had her back to the door. I tried to listen to what he was telling her, but all I could make out was the word *love* and him crying.

At first I felt on the verge of breaking down because he had never let the word leave his mouth in reference to me but I quickly remembered how healthy Minyah was. And it was okay if he didn't realize the gem he had, because her mother did. Back in my room, with her attached to my breast and her small hand cupped in mine, I contemplated our existence. An end and a beginning are constants, but death would always be replaced with new life, and as long as I had her in mine, I would forever have sunshine.

Vita

Marisa's death broke me down. I had escaped the Reaper by a few moments and still wasn't sure if it was coming for me any time soon. It seemed like death was always around me, and the only one who had survived was Quentin. But my dreams were telling me that his wasn't far behind either.

After I came back from South Beach I was more than willing to go on bed rest. If I had the choice I would've slept until I never woke up. Since Quentin was so busy worrying over me, his money was funny. He told me things were going to be okay and that he was going to be making some new moves, but I figured things hadn't gone right when he started drinking hard liquor. As long as I had known him, he drank water only unless he was at a party or out at dinner.

I felt like I was a burden to him and moved out. That way I knew I could be my own problem. Since I didn't have an appetite I doubled up on my prenatal pills, but they didn't help. I still went into early labor at seven months. My son weighed a little over three pounds.

I didn't like to consider him that since I didn't know if he would survive, and I hesitated even giving him a name. One day when he was having breathing problems, I couldn't take it. I wondered if it was possible for me to feel his pain, and slit my wrists.

Often people say they would never do this or do that, but I knew that shit wasn't real until it hit home. Of course, they saved me before I lost too much blood, but it didn't matter to me. The restraints didn't matter, and if I could have, I would've yanked the tubes that were feeding me.

I was hospitalized for two days before the attendants notified Quentin. He was the closest and only relative. I didn't want him to see me at my weakest, but it was all right because I saw in his eyes that he was already there too.

The nurses came everyday and asked if I wanted to see the baby, but I refused. I could tell that seeing him brightened Quentin's life a little, because he would come and tell me about his progress even if he only gained another ounce.

The day after they took me out the restraints I got a chance to look at my wrists. I had to turn my head to keep from crying. I laid my head over the edge of the bed and looked toward the window. I had to blink twice to make sure I wasn't seeing things.

"Violet, is that you?" I asked and lifted my head. The figure moved closer and I tried to prop myself up to get a better look. "Please tell me it's you. I need you right now."

The voice was barely a whisper but I recognized it. *"It's me,"* she said. *"I see you aren't feeling too hot, huh?"*

"No, my arms hurt and most of all my heart. I miss you everyday," I said, letting the tears roll down my cheeks and neck. "Why did you leave me?"

*"I didn't leave,"* she said calmly. *"I'm there with you everyday. You remember when you met Kristen in South Beach? That was me you felt when you sat across from her. I saw you looking around to see if what you were feeling was real. But that was me who touched your hair. I see you've been taking care of it. So nice and healthy... And who was that fine brother you ate dinner with later on that night?"*

I laughed at her observation. "Oh, just this guy who was all in my business."

*"I'm glad you let him in. That was real brave of you. I know your heart is important to you, but he was the real deal. You should get with guys like him more often. He stimulated that sharp mind of yours, didn't he?"*

"Yeah, and I kinda didn't want him to leave."

*"He'll be around. So what's up with this motherhood thing? Your little boy is gorgeous. He got that same honeydew skin, you see it?"*

"Nah, I'm scared to look at him."

*"Why? You scared he'll leave you?"*

I nodded yes since the tears were choking me.

*"Don't be scared to love, Vita. You weren't scared to love me and I'm still here. Maybe not in the way you want, but I'm here."*

"And it hurts so much. I'm so lonely, you know?"

*"I know. But look who you have now. Somebody to give unconditional love. Wouldn't you agree that's the best kind?"*

I nodded again.

*"Vita, I want you to remember that I'm here with you always. I'm not sure when I'll get a chance to talk to you like this again, but I love you. And I want you to love yourself so he'll know how to love. Will you do that for me?"*

"Yes. And Violet I never got to tell you this, but I love you so much. Thank you..."

*"You don't have to thank me. Thank you."*

"And one more thing. You still there?"

*"I'm here."*

"Tell my mother the same thing, okay?"

I waited for her to tell me something else, but she was gone. I sat up and reached out to the spot where she had been standing, but all I saw was a violet sitting on the windowsill. I slowly walked over to the window and held the bright flower in my hand as I watched the sun part the clouds.

I got dressed, walked to the nursery and asked to see my son. The nurse gave me a gown and showed me how to open the door when I was ready to touch him.

I sat in the rocking chair she brought out for me and looked into the small container that would be his bed for the next couple of months.

"Hey, little man. It's me. You are so strong, you know that?"

He moved his back, and I winced. "Don't be scared," the nurse said. "He's just responding to your voice. He knows you're his mommy."

"Your mommy, who would've known?" I looked at his little feet and hands and couldn't wait to kiss them. "I want you to know that I love you and my love will always keep you safe."

I sat there another two hours and then decided that I would go to the bookstore since the nurse said reading to him would improve his development. I wasn't supposed to be leaving the hospital but I wasn't the one to follow anyone's rules but my own.

I hadn't been to a *North Star* bookstore in months and wanted to get a book of baby names. Walking through the aisle, I almost passed by a familiar author. I picked up the thick book and it was Kahlil's self-published book—*Tough Love: The Black Male and Female Relationship*. So he had finished it. I laughed quietly as I thought about our conversation. I opened it to read the first paragraph, but my eyes stopped at the second page: *Dedicated to the woman who helped take me higher when all I had was assumptions... South Beach 2001*

I closed it and smiled wider than I had in months. I kept repeating what he had written and wished he knew that he had been the one who showed *me* that it was safe to fly—even with a broken wing.

Chelz

"Forgive me Father for I have sinned."

"When was your last confession?"

"Tenth grade, when I committed my first murder."

That was my last confession. I admitted to aborting my baby and murdering Smalls. I had asked for forgiveness and repented for wanting to commit the same against Charles, but it didn't help. The evils won over the good and a month later I took Charles to a similar place away from the city. The way I considered him a stranger when I heard him plotting to kill my best friend was the same way he stared at me when I put the barrel down his throat.

I had contacted an outside attorney and asked her about a wife's rights to her husband's property after he was dead. She said that as long as I had a will everything would be mine. I never gave my name, but I thanked her and typed up a will that night. I told Charles that I needed him to sign for some new furniture I wanted. He was still fucked up over Smalls so I knew his mind wasn't really there.

He got mad when I refused to go the funeral. I told him he could take Dana or one of his other whores because I wasn't pretending to like his fat-ass friend. He slapped me but I expected it. It only added to the fire burning inside me.

After Charles was gone, it was on! The best feeling was taking that estate from Dana. I looked her over the same way she had done me the first time I met her. Of course she called me a bunch of bitches, but I laughed. The same way I had done behind my veil at his funeral as all of his *girls* were falling over his body in the casket. They had all threatened to sue me. My response: "I got the papers to take those clothes off ya back."

I didn't expect them to hand over the jewelry, but I didn't want it anyway. The shit was symbolic for them, not me. When everything was auctioned off I would be getting a little over five million, and that wasn't bad at all. Us girls would never have to sell another piece of pussy.

I always wondered how a person's feelings could be so callous, but I realized that it's probably a result of the child's environment. That is, after I found out some things about my own family. I went back home looking for my father's acceptance again. We were sitting in the den again and he was watching his Sunday football.

"Why do you hate me the way you do?" I asked him with tears in my eyes after he had ignored me all day.

"I don't hate you Chelsea. I just don't like some of things I've found out. They've stayed with me and I can't let it go."

"Like what?" I asked and touched his beard where the stubble was growing in.

"Like, I'm not your father Chelsea, that's what."

That was worse than a slap in the face. I went back to Philly feeling like a *fatherless child*. I sat in the middle of the living room and scrolled through Charles' address book in his phone. He had an unknown number tracing to Bolivia and I knew who it was. I had talked to the connect days ago. I waited for the voicemail and left my message in Spanish, "I'm ready to do what we discussed. Let me know when the time is right to make the first trip."

Liquid/ 20

Nikola

So my liquid dreams turned out to be dry nightmares. I never intended for things to play out the way they did. There are times when I wonder how things would've turned out if I had never brought up the conversation that day in my basement. And the only thing that makes things better is knowing we had a chance to leave Baltimore and see what else was out there on our many trips to different parts of the world. Living a life rather than living a slow death through working. That was the one thing money couldn't buy.

I can't help but feel guilty about Chelsea. She has done a 360° two times around. *Was she forced to follow the road she's on or was it something within her all along?* Chanel came out okay, I guess. She's found love through Minyah, but she had to go through a rack of shit to get it. When I go to visit her, I see in her eyes that she won't ever be the same. There's something missing that was there that first day of school.

Chanel is in school studying chemistry and works as a part-time intern in the University's research lab. It doesn't pay anything but she isn't worried. My mother's lesson to her about saving for rainy days came in handy so she has more than enough to keep her comfortable until she starts making a chemist's salary.

Chelsea is another story altogether. She turned out to be the one woman we aimed to be in the beginning. After taking over "the business" where Charles left off, I can only imagine what's ahead for her. Chanel and me warned her that the drug game isn't the place for a woman. With the money she has, she can chill forever. She only looked past us with those green eyes of hers and handed us our separate account information with million-dollar balances.

On the flip side, I have to say that we have accomplished a lot at twenty-one. I finally own a salon simply called *Liquid*. It has one of the highest clienteles in the city. Thanks to KC and her real estate connections, I get the best prices when it comes to property.

And as far as me and love goes, I don't see it happening anytime soon. *Why?* Because I'm hooking up with one of the running backs from the Baltimore Ravens tonight and there's a gray Aston Martin Vanquish from the Bburago Gold Collection with my name on it. "You *know* I gotta make shit liquid."

226

# About the Author

Tiffany Womble, author of *Liquid Dreams* lives in Baltimore City with her Himalayan Chi Chi and her bird Mickey. The Aquarius enjoys living in a fanciful world where butterflies and artistic creativity can coexist. She finds that the harsh reality that is Life is best withstood with laughter and storytelling in the form of friends, books and music. Tiffany is currently working on the *Liquid Dreamer* series, the extended version of each girl's story.

To write Tiffany:

Blue Denim Press
P.O. Box 1181
Baltimore, MD 21203-1181

bluedenimpress@yahoo.com